PRAISE FOR *THE NEW AUTOMATION MINDSET*

"It's been decades since IT executives received a gift like this amazing book. At this moment defined by Generative AI, we need it more than ever. Vijay is the real deal—and he explains exactly how individuals and teams must operate to win in the modern era. It is put in clear, easy-to-understand, simple language. *The New Automation Mindset* is a "must read." Not tomorrow. Not next week. Now—pick it up, and crack it open. Your career will never be the same."

—Neeraj Agrawal, General Partner, Battery Ventures

"A proactive automation mindset is critical for every organization to develop to thrive in the future. This book provides practical guidance to CIOs on not only how to develop this mindset but also democratize that across the entire organization."

— Noni Azhar, SVP of IT at Podium

"No one in enterprise middleware has had a more impactful journey than Vijay Tella. We are so lucky, because, in this book, he shares his secrets. If you want to build an antifragile company that maximizes generative AI to overcome and thrive on challenges, *The New Automation Mindset* is your guide."

—Amit Bendov, CEO, Gong

"I've have known Vijay Tella for many years and was really waiting for him to write such a book. Vijay has the most comprehensive and yet concise views on the state of the enterprise integration & AI and the role these would play in digital transformation across industries. If you look back at the most transformative middleware companies of the last two decades, you'll find that Vijay had a significant role to play in them. The integration and automation markets will be upended by AI - but companies that leverage the New Automation Mindset are going to win and stay relevant. In a market with so much noise and hype, this book is a sincere effort to demystify. I will be referring to this book again and again over the next several years."

—Anand Birje, CEO, Encora, former President Digital Business Services, HCL

"Vijay Tella is undoubtedly one of the most impactful integration and automation pioneers of the past decade. Across Tibco, Oracle Fusion Middleware, and now Workato, Vijay has been years ahead of the trends. *The New Automation Mindset* is a foundational book for companies looking to harness generative AI and low-code automation to win in the new era."

—Andrew Chen, General Partner, Andreesen Horowitz and author of The Cold Start Problem

"*The New Automation Mindset* is a set of powerful insights to help enterprises get off the traditional automation treadmill and onto the transformation fast-track with true business adaptability."

—Arthur Hu, Global CIO, Lenovo

"There are plenty of books about automation software, but none of them provide the level of insights and practical advice that *The New Automation Mindset* does. That's because of Vijay's deep experience in the middleware space, which clearly comes out in this book. This is a book that every CIO should read."

—Kim Huffman, CIO at Navan

"Automation is the ultimate digital transformation. *The New Automation Mindset* is a must-read for everyone in Business Technology and IT. It provides a comprehensive guide to developing an enterprise-wide automation strategy from concept to driving business outcomes at scale."

—Natasha Irani, Senior Director of IT, Hashicorp

"I don't know of any entrepreneur who can speak better about the future of automation technology than Vijay Tella. If you're a current or aspiring company leader who wants to stay ahead of the curve, this book is for you. It provides a comprehensive view of the role automation will play in the next decade of business."

—Sean Jacobsohn, Partner at Norwest Venture Partners

"I have gotten to know Vijay and the Workato team over the past few years and was struck by the parallels between building a championship company and culture in professional sports with how you do the same in the dynamic technology industry. Systems thinking - the long-term vision and trusting the process, coupled with a culture that makes us stronger through the inevitable challenges, and having everyone in the organization be involved have been the core tenets for us in sports. The style of play where everyone gets touches, not just a select few is not just more rewarding, it is more resilient and fun. This is the book for business leaders who want to win."

—Bob Myers, 4 time world champion NBA President of the Golden State Warriors, 2 time NBA executive of the year

"*The New Automation Mindset* is the most important reference text for technology leaders today. It is packed with realistic, usable advice for any technologist or business executive. If you want your business to win in the next decade, it would be a mistake to not read this book."

—Amith Nair, CIO, Vituity

"AI is going to accelerate the change of the current landscape. *The New Automation Mindset* is a truly frame-breaking masterpiece that propels readers into the forefront of that revolution. With depth and precision, this book dives deep into the disruptive forces of AI, automation, and low-code tech. It empowers CIOs and other leaders to unleash efficiency, innovation, and competitive advantage. During my tenure as the CIO of Broadcom, I have personally seen all of these benefits. Brace yourself for a career-altering journey that will redefine the way you harness automation in the new AI era."

—Andy Nallappan, CTO, Head of Software Engineering and Operations, Broadcom

"The strategies that underpin success in the next 10 years are going to be completely different from the strategies that worked in the previous era. *The New Automation Mindset* is required reading if we are going to position our companies to win in the new era."

—Dan Rogers, CEO, LaunchDarkly (Also former President of Rubrik and CMO of ServiceNow and Symantec)

"This book should be read by all CIOs seeking a leadership role in transforming the internal operations of their companies. Vijay's Workato team is leading the integration and automation market into a new era of automation. His book is not simply a technology manifesto—it's a blueprint for building the world-class companies of the future."

—Mark Settle, 7x CIO and author of Truth from the Trenches: A Practical Guide to the Art of IT Management and Truth from the Valley: A Practical Primer on Future IT Management Trends

"Over the next decade every organization will be engaged in a massive reimagining of the way work gets done with the tasks that people perform increasingly augmented by automation and AI. This book does an outstanding job of explaining the essential three mindsets which will separate successful people and companies from those that fall behind: adaptability, systems thinking, and empowerment. A must-read for those who would be on the forefront of this transformation."

—Ted Shelton, Partner, Bain & Company

"In a world where technology and transformation are accelerating, this book will become the manager's essential guide to leveraging the power of automation. Every business use case will be impacted, and every leader will need a strategy; get ready to change your perspective!"

—Gary Survis, Operating Partner, Insight Partners

"Vijay Tella has successfully incorporated emerging technologies into the day-to-day operations across the enterprise. Across two decades, he has been a trusted partner to many in Silicon Valley. In this book, Vijay takes us into a not so distant future—where best of breed composable technology is woven together through automation forming the fabric of our planet's IT architecture."

—Eric Tan, CIO at Flock Security, and former CIO at Coupa

"We've entered an era of automation that's more than operational efficiency. This new book, *The New Automation Mindset*, shows leaders what it takes to achieve automation in multiple dimensions—process, growth, and scale. Moreover, the authors show how humans can thrive while operating at machine scale."

—R "Ray" Wang, CEO, Constellation Research, Inc. and two-time best-selling author of Disrupting Digital Business and Everybody Wants to Rule the World

"*The New Automation Mindset* is more than your average management consulting guide or book for roles with IT job titles. It should be read by everyone from venture capitalists to CEOs to aspiring leaders. This book will give them a completely new vision for what is possible in their companies. The three elements of the mindset, growth, scale, and process, are the new elements of every successful company."

—Bryan Wise, CIO, 6Sense, and former VP of IT at GitLab, Snowflake, and DocuSign

"*The New Automation Mindset* is a must read for every leader who recognizes how important AI and automation are to your company's future. I have known Vijay Tella for a few years and am excited he's sharing so much of his knowledge from building a culture of automation down to what processes and how to automate them."

—Pauline Yang, Partner, Altimeter Capital

THE NEW AUTOMATION MINDSET

THE NEW AUTOMATION MINDSET

The Leadership Blueprint
for the Era of AI-For-All

Vijay Tella

With Scott Brinker and Massimo Pezzini

WILEY

Published by John Wiley & Sons, Inc., Hoboken, New Jersey.
Published simultaneously in Canada.

For general information on our other products and services or for technical support, please contact our Customer Care Department within the United States at (800) 762-2974, outside the United States at (317) 572-3993 or fax (317) 572-4002.

Wiley also publishes its books in a variety of electronic formats. Some content that appears in print may not be available in electronic formats. For more information about Wiley products, visit our web site at **www.wiley.com**.

Library of Congress Cataloging-in-Publication Data is Available:

ISBN: 9781119898757 (Cloth)
ISBN: 9781119898764 (ePub)
ISBN: 9781119898771 (ePDF)

Cover Illustration and Design: Courtesy of Cathy O'Malley and Natalie Broussard

SKY10050288_071023

Contents

FOREWORD   xiii

Introduction   1

Part 1   The New Automation Mindset   15

1   The New Era of Automation   17
2   The Process Mindset   27
3   The Growth Mindset   39
4   The Scale Mindset   53

Part 2   Architectural Underpinnings   67

5   Orchestration   69
6   Plasticity   81
7   Democratization   95

Part 3   A Practitioner's Guide to World Class Automation   109

8   Mastering Your Automation Journey   111
9   The Back Office   121
10   The Front Office   137
11   The Employee Experience   153
12   The Customer Experience   169
13   Supplier Operations   181
14   The Platform-Driven Business   195

Part 4   Making it Happen   207

15   The Enterprise AI Platform   209
16   The Automation Ecosystem   217
17   Enterprise Automation   241
18   The New Operating Model   259

19 The Future of the Enterprise **269**

20 The New Career Paths **279**

APPENDIX A: KEY ROLES FOR DEMOCRATIZATION **291**

ACKNOWLEDGMENTS **297**

ABOUT THE AUTHORS **299**

INDEX **303**

Foreword

In my over 45 years in the IT industry, including the 25 I spent as a Gartner analyst, I was always intrigued by integration and automation. Many decades ago, when, after several days of work, I was finally able to connect an Olivetti system with an IBM mainframe, I realized how making different systems work together can deliver business benefits greater than the sum of the parts. In that case it was about helping a local public authority in Italy automate a particularly important business process, but since then I helped hundreds, if not thousands of organizations worldwide to devise what was the best way for them to sort out their thorny integration and automation problems to deliver business value.

My focus on this topic inevitably led me to cross paths with Vijay Tella, one of the pioneers in this space. As a Gartner analyst, I tracked Vijay's innovations at TIBCO, Oracle, and most recently Workato. Vijay's uncommon combination of entrepreneurship, business acumen, industry vision, leadership, open-minded attitude, and restraint made it very easy for me to establish a relationship with him that goes well beyond professional respect and the stereotypical love/hate rapport between an IT vendor and an analyst. It helps that Vijay and I share passions other than integration and automation: good food, fine wine, bicycles, and my home country: Italy.

In addition, Vijay and I also agree about many points of view about the role and the nature of IT, many of which are reflected in this work. One of the really strong convictions that we have shared for decades is that the modern, end-to-end model of automation requires integration. Automation is the goal; integration is the means. This book will give you an original perspective on the motivations, drivers, and benefits of automation and how organizations should get the most out of it by automating end-to-end cross-function processes, rather than individual tasks.

More and more user organizations are setting automation initiatives in motion, and a growing number of providers are describing themselves as automation vendors. However, "automation" is becoming increasingly associated with "integration" (as we think it should be). For example, several vendors, traditionally established in the integration technology market, are repositioning themselves as integration + automation providers. So how should you think about the concepts of automation and integration? And how do these two disciplines relate to each other? In my view the answer is simple: they are just two sides of the same coin. There is no automation without integration, and automation is the business outcome of integration.

What Is Automation?

In IT "automation" generally indicates the use of software technology to establish and execute a well-defined sequence of conditionally determined steps that must be performed to complete a business task (for example, issue a purchase order) or a business process (for example, originate a loan). The goals of automation are quite intuitive and include:

- Drastically shortening the time it takes to perform a task or process;
- Minimizing human activity;
- Improving accuracy by eliminating manual data reentry; and
- Tracking and reporting about the overall process activity.

From that perspective, therefore, most IT applications are indeed about automation. For example, a finance application essentially aims at automating tasks and business processes in areas such as general ledger, accounts receivable, accounts payable, and financial closure. Hence, it is legitimate to say that organizations have been automating since they bought their first computer system or application.

This classic form of automation is typically siloed within individual organizational units (for example, finance, HR, sales, procurement, supply chain, and manufacturing) by means of broad application suites (for example ERP or CRM suites) However, for many years now, organizations have been using integration technology, such as enterprise service buses (ESBs) or extraction, transformation and loading (ETL) tools, to synchronize data across different applications.

The need to break the organizational silos to automate cross functional business processes (for example, order to cash, procure to pay, and hire to retire) led to a new, end-to-end automation approach. According to this model, you should look at your application portfolio as a best-of-breed collection of business capabilities, exposing APIs that can be orchestrated via an external orchestration layer, thus defining and implementing more effective, impactful, and differentiated processes.

Progressive business executives want to rapidly automate complex—often inter-functional—end-to-end processes by orchestrating the business capabilities of multiple systems, increasingly including also "machines" (for example, 3D printers, drones, and industrial robots). You also want to be able to easily and quickly reshape, extend, or modify these processes in an agile way, as new requirements emerge. This quest for short time to value and business agility is the reason why the use of low-code orchestration tools is crucial.

To favor business agility, your automation strategy must enable more builders across IT, your business users, and potentially even business partners, to engage with these processes via a variety of channels (web, mobile, bots).

This is the technology that enables you to realize the orchestration, plasticity, and democratization concepts discussed in this book.

What Is Integration?

The modern, end-to-end model of automation requires independently designed systems to work together. This is not a trivial task as these systems are, more often than not, inconsistent in how they are built, the technologies they use, the way they deal with data, and how we interact with them. They have been developed by different vendors or development teams, years apart and with no up-front coordination among them. Consequently, their data models, external interfaces (whether APIs or events), interchange formats, communication protocols, technology platforms, and even data semantics are often quite different.

Luckily, there are technologies, architectures, and methodologies in the market that aim to tackle the "making independently designed systems work together" challenge, which is what is commonly referred to as "integration." Integration technology is used to connect different systems and enable them to exchange data by reconciling their differences in terms of data semantics, external interfaces, and communication protocols. Integration is the magic that makes it possible for your modern, cloud-based sales management system to exchange sales data with your 40-year-old on-premises ERP system, for example in the context of an automated, end-to-end order-to-cash business process.

Hence, the modern, end-to-end model of automation does, overtly or covertly, require the use of integration capabilities that assist and complement the orchestration capabilities.

It doesn't make a lot of sense to have an automation strategy without a closely aligned and coherent integration strategy. Vice versa, an integration strategy that's not designed to support automation needs is poor and incomplete.

Consequently, your organization's automation and integration strategies should be designed together as two sides of the same coin, a coin I call "enterprise automation."

The business value of a unified enterprise automation strategy vs. distinct integration and automation strategies leads to valuable business benefits measured in terms of:

- Reduced costs and improved efficiency, by streamlining processes, minimizing manual errors and liberating human resources from mundane, repetitive, and low-value tasks;
- Improved business agility, by making it possible to incrementally reshape and extend established processes while reducing time to value;
- Business differentiation, by enabling you to creatively assemble "commodity" IT systems and devices to implement innovative products and services;
- Improved customer/employee experience, by providing them an integrated, consistent, intuitive, and conversational UI for the business processes;

- Real-time business insights and improved situation awareness, by collecting, aggregating, analyzing, and acting in real time upon business-event data.

The business value of the combined strategy is compelling per se but also because enterprise automation:

- Enables a wide range of strategic initiatives, including AI and advanced analytics, digital transformation, API economy, hyper-automation, application modernization, transition to the cloud and the composable enterprise
- Optimizes technologies, skills, and costs by defining a clear set of common goals technologies and methodologies across the automation and integration disciplines, by improving your ability to tackle complex scenarios, by promoting technology and skills synergies and by making planning, management, monitoring, and governance of integration and automation initiatives much simpler.

Implementing a Single, Unified Strategy

Aligning your integration and automation approaches according to a unified enterprise automation strategy may not be easy for you. Typically the integration strategy is IT-owned, whereas the automation strategy may be a responsibility of a business team, for example, finance or HR. Their unification can lead to friction, organizational resistance, and turf wars. But it can be done—many large organizations, such as Atlassian, MGM, Kaiser Permanente, Adobe, HubSpot, and others are living proof.

Separate integration and automation strategies usually lead to the establishment of different "centers of excellence" (CoEs). Therefore, the first step in your unification journey is to combine your integration and automation CoEs into a single enterprise automation team.

Unfortunately, my experience suggests that organizational, political, and technological factors can significantly hinder, if not completely prevent, the establishment of a unified enterprise automation strategy. Therefore, building consensus around such a unification is critical for success. This is not easy and requires a methodical and well-thought-through process meant to help you get buy-in from your business leaders. This process should include the following steps:

- **Educate** IT and business leaders on the notion that automation and integration are two sides of the same coin.
- **Demonstrate**, through exemplary real-life projects, how combining integration and automation skills and technologies makes you achieve better results in terms of efficacy, costs, and time to value.
- **Look for economies of scale** by reducing technology and skill redundancies across the two disciplines. Bring the distinct teams together to brainstorm on how the tools and approaches could be brought together to create something more powerful.

A decisive thrust toward unification will come from the quantum leap in productivity stemming from the use of generative AI in enterprise automation, which will make the distinction between the two disciplines to de facto disappear. The idea is to basically "describe" in natural language how the task or process looks like and then use generative AI technology to create the automation and integration artifacts that actually implement the task/process itself and all the necessary integrations. Not only will this approach dramatically improve developers' productivity, but it will also contribute to further democratizing enterprise automation: Without needing support from IT personnel and with minimal or no training, businesspeople will be able to automate tasks and business processes by basically telling the system the business outcomes they aim for. Will they think in automation or integration terms? Most likely neither. They will just focus on the business value that the new integrated approach enables them to deliver.

Does it sound too good to be true? Undoubtedly generative AI is in its infancy, let alone its use to support enterprise automation. A number of security, compliance, privacy, reliability, trust, and intellectual property issues must be sorted out before it reaches enterprise-grade.

However, the initial POCs delivered very, very promising preliminary results. I wouldn't be surprised if, in two or three years' time, generative AI became the most popular approach to enterprise automation development.

With the new world of SaaS, cloud, and app specialization, the world of automation has needed to shift from single-domain activities to end-to-end multisystem business processes. This shift made integration a core capability required to achieve our desired outcomes. Some organizations choose to turn a blind eye and pretend integration and automation are separate disciplines. This only causes problems for the teams on the ground who are trying to accomplish the same thing but under the banner of two different names. By unifying your integration and automation strategies, you will help your organization address a wide range of end-to-end process automation needs effectively and efficiently over the next several years.

In the book you'll find actionable insights and valuable examples about how and why business and IT leaders should think about enterprise automation, AI, and the future of business. Enterprise automation can help you and your organization not only stay in business but also build competitive differentiation. However, this requires a radical switch from a short-sighted, task optimization focus to a holistic, strategic, enterprise-wide automation mindset. This book is meant to provide you with the compass that you need to navigate through this journey.

—*Massimo Pezzini*

Introduction

AI is expected to have an extraordinary impact on our economy, adding 1.5% to our productivity annually, according to Goldman Sachs.[1] Despite high investments and hype, digital transformation has proven unsuccessful for 90% of companies.[2] Will AI be the savior? Will it be different this time in the era of AI-for-all?

Yes and no. Much of the emphasis of business transformation initiatives has been on technology. We believe an organization's mindset around transformation was always important and will matter more in the future. It will dictate *how* we choose to apply AI—whether we think about our business and our processes holistically from first principles or pave the cowpaths by automating existing practices.

We find ourselves at a crucial juncture in computing and the future of work. With the advent of generative AI, the barriers between ideators and automators have been eliminated. The emergence of cloud-native, low-code platforms in the enterprise domain offers unparalleled transparency, utility-level ease of operations, and governance. Together, these technologies have the potential to unlock an astonishing level of continuous innovation and automation within organizations.

During my career at TIBCO, Oracle, and Workato, I have had the honor of working with pioneering companies such as FedEx, Amazon, Nike, and Grab during their transformational journeys. They possessed a unique organizational mindset that embraced challenges, characterized by what writer Nassim Taleb calls antifragility.[3] Additionally, they had the advantage of ample resources—both in terms of technology and human talent, which allowed them to execute their plans effectively.

One of the most promising developments of this digital age is that any organization can now achieve this level of transformation. With the right mindset, we do not need the same level of extraordinary resources of prior generations of leaders. With the emergence of generative AI and low-code automation technologies, any business can now achieve the speed and scale to transform and thrive.

But, as Professor Louis Hyman, who leads the Institute of Workplace Studies at Cornell, puts it, "The huge productivity gains of the industrial age didn't happen just because someone invented a new technology; they happened because people also figured out how best to reorganize work around that technology . . . [It was] as much organizational as technological."[4]

My hope for this book is that it provides CEOs, CIOs, and other business and technology leaders a blueprint to embrace a new way of working, one that is focused on the big picture, thrives on change, and engages everyone. This new way of working results from adopting what I call the new automation mindset.

To assess if our organizations have such a mindset, we can ask three key questions.

- Do we approach problem-solving and decision-making by considering the broader context and the vision (systems thinking), or do we primarily concentrate on streamlining individual tasks and processes through automation (task thinking)?
- Do we think from first principles and embrace change, or are we afraid to break things? When challenged, do we rethink or merely adjust to get by?
- Do we rely mostly on technical experts or empower everyone in the organization to contribute? Are those closer to the business given the authority to initiate and lead changes?

The next three sections will explore each of these questions that form the basis of the new automation mindset.

Do We Follow Systems or Task Thinking?

Research shows a direct correlation between the number of apps in a company and the amount of manual work for employees. It is ironic. Individual applications exist to automate business processes and functions and replace manual work. Yet, with all the data fragmentation and context switching, we are piling busywork onto every part of our company. There's been an exponential increase in the application "toggling tax."[5] It is not just that we have reached the point of diminishing returns with explosion of applications. Research shows that deploying more apps on top of the hundreds we already use now *increases* the total time we spend on context switching rather than decreasing it:[6]

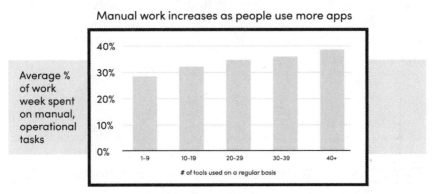

Manual work increases as people use more apps

Average % of work week spent on manual, operational tasks

# of tools used on a regular basis

ChiefMartec, "Wait, more martech tools create more manual tasks?!," 2021

The bigger issue is that we focus on incremental improvements in our business at the margins. We have been organized around and operate in terms of discrete applications and tasks rather than considering the bigger broader picture. The dominant paradigm for automation is to look for manual tasks and automate with bots.

While automating tasks results in cost savings in the short term, they also lock in place how our processes work today—which is the opposite of transformation! This tunnel-vision focus on tasks drowns our organizations in the minutiae and causes us to miss the big picture of strategic pivots. As the management guru Peter Drucker put it, "There is nothing so useless as doing efficiently that which should not be done at all."

As generative AI storms into this world of fragmented IT and task-centered work, our instincts may again be to apply AI to automate tasks we are currently doing manually. It makes sense. It saves us labor costs. The Goldman Sachs estimate of the impact of AI on our economy was also based on the percentage of manual tasks being performed today that they estimate can be automated with AI. But if that is the extent to which we apply AI, we would be cementing how our businesses operate today and will again fall well short of the transformational impact it promises.

We have already seen this happen with the glut of technology in companies today. In a world of extreme fragmentation of our IT and the resulting piecemeal work, productivity peaks and eventually starts to regress. But if we apply systems thinking and orchestrate our people, processes and technologies holistically toward a larger vision, the whole of our impact from productivity gains becomes greater than the sum of its parts.

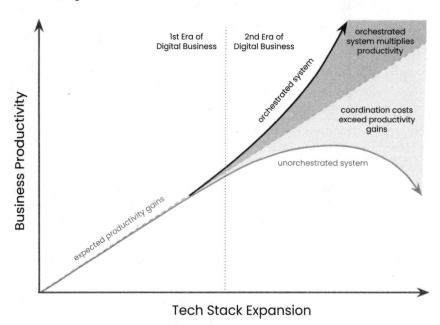

The most groundbreaking technologies in human history, such as the automobile, the steam engine, and the printing press, transformed how people traveled, worked, and learned. They propelled enormous gains in productivity, disrupted jobs, created more rewarding jobs, and changed the trajectory of human existence. AI has a similar potential, but to achieve it, companies will need the new automation mindset. They will look at the big picture around customer needs, first principles, and end-to-end processes. From that starting line, they will begin to transform.

Even with a good understanding of the big picture of where we want to take our business, there can be significant friction to make changes happen. This brings us to the second question around the new automation mindset.

Do We Embrace Change or Fear Breaking Things?

Companies with the new automation mindset embrace change, embodying the concept of "antifragility." Writer Nassim Taleb describes antifragility as the ability to not only withstand shocks but even thrive and grow in response to these shocks.

He says, "Wind extinguishes a candle and energizes fire." Some businesses crumble in adversity, some survive, and others thrive. In response to system shocks such as economic downturns, global pandemics, or disruptions from technologies such as cloud, big data, and AI, most companies adapted. For example, during the pandemic, most of us got on Zoom, Slack, and other remote work tools. Companies with this new mindset know that mere adaptation just delays their demise. Rather, they look to system shocks, technology disruptions and challenges as the impetus to rethink their business to take on new markets, and new opportunities.

Nearly every company will *adapt* to AI disruption. But antifragile companies will use the disruption to rethink their goals and how they will get there. They are not afraid to break things down and build them back better.

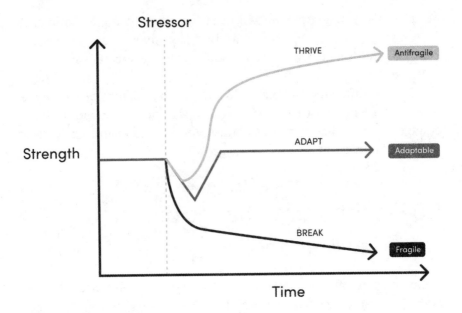

Every category-dominant company I have seen emerge in the last 30 years has been and continues to be antifragile. Amazon, Toast, FedEx, Grab, Airbnb, Navan, and more have exhibited this trait over and over.

When the pandemic challenged everyone, the antifragile companies showed their true colors: The rideshare business vanished, so Grab morphed into a super-app offering an array of services from food to financial services to their customers in Southeast Asia. When their restaurant point-of-sale business hit a wall, Toast morphed into delivery, finance, touchless ordering, and more. When business travel disappeared, TripActions (now Navan) remade itself into a spend management and finance company.

Generative AI dramatically speeds up coding up new solutions and evolving them rapidly, so organizations that embrace antifragility and the new automation mindset can more easily break down their current processes, reimagine new ones, and build them back better.

The challenge is that there are thousands of processes in every company—which brings up the question: Who is going to do all the breaking down and building?

Is Automation a Team Sport or Exclusive to Specialized Experts?

A business consists of thousands of processes, small and large. Collectively, they define how the business operates. The sheer number of all these processes makes it impossible to dictate them—much less transform them—top-down.

Steve Jobs said it well: "Authority should be vested in the people doing the work to improve their own processes."[7] Enabling such bottom-up invention at scale, forged by talented individuals at all levels within our organization, not just technical experts in IT, lets us differentiate from our competition across hundreds and hundreds of processes, small and large.

This empowerment of our teams must be done with governance and guardrails. Without it, we load up on risk and technical debt. A democracy without governance becomes an anarchy. There's a need and opportunity for the role of IT to shift. They will evolve from a service provider to an enabler. Before, the business side of the company sent their process requirements to be implemented, but now, they become a player-coach to our business teams. Hence, in this new era, CIOs will become more central to business and more strategic to their transformation agenda.

An interesting side effect of the democratized automation, accelerated by generative AI, will be bringing more of the cross process work back to internal teams, a trend that Forrester analyst Leslie Joseph calls "insourcing."[8]

Generative AI + Cloud-native Automation Changes Everything

Low-code, cloud-native technologies have made it possible for a broader range of people in our organizations to automate. What took weeks or months to automate can get done in days, and more of our team can participate in the process. The low-code creators, even if they don't need technical coding knowledge and skills, still need to think like a coder. This blocks a broad swath of people with ideas in our companies from engaging productively in automation.

Generative AI eliminates these coding barriers, enabling anyone with ideas about any aspect of our company—customer experience, employee experience, business operations, sales, or marketing—to automate processes with the assistance of AI. At the same time, the transparency, utility-level consumer-like operations, governance and security of cloud-native, low-code automation platforms in the enterprise make it possible to understand, confirm, deploy, and continuously improve AI generated automation.

Together, AI and cloud-native platforms open the aperture of automations in our companies wide, opening the floodgates for new ideas to be automated and see the light of day. This moment where automation and AI are converging is analogous to the world of search before and after Google. With Google, search became ubiquitous in our lives. The world of automation today, even low-code automation, is akin to that of a world where Google works offline to get you results in days. We'd be searching dramatically less. Similarly with "off-line" automation that takes days to weeks, we automate a small fraction of processes and act upon a small fraction of our ideas to improve what we do and how we operate. Generative AI with cloud-native automation will help us get to the remaining 99% and help us continuously iterate and improve. This will have a game-changing impact on how we work.

Organizations that embrace the AI and automation movements along with the key tenets of the new automation mindset—the systems thinking, the adaptability and making work a true team sport—will become unstoppable and separate themselves from the rest.

The Blueprint for the New Automation Mindset: Enterprise Automation and Generative AI

The new automation mindset is not really new. Leading companies of the earlier generation fully embodied its core principles of systems thinking, antifragility, and engaging everyone in their companies. This mindset feels new and novel in the context of the current paradigm for automation, which is to primarily look for and automate manual tasks.

The earlier generation of trailblazers all had access to extraordinary resources in terms of people and technology. The reality of enormous transformation projects was that they required a resource expenditure on a different level than most companies could afford.

As we mentioned, with the right mindset, we don't need the resources of the earlier generation of leaders to achieve our vision. Dramatic advances in and the convergence of generative AI, cloud-native platforms, data cloud platforms, and low-code automation are forging a modern blueprint for path-breaking transformation. This blueprint is within the reach of the rest of us.

Low-code automation significantly lowers the level of technical skill required to execute complex transformation projects.

Cloud-native deployments and utility-like consumption models make enterprise software nearly as easy to adopt and operate as the best consumer technologies.

A versatile, low-code, cloud automation platform backed by the governance and security guardrails that enterprises need, is what we call enterprise automation.

Enterprise automation platforms significantly lower the barrier for companies of any size and industry to be able embark on and execute meaningful transformation initiatives.

Generative AI lowers these barriers even further! With low code, one does not need technical skills to code. Generative AI does away with even these barriers by completely removing the need to code. It is possible for our business teams to create automations and solutions by conversing with LLMs.

However, for generative AI to be applied in the enterprise and achieve its potential:

- It must be supported by an execution capability, like those found in enterprise automation platforms, that matches the power, versatility, and expressiveness of LLMs.[9]
- Solutions that LLMs generate must be explainable and transparent, so we can confidently put them into production use. Low-code platforms are designed to be inherently transparent to business users—it is part of what makes them low code.

- Cloud-native deployment means the less-technical people that use LLMs to create solutions can deploy as easily as if they were using their favorite consumer app.
- Security and governance of enterprise automation makes it safe to adopt AI at scale within our companies.

In the coming years, generative AI and enterprise automation will be a tight synergy for organizations on their transformation journeys.

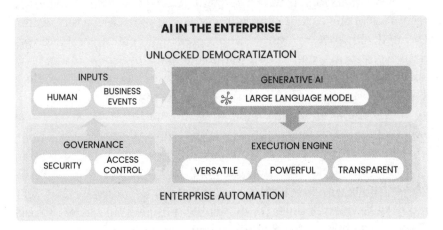

Whether you are coming at transformation from a modern automation perspective or an AI perspective, the blueprint to adopt and apply the new automation mindset is the same. AI opens the doors wide, so more people can automate than ever before. Enterprise automation provides the versatility, transparency, consumer-like ease of use and the governance that makes it possible for any company to transform at scale.

The New Era of Digital

Many of the most impactful companies in the last 10 years have already started this journey. These aren't just the usual suspect digital native tech companies. These include incumbents in traditional industries competing digitally—companies such as Broadcom, Disney, Nike, Lego, DHL, Caterpillar, IKEA, and Capital One/ING Direct. In the new era, every company will need this mindset. It's an era where we tailor the software to fit our business instead of forcing it into cookie-cutter applications.

Throughout key inflection points in the history of software, the big winners adopted a collective growth mindset within their organizations that allowed them to emerge from periods of upheaval in a stronger position than when they went in. It was only in hindsight that we realized that these companies were championing a new era and mindset.

Bain & Company studied 3,900 companies before and after the Great Recession of 2008. While the companies grew at comparable rates before the crisis, their performance showed a sharp contrast when the recession hit.

The research notes, the winners grew at a 17% compound annual growth rate (CAGR) during the downturn, compared with 0% among the losers. What's more, the winners locked in gains to grow at an average 13% CAGR, nearly quadrupling their business in eight years after the downturn, while the losers stalled out[10] As researchers at MIT put it: "The worst of times for the economy as a whole can be the best of times for individual companies to improve their fortunes."[11]

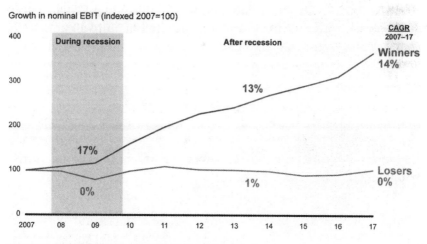

Growth in nominal EBIT (indexed 2007=100)

Sources: S&P Capital IQ; Bain Sustained Value Creator analysis, winners (n=415) losers (n=3,449)

In other words, if we can build our companies to thrive on challenges, we can achieve greatness and separate ourselves.

We have a chance to build companies that can propel themselves to lead in challenging times and excel in the good times. We have a chance to build upon the foundations laid down in the previous era and to fulfill its promises. This book will show you how.

A Roadmap to the New Automation Mindset

This book has four sections designed to walk you through the new automation mindset and an approach to realizing it in our companies.

This book is designed for a wide audience, including C-suite executives, IT leaders, and automation practitioners, to ensure that automation becomes a collaborative effort. The content is structured to be easily consumable based on the reader's role and interests. Section 1 and relevant parts of Section 4 cater to the C-suite and board level professionals, while Section 2 is beneficial for CIOs, chief digital officers, and enterprise architects. Section 3 is specifically tailored to automation practitioners.

In Section 1, "The New Automation Mindset," you will find a deep dive into the three essential mindsets required to build an antifragile company. We walk you through a new way of thinking about automation and highlight the need for a paradigm shift away from the current model.

In Section 2, "The Architectural Underpinnings," we discuss how the right mindset must be combined with a strong tactical approach to automation. This section provides an overview of the architectural underpinnings that can be implemented for successful enterprise automation.

Section 3 is for the practitioners in our companies. In this section, we share stories and best practices for automations and innovative automations that can be applied across nearly every aspect of our business—the front office, back office, customer experience, employee experience, and supplier and partner operations. Senior execs may skim this section or skip forward to Section 4. Business and IT practitioners can focus just on chapters in this section for the functional areas that they are closest to.

And finally, in Section 4, we discuss how all of this comes together in our companies. How the mindset and architectural underpinnings work with our existing integration and automation technologies. We then discuss the operating models and the impact of automation on future careers.

Notes

1. Goldman Sachs, 2023, "Generative AI Could Raise Global GDP by 7%," (April 5), **https://www.goldmansachs.com/insights/pages/generative-ai-could-raise-global-gdp-by-7-percent.html**.
2. LaBerge, Laura, Kate Smaje, and Rodney Zemmel, 2022, "Three New Mandates for Capturing a Digital Transformation's Full Value," McKinsey, (June 15), **https://www.mckinsey.com/capabilities/mckinsey-digital/our-insights/three-new-mandates-for-capturing-a-digital-transformations-full-value**.
3. Taleb, Nassim, 2014, *Antifragile: Things That Gain from Disorder*, New York: Random House.
4. Hyman, Louis, 2023, "It's Not the End of Work. It's the End of Boring Work," *New York Times*, (April 22), **https://www.nytimes.com/2023/04/22/opinion/jobs-ai-chatgpt.html?searchResultPosition=2**.
5. Murty, Rohan Narayana, Sandeep Dadlani, and Rajath B. Das, 2022, "How Much Time and Energy Do We Waste Toggling Between Applications?" *Harvard Business Review*, (August 29), **https://hbr.org/2022/08/how-much-time-and-energy-do-we-waste-toggling-between-applications**.
6. Brinker, Scott, 2021, "Wait, More Martech Tools Create More Manual Tasks?!" *ChiefMartec*, **https://chiefmartec.com/2021/04/martech-tools-manual-tasks/**.
7. American Society for Quality, "Steve Jobs on Joseph Juran and Quality," YouTube Video, Uploaded January 24, 2014, **https://www.youtube.com/watch?v=XbkMcvnNq3g**.
8. Joseph, Leslie, 2022, "Take the First Steps Toward an Automation Fabric," *Forrester*, (May 19), **https://www.forrester.com/report/take-the-first-steps-toward-an-automation-fabric/RES177540**.
9. Cai, Yuzhe, Shaoguang Mao, Wenshan Wu, Zehua Wang, Yaobo Liang, Tao Ge Chenfei Wu, Wang You, Ting Song, Yan Xia, Jonathan Tien, and Nan

Duan, 3023, "Low-code LLM: Visual Programming over LLMs," *Microsoft Research Asia*, (April 20), **https://arxiv.org/pdf/2304.08103.pdf**.

10. Holland, Tom, and Jeff Katzin, 2019, "Beyond the Downturn: Recession Strategies to Take the Lead," *Bain & Company*, (May 16), **https://www.bain.com/insights/beyond-the-downturn-recession-strategies-to-take-the-lead/**.

11. Sull, Donald, and Charles Sull, 2022, "Preparing Your Company for the Next Recession," *MIT Sloan Management Review*, (December 6), **https://sloanreview.mit.edu/article/preparing-your-company-for-the-next-recession/**.

PART 1

The New Automation Mindset

CHAPTER 1

The New Era of Automation

"'Automation-native' companies will emerge and enjoy tremendous growth and profitability at the expense of their competitors."

—Leslie Joseph, Forrester Research

The word "automation" covers a lot of ground. For some, it's a way to replace manual work with bots. For others, it sparks worry. It's important to think about automation in a new way so we don't miss out on its benefits. In the future, companies with the right mindset about automation will thrive in the face of challenges rather than succumb to them. This mindset will determine whether they tap into exciting opportunities such as generative AI (GenAI) or are disrupted by them. In other words, how we think about automation and AI will decide if we succeed or fail.

Companies with the right mindset apply the advances in automation and generative AI to become unstoppable. They look at the big picture, with an ethos that embraces challenges and an approach that is inclusive of all of the talent in their companies.

That sentiment might sound like wishful thinking in tough economic times. But I think it is needed precisely when we're "up against the wall." How we respond in times of challenge and fundamental change will dictate our future. To understand, let's look at the company Toast.

Many Restaurants Would Have Been Toast Without Toast

When Wayne Carrington left the New York Police Department after 18 years to open a ramen shop, he didn't expect to be furloughing all his employees due to a global pandemic six years later. "It was a scary time," he said. "I really had no idea if I would stay in business."[1] At its lowest point, his business dropped 75% from its pre-pandemic levels.[2] He said, "We had a sense of urgency that we had to pivot quickly."

The pandemic was particularly hard on the restaurant industry. The National Restaurant Association estimates the industry lost $280 billion in sales during the first 13 months of the pandemic, and a sixth of all restaurants permanently closed.[3]

Thankfully, the ramen shop survived. Carrington is one of the thousands of restaurateurs who acknowledge restaurant tech company Toast for helping them make it through. "[The restaurant] was a 95% dine-in restaurant, and we had to flip that whole platform. Honestly there would have been no way to do with without Toast," Carrington said.[4]

Before the pandemic, Toast was a restaurant technology platform with a bright future. But in the spring of 2020, they were in a similar boat as their restaurant customers: revenues had drastically declined, and it felt as if they were sinking. But Toast took stock of the situation and sprang into action.

Toast CIO Anisha Vaswani recounts some of Toast's rapid work to save themselves and their customers: "What [we] did is very quickly pivot the product. For example, we launched products like Toast Now for our restaurant customers, which created a digital or e-commerce-only presence. A lot of restaurants likely didn't think of doing that pre-pandemic, or weren't incentivized enough to invest in it," said Anisha. "Our mission has always been to serve people who open restaurants because of their passion for hospitality and food. We wanted to make sure we helped them survive the crisis and come out of it thriving."

Toast also started Rally for Restaurants, a grassroots movement to support restaurants through ordering gift cards and takeout so that restaurants could continue to support day-to-day operations and staff wages. And the company supported lobbying efforts to pass the RESTAURANTS Act, helped provide customers access to loans through Toast Capital, and launched many new products and features that helped its customers quickly change with each new challenge thrown at them.

Their push to support restaurants in their darkest hour was a success, and the company went on to IPO in late 2021. Toast is now a hero to many in the restaurant industry. There are thousands of grateful restaurateurs like Mr. Carrington, who, in his own words, would not be in business today if it weren't for Toast's own transformation journey.

Going Beyond Adaptation

Adaptation is a word we use a lot, but it is not sufficient to describe the Toast story. We all adapted to the pandemic in our own way. Knowledge workers adapted to remote work, doctors switched to telehealth, and our kids joined online classes. Companies implemented Zoom, Teams, Slack, and other remote collaboration tools. These adaptations were needed to keep us running.

Toast belongs to a different class of company. In the face of an upheaval, they rethought their strategy and used the challenge to emerge stronger. While others were struggling to stay alive, they quickly adapted and focused on delivering for their customers at a critical time.

These companies more than merely adapted. There isn't a good word in the English language to describe this situation. It is a situation where something gets stronger *because* of systemic shocks. In the introduction, we mentioned that author Nassim Taleb saw this gap and coined the term "antifragile" to describe the phenomenon.[5] He points out that antifragile systems exist everywhere in nature. Antifragile systems paradoxically require their components to be breakable. Only then can they be reformulated into something better and different. They are behind the biggest transformations in human history, from the industrial revolution to the human genome project.

> "Antifragile is a property of systems in which they increase in capability to thrive as a result of stressors, shocks, volatility, noise, mistakes, faults, attacks, or failures."
>
> —Nassim Nicholas Taleb

It is an important idea that also applies to companies and organizations. Toast is a great example of an antifragile company:

- **Willingness to break things and rethink:** First, Toast was not afraid to break things even further and build them back better. For example, their core competency was point of sale, and yet they pushed into new technologies and territories. Moves like these opened the aperture of possibilities for their business and their struggling customers.

- **Culture of change:** Second, Toast created a culture that embraced change. Taleb points out that when systems or societies squeeze out randomness and change, they become more fragile. It's the basic difference between playing defense and playing offense. One tries to preserve and conserve stability, while the other takes an optimistic and constructive view to create a better future.

- **Collective engagement:** The third thing that Toast did was to engage their entire team—from product to business teams to IT—in the journey. As Taleb would say, democracies where everyone is engaged are stronger than autocracies with their fragile command-and-control style.

Toast used systems thinking, embraced change, and worked at scale. These three basic building blocks are an example of what every company must do to be antifragile.

> Antifragile or anti-anything can be a tough concept to get our heads around. You could also call these companies unstoppable. If economic challenges, system shocks, and even potential black swan events all only make these companies stronger, then by definition they are antifragile.

A New Organizational Mindset

It is not just tech companies such as Toast but iconic mainstream companies such as Caterpillar and Ikea that are already on this path. They are taking a fresh approach and thinking about their own transformation in a new way. Automation and AI are central to this new way of thinking, so we call it the new automation mindset.

When we look at these companies, their transformation did not come from optimizing existing operations. To become antifragile requires looking at the bigger picture and the long term of our business and market. It requires AI and automation to expand the possibilities. Automating and optimizing existing operations reduces costs and improves margins but does not change our position in the market. Transforming our business requires *big-picture and long-term thinking, what we call the process mindset.* Companies with a process mindset go beyond looking at automating tasks to looking at processes end to end and how they can be transformed to address the needs today and for the future. AI plays a critical role in this from understanding the entire process, identifying the opportunities for automation in the process, building out the automation using generative AI, and then helping understand the value by measuring the ROI of automation.

Big-picture thinking or process mindset is just the start. To transform deeply, we need a high degree of adaptability and malleability in our systems and processes. We also need teams that are in the mindset of embracing challenges and change. *We need a collective growth mindset in our companies.* Companies with a growth mindset take an agile approach to their transformation initiatives. They continuously seek to understand and adapt their approach based on what's happening at the macro market level and internally within their company.

Having the big vision and the potential to change in our team is not enough to transform at the scale and speed needed to achieve our transformation goals. If we are relying only on a small handful of technically skilled people to do the work, we'd again be stuck. Business transformation today is complex, and it must be fast and dynamic. To keep up, the entire team—from IT and technical experts to business and operational experts—must be brought to bear, with a low-code, AI-powered approach, empowered by governance. To achieve this scale, *companies need democratization, or what we call the scale mindset.*

To become antifragile, to achieve transformative change at the scale that is required, you need all three things. It is not enough to just have big-picture thinking, adaptability, or democratization alone. You need to have all these—the process, growth, and scale mindsets—working in unison in your company. When that happens, we call it the new automation mindset.

When all three mindsets fall into place, our organizations can become unstoppable.

Thus, to become antifragile or unstoppable, we must adopt the new automation mindset.

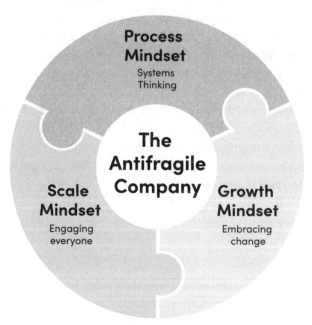

The New Automation Mindset

These three ideas are deeply connected and reinforce each other. In theory, these concepts may sound obvious, but in practice, there are some foundational problems that prevent many companies from realizing them today.

Applying the new automation mindset requires new architectural and technical underpinnings that help us orchestrate our processes end to end, make it easier to refactor or adapt these processes, an ability called plasticity, and to be able to do this with scale and security by democratization. Section 3 covers in detail these three technical underpinnings of the new automation mindset: orchestration, plasticity, and democratization.

Unleashing the New Automation Mindset

When we implement the new automation mindset, we find that several things happen. Let's see how this looks in one such company.

In the bottom line of the figure below, we can see that the number of people engaging in automating grew over time. The company started with IT, ops, and HR and is currently expanding into finance, marketing, and customer support.

Each of these growing groups of creators is connecting to or integrating more systems each month. So the number of connected systems grew even faster than the number of creators, represented by the middle line.

As more people became engaged, more systems were connected, and AI was used to generate, learn, and leverage these connected systems, the number of end-to-end orchestrations grew exponentially.

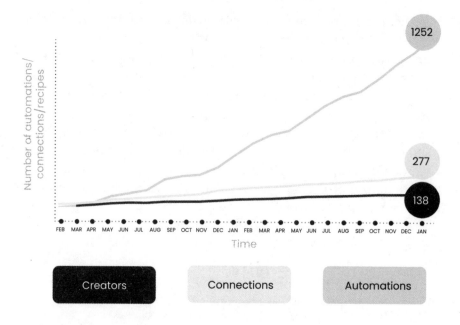

While these numbers are impressive, it is this pattern that matters. They are leveraging their people, they can adapt their business rapidly, and they are able to address the scale of the automation opportunity in front of them. They have the DNA of an antifragile company.

Walking the Walk

We all want our businesses to have this amazing characteristic—to be built to become stronger because of change, stronger because of challenge.

Over the past three decades, I have seen breakthroughs in leading companies when they are built to be antifragile. They have certain strategies, mindsets, and practices in common. Over my years at Tibco, Oracle, and now Workato, I have seen patterns in how the unstoppable companies build and evolve their businesses using automation.

Humans have a long history of applying technology to do things in new ways. Automation is so much more than saving costs by automating manual work or optimizing in place. The antifragile companies have figured out how to leverage technology advancements to execute at the highest level *and* transform when the moment calls for it. They are built purposefully to do both.

These patterns, consisting of the process mindset, the organizational growth mindset, and the scale mindset for winning as a team compose the new automation mindset.

Over the course of this book, I share these lessons. I show how these incredible companies, sometimes in extreme circumstances, used the new automation mindset to become unstoppable.

The new automation mindset is not that new. I have seen companies going back 30 years that used these practices to achieve amazing things. However, there are two things that are different today. The speed, scale, complexity, and dynamism of modern transformation journeys makes applying this mindset more relevant than ever. AI technologies, especially generative AI, is enabling businesses to leverage a vast amount of knowledge to create an even playing field for small and large companies alike where businesses don't need the resources of companies like FedEx, Amazon, or Nasdaq to be able to apply this mindset at scale. I believe that any company—from the newest grocery delivery start-up to the car dealership down the street—can apply the new automation mindset and become antifragile. This book shows you how.

Notes

1. Muchnick, Jeanne, 2022, "How a New Rochelle Ramen Restaurant Stayed in Business During the Pandemic," *LOHUD*, (October 22), **https://www.lohud.com/story/life/food/restaurants/2020/10/20/roc-n-ramen-expands-new-york/5967309002/**.
2. Leenas, Maggie, 2022, "Retired NYPD Officer Brings His Own Take on Ramen to New Jersey," *New Jersey Monthly* (January 10), **https://njmonthly.com/articles/eat-drink/table-hopping/retired-nypd-officer-brings-his-own-take-on-ramen-to-new-jersey/**.
3. National Restaurant Association, n.d., "Reopening and Recovery," last accessed December 31, 2022, **https://restaurant.org/education-and-resources/learning-center/business-operations/**

coronavirus-information-and-resources/reopening-and-recovery/.

4. Toast, Inc., 2021, "How Roc 'N' Ramen Increased Average Check Size by 15% with Toast Order and Pay," YouTube Video, (Uploaded March 18), **https://youtu.be/V31pdiCHTeo**.

5. Nassim Taleb, 2014, *Antifragile: Things That Gain from Disorder*, New York: Random House.

CHAPTER 2

The Process Mindset

"If you just focus on the smallest details, you never get the big picture right."

—Leroy Hood

Wwe buy apps to solve problems and add capabilities. They complete tasks or make groups of tasks easier. But the tasks are not isolated; assembled together they make up processes, which make up businesses. We're all buying apps for tasks, but is anyone thinking about how they affect the whole? To understand how the tasks fit into the big picture, we need to apply systems thinking.

In Peter Senge's *The Fifth Discipline*, he describes systems thinking in this way: "Business[es] . . . are bound by invisible fabrics of interrelated actions, which often take years to fully play out their effects on each other. Since we are part of that lacework ourselves, it's doubly hard to see the whole pattern of change. Instead, we tend to focus on snapshots of isolated parts of the system, and wonder why our deepest problems never seem to get solved."[1]

If one phrase can describe the last 15 years of technology, it might be "There's an app for that!" It captures the prevalence of a task-centric technology mindset. In the US, companies have loaded up on software for tasks, yet average productivity increases at a meager 1 percent per year. For comparison, during the period between 1996 and 2004, productivity grew on average more than 3 percent per year, and in the postwar boom of the 1950s and 1960s, 3.8 percent per year.[2]

A recent study unearthed something that many of us intuitively already know—more apps correlate with more busywork. In the 2021 Airtable/Lawless Research study referenced in the introduction of this book, an increase in a marketing team's application stack correlated with an increase in hours spent doing manual, operational tasks.[3]

Researchers assign the blame for this phenomenon to "context-switching," a term used to describe the cost imposed on our brains when we change from one task (or application) to another. It leads to lost time, as our teams navigate from app to app, resulting in continuous interruptions to our natural thought processes. A study out of Cornell University found that, on average, the cost of navigating across apps takes an employee away from productive work for nine and a half minutes each time they switch. Nearly half of the participants also admitted that changing apps throughout the workday fatigued them.[4]

It seems we are caught in a lose-lose situation. Our productivity is flat or declining, and our people are fatigued and drained. The cheery optimism of "There's an app for that!" is giving way to the sarcastic "Oh great, another login." To paraphrase my favorite infomercial, "There has to be a better way" than the task mindset. That better way is systems thinking, or the process mindset.

The Task Mindset vs. the Process Mindset

My team and I are fond of a famous parable about an elephant. It goes something like this: A group of people encounter an elephant for the first time in the dark of night and attempt to describe the animal based only on touch. The problem is each person is touching a different part of the elephant. The one touching the leg insists it's a tree, while the one touching the trunk is certain it's a snake. While each believes they are correct, they all come to the wrong conclusion. Each person's limited perspective makes them miss the big picture.

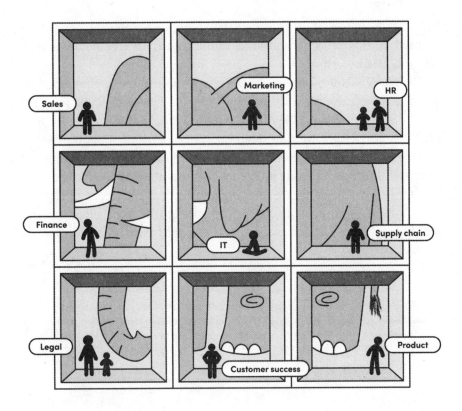

The state of affairs in most companies resembles this parable. For example, each of our departments may only be seeing the customer from a certain perspective and lack the bigger context. A customer support agent may be aware that the customer is very unhappy due to current issues they are experiencing, but a sales team member may unfortunately ask the customer for a referral completely unaware of the issues.

The task mindset made sense during the Industrial Revolution, when most work consisted of repetitive, manual tasks. But despite work becoming exponentially more complex, this task mindset remains deeply entrenched. Automation is viewed as a CFO project, with the goal of whittling down hours and costs over time in each individual segment. The vision is limited to a leaner, cheaper version of the same business.

You can see the mindset at work in the use cases discussed about generative AI. They are often tasks. Most do not think about how it can fit within a process. If we approach it with the same mindset, generative AI tools could become yet another context shift for employees as they navigate their work.

While CFOs are looking to optimize staffing costs, they are also mindful of increasing technology budgets. The app stack in companies is growing fast. The quantity and diversity of automation tools is growing too. Each new automation and integration tool promises to reduce fragmentation and transform the enterprise, yet the patchwork approach has now become a new layer of fragmentation. Rather than breaking down silos, we are creating new ones.

It's as if we are buying tools for each part of the elephant but still failing to see the big picture. In turn, that creates elephant-sized problems.

Let's look at a real example. Today, most automations look like the example on the left of the figure below, where a bot extracts details from a signed contract and enters it into the ERP. Someone was spending hours of their day copying and pasting that data from PDF files, and now with the new bot in place they can focus their energy on something else. The CFO is happy, so what's not to like?

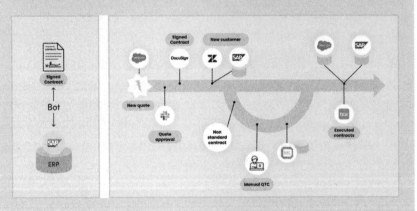

There is nothing wrong with finding efficiencies, but the task mindset leaves us with a narrow view of what needs to happen to resolve a customer order. When we zoom out and understand the bigger picture around the quote-to-cash process, the goals are to reduce the amount of time to execute orders, reduce the time to get paid (or reduce days sales outstanding), increase the percentage of orders that are touchless, and shrink the error rate. On the right, the entire workflow is automated. This includes edge cases such as a nonstandard order that is automatically routed to an expert via Microsoft Teams to process manually. To construct an automation like this takes bigger-picture thinking, using technology to optimize for the real outcomes that matter. Reducing this manual copy/paste effort is nice but improving the experience for customers and the speed of the company is when we see the top line impact of automation.

The Power of the Humble Checklist

In practice, processes are checklists that describe how our employees must work with each other. To understand the power of process to drive predictable excellence in our business, let's take a closer look at this idea of the humble checklist, the real-world counterpart to business processes.

In 2009, physician Atul Gawande published a book called *The Checklist Manifesto*.[5] It told the story of how basic checklists led to, among other things, stunning improvements in patient outcomes. The medical culture at the time did not embrace checklists. Instead, it prioritized doctor autonomy to practice the art of medicine. The book was a critique of this "rock star culture" with a "central belief that in situations of high risk and complexity what you want is a kind of expert audacity" to make the right decisions.[6] Rock star or not, all too often, split-second decisions made by humans are the wrong ones.

When the stakes are high, we want experts to make rational decisions. In this way, ICU doctors could learn from experts in another field: airplane test pilots. In the ICU, there are thousands of variables to consider when caring for an ailing human body. Flying and maintaining an airplane is also extremely complex. Over time, the test pilot industry learned that anyone can be error-prone—even the rock stars—when making split-second decisions under pressure. They discarded the rock star culture decades ago. Today, all pilots follow universal checklists, ones that are updated based on disasters and new learnings—making flying one of the safest ways to travel.[7] Taking the same approach in hospitals, Gawande has seen dramatic results. He estimates that millions of lives could be saved if all hospitals used checklists.

Years ago, a woman went to a well-known hospital where one of the studies took place that Gawande cites in his book. She needed surgery on one of her knees. The surgeon worked in a different team than the one studied by Gawande that adopted checklists. The surgeon was renowned for his expertise in knee replacements. Despite his expertise, he left behind suture retentions in her knee. He did not remember to follow up to remove it. Nor did he let the physician attendant know about it. This is exactly the kind of thing that checklists are designed to catch. It took threatening phone calls from her family to do a follow-up appointment, because those are expensive and cut into hospital margins. Unsurprisingly, the knee had become badly infected by then, causing significant damage to her knee tissue. She has been living in pain since, with her ability to walk impaired for the rest of her life. That woman is my mother. She makes do today, as a more complex corrective surgery helped her regain some function, but in the end, the hospital spent a lot more on her care than they needed to.

This is not the only time I have seen this happen. Sylvia, a nine-year-old family friend, had an infection in one of her eyes that caused vision loss in that eye and required surgery. Unfortunately, the surgeon operated on the wrong eye. Sylvia has been wholly deprived of her vision since.

I often wonder how Sylvia's and my mother's lives would have been if Gawande's checklist approach had been in place as standard operating procedure for surgeons as it is for airline pilots. We now know that these types of checklists help people avoid these kinds of errors *every single time*. Even a 1 percent error rate does not seem acceptable for basic mistakes during surgeries, and, per Gawande, easily avoidable errors or oversights happen across medical teams much more often than that.

Not all businesses deal in life-or-death outcomes. But the truth is, we all can benefit from less rock star culture and more predictable and best-in-class outcomes. *In business, an operationalized checklist is an automated process.* They are a series of actions that get done right every time.

Twenty years ago, IT teams could track the number of business applications they supported in a simple spreadsheet. They would use a few dozen apps at most. Today, the average company uses hundreds or even thousands of apps to keep their company running. There are now apps designed entirely for businesses to inventory and keep track of their applications.

This is a new era. With all these apps and data sources in our organization, *focusing on individual technologies and individual tasks neglects the bigger objectives of the company*. Driving tangible outcomes for the business requires thinking at the level of the end-to-end business process (or checklist), not the level of the app (or task). Those who transform entire processes rather than single tasks will emerge on top.

From Fractured Parts to a Connected Whole

You may recall an incident involving the container ship *Ever Given*, which seemed to stop the world when it got stuck in the Suez Canal for six days in March 2021. About 90 percent of all consumer goods travel by sea.[8] A ship getting stuck for six days might not seem like a long time, until you consider that for each day the *Ever Given* blocked traffic, it held up $10 billion worth of cargo.[9]

Supply chains are expansive, complex end-to-end processes that must be orchestrated in harmony to succeed. Broad-impact disasters like the *Ever Given* incident are uncommon, but smaller disasters like containers lost at sea, closed ports, or broken-down railways happen almost daily. In every case, they are tackled by logistics firms that need to get the goods and materials to their destinations.

As the route for a shipment changes, the interfaces each firm needs to interact with changes too. For example, containers may be moved from one ship to another, and suddenly the logistics firm needs to interact with a different shipping company. While the original shipping company may be a global conglomerate with sophisticated systems, the new shipper might be a smaller company that still relies on ancient email or even paper-based processes. Logistics firms never know who they are going to have to interact with and need to be prepared for all scenarios to keep the supply chain healthy.

One of the largest logistics railway firms in Germany recently searched for an approach to automation that would work for such a dynamic environment. For them, there was little value in automating a single task in their process. They work with hundreds of partners, each with a completely different method of interaction: the way one automates a task with one partner will not scale out to the others. Additionally, with such a dynamic, ever-changing environment, automating tasks one at a time is simply not a smart strategy. As they evaluated automation approaches, their goal was to focus on technology platforms that supported their entire process and allowed them to rapidly interact with the diverse requirements of other firms.

(continued)

(*continued*)

For example, many of their shipping partners are starting to roll out GPS tracking for containers. Each partner takes a different approach. On refrigerator containers, which already have electrical power, technologies such as GPS or Bluetooth are an option. On containers without a power source, RFID tags are used. Each of the shipping partners develop their own software to go with their chosen tracking technology. The railway company must be able to set up solutions for each of these options quickly. A similar story plays out across every partner the railway company interfaces with: customers, suppliers, transportation companies, truckers, and even manufacturers.

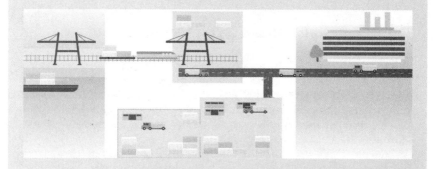

On top of all the complexity, the company has to offer software portals for their customers to track and book capacity. If a raw materials vendor is looking for capacity to ship their wares across the country, the railway needs to keep a competitive edge by offering an easy-to-use portal for booking. The business logic underlying such a program is extraordinarily complex.

"It's important to keep in mind that digital transformation shouldn't be seen as a plateau to be reached or some kind of end state," says the railway's head of IT, "rather, it is a state of transformation." This approach allows them to keep pace with the rapidly changing supply chain. It is important work. Modernizing the supply chain not only creates value for logistics companies, but it also has far-reaching implications for millions of people who rely on the supply chain for goods, jobs, and more.

It took a global pandemic for many businesses in logistics and beyond to shift their perspectives and put a process mindset in motion. But even as some pandemic pressures have eased, the need to evolve and react quickly in the face of change remains. Providing customers with reliable service in an unreliable world is what sets the winners apart.

The Integration Fragmentation

Our "there's an app for that" world means more specialized and purpose-built tools, but it also means we are slicing our companies into tiny parts. To stitch it back together, companies are forced to take a piecemeal approach to automation and surround themselves with a patchwork of tools.

Each of these tools can deliver specific discrete functionality well. Integration platforms (iPaaS) sync data between apps, extract, transform, load, and extract, load transform (ETL/ELT) loads data in bulk from apps into a data warehouse such as Snowflake, robotic process automation (RPA) automates the work of call center or invoice-processing staff, API management enables mobile or custom apps, business process management (BPM) automates onboarding workflows, and chatbots enable products such as Slack and Microsoft Teams to be a unified user experience.

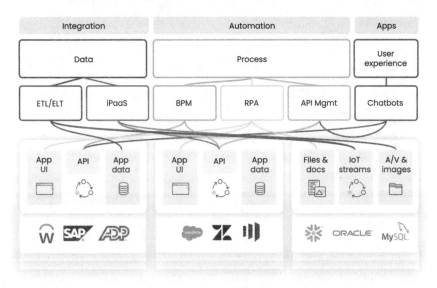

The figure above looks clean and tidy. The reality when this is deployed in our companies is much different. The next figure is a simplified view of a real company's deployment of integration technologies across their organization. Each of these tools integrated apps or data to address needs of specific projects and made sense at the time. Unfortunately, the technical term for this architecture is *a mess*.

Too many tools create point projects. These become islands of automation, disconnected from each other. Instead of creating a more connected enterprise, it has led to new silos. As a new generation of generative AI approaches are added to the stack, new silos may crop up.

In addition to the complexity, it also becomes hard to know the status of your core operating flows such as the status of orders. Which tool or underlying app do you investigate? In this environment, such a question creates anxiety for even the most seasoned technology leader.

Companies need a cohesive, unified foundation of data, workflows, and user experiences to be able to begin to drive successful transformation across their business.

Despite the massive investment in platforms, apps, and the corresponding experts, our productivity is not getting better. At the same time, employees are becoming more fatigued, and we're falling short on company results. It's time we recognize the missing piece in the enterprise and do something about it.

Automation and AI are not simply about saving a few hours; it's about bringing the big picture back into focus and rediscovering our productivity.

- The real value in automation is connecting all our apps and weaving together our existing investments. To solve the ever-growing problem of fragmentation across our processes, we need something that enables a holistic cross-functional view of the different processes that support our organizations.

- The real value of AI is a significant catalyst in accelerating this value chain. With generative AI you can build the code to connect to applications, you can design workflows to automate processes across them, use the large language models (LLMs) to understand and intelligently use the data to accelerate insights and decision making, and use a ChatGPT-like interface to enable everyone in the enterprise get answers to their questions—no more getting stuck waiting for help desk or any other person.

In this "process mindset" world, automation and AI with strong governance are the technical underpinnings to achieving end-to-end orchestration. It not only puts the pieces of our company back together into a cohesive whole but enables us to make a leap in productivity across the entire company. We explore this in detail in Part II of this book.

Orchestrating our systems is not enough. The ground is rapidly shifting in the market; change is constant, and uncertainty is the norm for every company. We need to be highly adaptable and malleable to leverage these changes to our benefit. In the next chapter, we look at how that plays out in companies with the growth mindset.

Later in this book, we cover the five key areas of every company that benefit from automation and AI. Each of these categories has major apps surrounded by ecosystems of thousands of smaller apps. With the new automation mindset, our companies will need to find a way to overcome fragmentation across each of these areas:

- **Front office:** the revenue-generating and customer-facing parts of the company. Important front office processes include lead management, sales operations, and deal desk.

- **Back office:** the operations that keep the company running, including finance and information technology. Important back-office processes include accounts payable, payroll processing, and security orchestration.

(continued)

(continued)

- **Customer experience:** how the customer perception of the company and product is captured and put into action. Important customer experience processes include customer 360, reporting, and product-led growth.
- **Employee experience:** how a company crafts and shapes the engagement and experience of their employees. Important employee experience processes include hire-to-retire, employee onboarding, and feedback capture.
- **Supplier and partner efficiency:** how a company works with suppliers and partners crucial to their business. Major supply chain processes include order-to-cash and procure-to-pay.

Notes

1. Senge, Peter M., 1990, *The Fifth Discipline*, New York: Penguin Random House.
2. Lohr, Steve, 2022, "Why Isn't New Technology Making Us More Productive?" *New York Times*, (May 24).
3. Brinker, Scott, 2021, "Wait, More Martech Tools Create More Manual Tasks?!" *ChiefMartec*, **https://chiefmartec.com/2021/04/martech-tools-manual-tasks/**.
4. Newport, Cal, 2016, *Deep Work*, New York: Grand Central Publishing.
5. Gawande, Atul, *Checklist Manifesto*, New York: Metropolitan Books.
6. Gawande, Atul, 2007, "The Checklist," *New Yorker,* (December 10).
7. "Is Air Travel Safer Than Car Travel?" *USA Today*, Accessed September 22, 2022 **https://traveltips.usatoday.com/air-travel-safer-car-travel-1581.html**.
8. OECD, n.d., "Ocean Shipping and Shipbuilding," last accessed September 22, **https://www.oecd.org/ocean/topics/ocean-shipping/**.
9. Clark, Aaron, 2021, "Suez Snarl Seen Halting $9.6 Billion a Day of Ship Traffic," *Bloomberg*, (March 24).

CHAPTER 3

The Growth Mindset

"An organization . . . might embody more of a growth mindset, conveying that people can grow and improve with effort, good strategies, and good mentoring."

—Carol Dweck

I n an environment of constant change, we are left with little choice but to embrace it. At any moment, customer demand, market dynamics, and other factors can shift. Groundbreaking AI technology, like ChatGPT, can burst onto the scene at any moment. When this happens, fixed or rigid processes are a liability. But some companies have embraced change as part of their processes and pulled ahead. Soon, every company will have to build processes for change.

Those who choose to embrace change have what psychologist Carol Dweck calls a growth mindset. While Dweck's writings primarily focus on individuals, she says that organizations can also have a growth mindset. They don't just adapt to challenges; they relish and eagerly welcome them.[1]

Built to Last vs. Built for Change

Over the last 30 years, video content has taken many forms. From antennas on our TVs to VHS cassettes and LaserDiscs, then MiniDiscs,

DVDs, BluRay, and now Netflix and TikTok. Many companies profited, and others catastrophically failed as a result of this constant evolution (do you know any Betamax fans?). Companies in the sprawling content ecosystem, such as Technicolor or MGM, have watched their business model continuously flip on its head.

Not every industry undergoes such a roller coaster, but the rate of change is increasing for everyone. Technology is to blame, as it spreads into every corner of the business. For companies everywhere, this constant change can be an opportunity or a destructive force. The difference in outcome is a direct result of whether an organization has a growth mindset.

Joey Wat, CEO of Yum China, describes it as continuous innovation: "I have always believed that the companies that survive and prosper in dynamic, competitive markets are not necessarily the strongest or the smartest; they're the ones that can respond quickly and adapt effectively to changing circumstances. That requires empathy for those we're serving, resilience, and creativity."[2]

Wat explains that agility and a continuous drive to innovate and improve outweigh many other factors. "In times of comfort, many companies stop innovating because they lack a sense of urgency, and as Professor Clayton Christensen demonstrated, in doing so they open themselves to disruption. In times of crisis, innovation is even more important, as the pandemic showed us. In my industry, the firms that quickly adopted new health and safety measures for employees to keep their restaurants open and designed new solutions like contactless ordering and pickup were the ones that came out stronger."

The growth mindset is not only about our ability to react to major events such as the pandemic, market downturns, or global supply chain issues. It's also about our response to everyday challenges that persist in our companies. We might have a new competitor entering the market, a customer who is unhappy, an employee morale issue, or a delay in an important project. Our businesses need to be equally as effective at responding to both daily challenges and company-threatening crises.

For most people in the average company, a growth mindset requires a big shift in thinking. However, it is not completely new to the business world. In fact, most IT teams and developers have been exposed to the principles of the growth mindset for the last 10 years, whether they realized it or not. Agile methodology, a popular approach to software development and project delivery, is behind many successful products we all know and love today.

The Value of Agile

Historically teams have relied on more rigid approaches to building solutions and delivering large-scale projects. This is typically referred to as waterfall-style management. These older methods involve up-front planning, sequential steps with siloed functional experts, and product or project delivery at the very end.

At its core, Agile is a method for expecting, managing, and embracing change. It divides tasks into short phases of work called "sprints." Scrum is a common form of Agile delivery where each sprint begins with a planning meeting. During the planning meeting the team members decide what each of them will work on during that sprint. The team then proceeds to work on their activities and concludes the sprint by demonstrating their respective progress to the rest of the team. This simple process enables the team to continuously assess what has been created to date, learn from it, and decide on the next best step. At every step, agile teams are testing their progress and determining if the original intended path forward is still the best one. In this way, Agile helps companies adapt to changes in the environment quickly while enabling innovation. The incremental progress minimizes risk by checking if we are on the right track frequently. We get to continuously check if the environment around us has shifted, resulting in a need to change approaches.

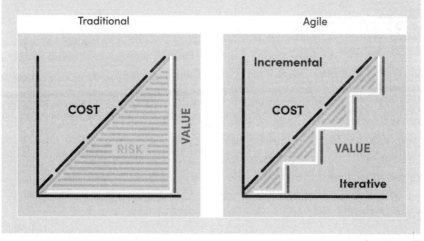

(continued)

(continued)

>   While Agile has made inroads in some companies, many business projects still happen waterfall-style. A great example of this is the difficult enterprise resource planning (ERP) implementations of the past that tested everyone's patience. Still today, major IT, HR, or finance projects can last six months to multiple years, making it feel as though our companies are moving at a snail's pace.
>
>   Perhaps one of the culprits for this lengthy delivery time is that processes are still managed sequentially:
>
> - Business managers have an idea.
> - They hand that idea off to IT.
> - The technology team develops it and then hands back a solution to the business to review.
>
>   From the time the idea was conceptualized to the point when a solution was implemented, months or even years have gone by. When the intended business outcome of that idea isn't achieved, we act surprised, and often a finger-pointing exercise ensues. We shouldn't be surprised. If ideas take months or years to be realized, it means that every decision made is on a massive delay. It is like trying to control a car with a 30-second delayed brake pedal—we pump the brakes, blow through the stop light, and end up in a ditch, because the response time was too slow. Today's markets are too unforgiving for this style of work.
>
>   Whether we want to call it the growth mindset or Agile, the evidence is clear: the old way of doing things is no path to a high-performing company. Rather, embracing change to continuously learn and innovate is the way of the future.

Process Variance vs. Adaptability

We've inherited much of our current thinking about process management from the days when all that mattered were people and things moving about in the physical world. We designed processes to optimize those moving parts. As old processes are brought into the digital age, we are finding they aren't as adaptable as they need to be, and it will continue to get worse in the new world of AI.

Since implementation or change of processes was expensive, we didn't think of them as flexible. In fact, the rigidity of a process was a feature, not a bug. We took comfort in the phrase "This is the process." Follow the process. Don't deviate from the process. We eliminated variance. But variance and adaptability are two very different things.

Eliminating variance with a fixed, repeatable process gives us a certain *internal* predictability. It's like a deterministic function, such as $y = x + 1$. Every time you plug in $x = 2$ as the input to that process, you'll get $y = 3$ as the output on the other side. (I assure you this will be the extent of the mathematics in this book.)

But it does nothing about *external* predictability, of which there's very little these days. We are operating in an environment of rapid and continuous change. Technology, competitive dynamics, and—most of all—customer behaviors and expectations are continually shifting around us.

Whether those changes are a threat or an opportunity largely comes down to adaptability. How quickly can we adapt our business to new circumstances?

Adapting our business means changing our processes. It doesn't work to have our old process of $y = x + 1$ take $x = 2$ and suddenly output $y = 5$. That would be chaos! Instead, we need to swap out $y = x + 1$ with a different process. Maybe a slightly modified one, $y = x + 3$. Or maybe an entirely new one, with additional steps and variables, $y = 2x^2 + 5z + 7$. (Okay, seriously, no more math equations. I promise.)

We still want this new process to be as predictable as the old one. But the key is that it's a *new process* that's been adapted to new circumstances.

And here's the beautiful thing: because almost all our processes today are—or can be—digital or digitally orchestrated, they are extremely malleable. It's bits, more than atoms, flowing through them.

Overbuilding the Swing Set

We like to say that when someone automates a process permanently, they "brought the skyscraper construction crew to build the swing set." It is a play on the famous tree swing analogy from project management and our way of (lightly) poking fun at the way many companies harden their processes.

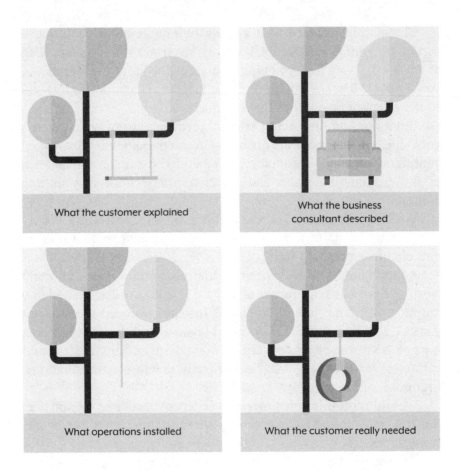

| What the customer explained | What the business consultant described |

| What operations installed | What the customer really needed |

Often, automation is solely owned by the IT department, and IT is called in on a by-request basis to automate activities or processes. It is a centralized operating model built around a service queue, where requests wait in line until someone has the time to take them on. This model involves experts with computer science degrees (and sometimes wizard hats) using complex and powerful technology to automate each process.

This model is the opposite of a growth mindset. It is a fixed mindset. It presumes that:

1. The technical capacity to automate our processes is a fixed, limited, and precious resource;

2. The precious resource of automation skills should not be wasted on maintenance or support of past projects;

3. The precious resource of automation skills should be carefully spent on the most important 1% of processes in the company.

It is not hard to see how this model encourages us to bring the sky-scraper crew to the swing set. We don't have time to change it later, so we build a swing set that will last for 100 years. IT teams know they need to get it right the first time. The automation specialists need to move on to the next project; otherwise, nothing will get done. The fixed mindset treats them as a scarce resource, creating an organizational bottleneck.

In a world of accelerating change, this fixed mindset is no longer effective, if it ever was. In fact, companies that want to win must run the opposite way from this approach. You never know when the rug will be pulled out from under your customers, your market, or your employees. Teams and processes must be ready to thrive in the world of new and ever-changing demands.

Wendy Pfeiffer, former CIO of several companies including Nutanix and GoPro, has shown how this can be done. She implemented a three-month process improvement cycle that applies to everything that the IT department touches. Every quarter, the organization spends an entire month assessing processes: gathering information, thinking about what can be improved, and looking for opportunities. The following month is for requirements gathering. This involves determining which approval steps are the most important, assessing security needs, and determining which steps can be eliminated. The final month is the build/rebuild phase, where the processes are torn down, rebuilt with automation at the core, and implemented/tested. In this way, every process in the Nutanix organization is undergoing continuous evaluation and change. No solution will be expected to last 100 years, because a culture of continuous improvement has been created. Therefore, teams focus on what is needed now, knowing that they can rapidly change course at any time.

When Stuff Hits the Fan

Business travel and expense management company Navan (formerly known as TripActions) had ambitious plans for 2020. With more than 3,000 customers, 2019 was a banner year for the company.[3] They had hired over 700 new employees and set their growth target for the following year at a "modest" 400%. Things were looking great for the first few months of 2020—that is, until March.

The Covid-19 pandemic had a disproportionate impact on different industries. Some ballooned, like video conferencing, home fitness equipment, and food delivery. Others cratered, like in-person dining, retail, and travel—especially corporate travel, as companies' duty of care responsibilities restricted the ability to allow employees to travel if they were unable to do so safely. The impact on each company was based on how dependent their business model was on in-person interactions. Unfortunately, Navan fell on the wrong side of that spectrum. Business travel evaporated. Their revenue projections quickly dropped by 95%. Their marketing budget and employee count got cut in half. Things were looking bleak. Their former CMO, Meagen Eisenberg, described it as a "wartime" experience.

Rather than crumble under pressure, Navan got to work on changing its business. They rapidly refocused how they could provide value to their customers. The company knew that employees—newly distributed—would need to be empowered to spend company money in new ways: for home office equipment, software subscriptions, and even food delivery. And so the company doubled down on Navan Expense, their spend management product. They quickly expanded the product's ability to process all employee expenses, not just travel. It turned into a huge success. Navan took a disaster and turned it into an opportunity. This is the growth mindset in action.

It wasn't only about the way they thought about the problem. Navan had also implemented the architectural underpinning of the growth mindset—plasticity. *This means that they implemented their automations in such a way that it didn't cement their existing processes into place and instead enabled them to refocus the team and the company.* We share the methods they used to achieve plasticity in an upcoming chapter. Without the speed and agility that their unique approach to automation afforded them, they would not have been able to rapidly refocus, and there would be no Navan today.

Navan is not the only story like this. Another great example is Airbnb, which quickly refocused on its core business and adapted its policies to address customers' new concerns about cleanliness and last-minute cancellations.[4] It takes a special type of grit for a company to overcome these kinds of challenges. It takes an organizational growth mindset: the willingness and ability to embrace the challenges as part of their very nature. To quote Airbnb's CEO Brian Chesky: "In a world that is fast changing, one of the things we know is that things that survive in the world are the things that are most adaptive. The things that are most adaptive are things that constantly change."[5]

The Growth Mindset in Action

It is all good and well to look at successful companies from the outside and say, "We should be like them!" But what does this look like in action? Let's take a closer look. Here, we see a quote-to-cash process showing the various systems and interactions from end to end.

This quote-to-cash example illustrates a company that has applied the process mindset from the previous chapter, thinking about automation beyond a single task.

- When a new quote is created by the account team in Salesforce, the quote immediately triggers a Slack notification for deal desk approval.

- Once the approvals are done and the customer has signed the contract, the completed Docusign leads to a new customer record being generated in the customer support platform (Zendesk in this case) and the ERP (SAP here).

- All along the way, the documentation is being saved, and the data is being updated for consistency throughout.

As the business evolves and uncovers new market segments, they might start to notice that quite a few nonstandard orders are coming in that simply don't fit the process. Perhaps the deal sizes are too large, and customers need multiple support requests and ERP record updates. If we were talking about a company with a fixed mindset where IT simply built the processes and left them to run for eternity, the teams involved in this process would be out of luck. They'd have to deal with whatever duct-taped solution they could muster.

In growth mindset companies, however, processes are built for change. In this example, the company added a human-in-the-loop step to route the nonstandard orders to the resident expert on the subject. Additionally, they've included an AI engine that continuously monitors the expert's actions, recognizes patterns, and generates the appropriate set of actions using generative AI. Apart from the nonstandard order patterns, it can also start recognizing patterns with delayed or non-approvals and start informing the people creating the orders to set expectations correctly. The possibilities of how the process can be improved are endless. All of this happens without the need for duct tape or a six-month IT project to adapt to the new order type.

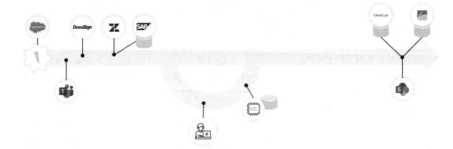

Perhaps, as the process continues and our hypothetical company grows, we realize that these large customers need a more white-glove, hands-on approach. So we add a series of steps for customers spending more than $400,000 annually to send alerts to the service and account teams, automate gifts of high-end wine, and enable a VIP field in Zendesk.

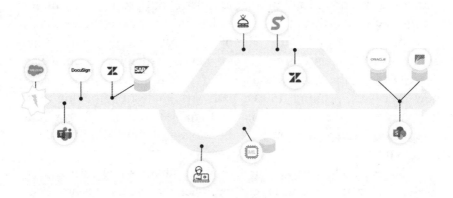

Leveraging a growth mindset, you see, the process evolves with the needs of the company but remains a highly efficient and results-oriented process. The process doesn't exist only in the minds of a few team members; it's well defined but still highly dynamic.

In her book *Mindset*, Carol Dweck writes that "our findings tell us that it's possible to weave a fixed or growth mindset into the very fabric of an organization to create a culture of genius or a culture of development. Everybody knows that the business models of the past are no longer valid and that modern companies must constantly reinvent themselves to stay alive. Which companies do you think have a better chance of thriving in today's world?"[6]

Dweck reminds us that we have a choice as company leaders. Either we can pursue what she calls a "culture of genius" that relies on a handful of rock stars to get the important work done, or we can implement processes and technologies that lead our organizations to take on the growth mindset, embracing change, challenge, and hard work. The choice is ours.

An Epic Scale of Change

Today, when we step back and look at the grand scale of processes that need to be automated, hundreds, and perhaps thousands of processes emerge. The sheer size of the opportunity can be hard to grasp.

So far, we have used psychology and the growth mindset to understand how our organizations should think about processes. To understand how we do this at scale, it is helpful to change the lens from psychology to neuroscience. One of the most exciting recent discoveries in this field is the concept of neuroplasticity. Neuroplasticity describes how the brain is constantly reinventing itself by wiring up new processes, pruning unused pathways, and strengthening existing ones over time. This trait is what enables us to learn, grow, and improve as human beings. It is the biological underpinning of the growth mindset.

I believe finding ways to make our companies neuroplastic, like the human brain, is a smart strategic choice for leaders. It is how companies like Navan, Airbnb, and Toast (from Chapter 1) were able to quickly break down and reform themselves in response to existential threats. In some ways this is a perfect fit for AI and automation. AI is built on the premise of learning from large sets of data, taking action, and then continuously monitoring for new things to adjust accordingly. As described in the order-to-cash example earlier, AI is a great way to monitor, visualize what is happening across all the processes in the organization, learn and inform the key stakeholders of the process as new patterns emerge, and even make adjustments to the automations in all the processes across the company.

Neuroplasticity hinges on the ability of the brain to be completely interconnected. In fact, research into cognitive decline has found that one of the first signs of the disease is that neurons stop flowing between the different portions of the brain, leading to a heartbreaking loss of function.[7] In the same way, impenetrable business silos are kryptonite to enterprise-wide automation strategies; if important data, such as customer data or product usage data, is trapped, AI will not be as effective and any related automations will suffer. Therefore, the growth mindset must be pervasive across the company and, when driven from the top, can actually be leveraged as a means to work with the silos in unity.

Many of today's businesses still have a rock star mindset, empowering the few, such as executives, or technologists, to determine how processes are automated and improved (if at all). But if our organizations are going to thrive in this volatile world, our business systems need to be neuroplastic, just like the human brain. We need to be able to adapt and react on the "neuron" level rather than at the executive level. The brain doesn't just think differently; it continuously remolds itself—and our organizations must do the same.

Notes

1. Dweck, Carol, 2007, *Mindset: The New Psychology of Success*, New York: Ballantine Books.
2. Wat, Joey, 2022, "The Ideas That Inspire Us," *Harvard Business Review*, (November), **https://hbr.org/2022/11/the-ideas-that-inspire-us**.
3. Shankman, Samantha, 2019, "2019: An Incredible Year at TripActions," *TripActions Blog*. (December 18), **https://web.archive.org/web/20220520071557/tripactions.com/blog/2019-an-incredible-year-at-tripactions**.
4. Yohn, Denise Lee, 2020, "How Airbnb Survived the Pandemic—And How You Can Too," *Forbes*, (November 10), **https://www.forbes.com/sites/deniselyohn/2020/11/10/how-airbnb-survived-the-pandemic--and-how-you-can-too/?sh=6612f96b9384**.
5. Manyika, James, 2021, "The 21st-century Corporation: A Conversation with Brian Chesky of Airbnb," *McKinsey & Company*, (July 23).
6. Dweck, Carol, 2007, *Mindset: The New Psychology of Success*, New York: Ballantine Books.
7. Jackson, Johanna, Enrique Jambrina, Jennifer Li, Hugh Marston, Fiona Menzies, Keith Phillips, and Gary Gilmour, 2019, "Targeting the Synapse in Alzheimer's Disease," *Frontiers in Neuroscience*, (July 23).

CHAPTER 4

The Scale Mindset

"The potential for employee-driven digital innovation . . . cannot be accomplished by small groups of technologists and data scientists walled off in organizational silos."

—Satya Nadella & Marco Iansiti

Automation is not a new concept. Most understand its value and are aware of ample opportunities for automation in their business. So what's stopping them? Why not automate every process in every corner of the business? Many leaders would say it's impossible.

Say a midsize company has 200 apps (a conservative estimate).[1] The company has 1,000 employees. Each employee uses three apps and three processes every day. The scale of processes in the company is some multiple of those numbers. It can come out to thousands of processes and subprocesses. The top processes have names and established checklists. Most others do not.

In most companies, nameless processes are manual ones. They typically exist only in the heads of the team members involved. These processes very rarely get automated. These can include:

- Data entry into the customer relationship management platform (CRM);
- Reporting on quarterly performance;
- Project requests between teams;
- And thousands more.

It would make no sense for an average IT team, which is understaffed and overworked, to prioritize these unnamed processes. As a result, only the most critical and high-profile processes in the company get automated. The remaining 99% of processes go unaddressed. When thinking about automation in the traditional way, this makes perfect sense. If an automation takes the IT team one month to build, and there are 1,000 processes to automate, the timeline to completion is just over 83 years.

The scale of need is out of sync with the available resources. In other words, *there is a scale problem with the traditional approach to automation.*

Working in the Shadows—Without IT

Eight in ten workers use software without IT team knowledge.[2] They have good intentions; they want to succeed, and the software they buy helps. This is not new. When laptops replaced desktops, offices provided wired internet but no Wi-Fi. Employees solved this by bringing in personal Wi-Fi routers and plugging them into the local network port. Mobility inside the office wasn't an IT priority at the time—so employees found their own solutions. These are examples of what is called shadow IT.

Shadow IT is a problem. In bad cases, it morphs into rogue IT, where employees use important business data in unauthorized ways. Sensitive data falling into the wrong hands can create even bigger problems. With the maturing of AI technologies, it is now becoming even easier to automate without IT help. All someone has to do is tell a generative AI tool what they want to automate, and the automation is created. On one hand, this helps accelerate how fast a company is able to transform itself. On the other hand, it increases the risk of sensitive data falling into wrong hands.

When business teams try to automate without IT team help, the shadow IT problem is a threat to your business. Unrestricted automation has enormous damage potential. From business outages to poor customer experiences to security and compliance issues, the possible impacts are serious. Undoing the damage can create significant technical debt that just adds more work to the IT team's extensive backlog, which compounds the strained relationship between IT and business teams.

As leaders, we see shadow IT as a problem to solve. But it is also a sign of an IT model that can't support what our companies need. Our business teams are trying to solve issues that are not IT team priorities, so they look elsewhere for answers. A change in mindset is needed to solve the root of the problem.

Transformation Cannot Be Limited to IT

In the past, companies tried to scale by adding more. They would add new people to the automation team or hire external consultants. Best practices suggest one IT expert for every 100 employees.[3] But continuously increasing headcount is not a realistic or cost-effective choice. The sheer number of processes means we can't ask a small handful of technical specialists to drive the automation revolution alone. There will never be enough specialists to keep up with demand.

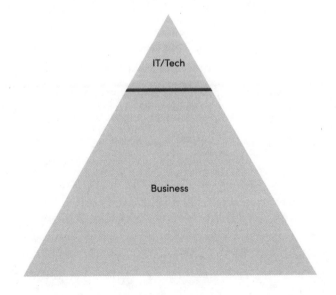

Business teams are creative, thoughtful, and eager to solve problems. In many instances, they are well versed in the data, applications, and business logic that underlie core processes in their domain. Collectively they know the vision and mission of the organization well. Each new generation that joins the workforce grows more technically savvy.[4] When business teams are not empowered to solve their problems, it is a lost opportunity. Business teams are a proverbial mountain of untapped potential for automation.

When IT teams own automation alone, shadow IT grows. Business teams step in to create automations themselves, often creating risk and technical debt for the company. As described above, this is going to further accelerate as generative AI technologies become more pervasive.

The automation opportunity looks like this pyramid. The IT team keeps the company alive, and creative people build in the shadows. Most automation potential remains untapped. Generative AI has the potential to invert this pyramid, but without proper controls it creates a big risk for all organizations. ChatGPT adoption is already showing signs of this; companies are devising strategies on what to do about it and how to protect their data. It has reached a point where some companies have even blocked access to it.

Keep the lights on

Shadow IT projects taken on by entreprenurial people

The rest of the opportunity

It's Time to Update Our Mental Model of Technical Skill

Many of us still separate workers into dated mental models: technical and non-technical. Apps and information systems managed through code, complex config files, command-line tools, and SQL queries have been the norm. These complex technologies required deep technical expertise and segregated specialists from the average business user.

People and technology have evolved. Tech literacy is growing, but technology is also more accessible. Packaged cloud offerings, self-service analytics tools, low-code/no-code, generative AI, and better user experiences have helped. Consumerization of enterprise software is underway.

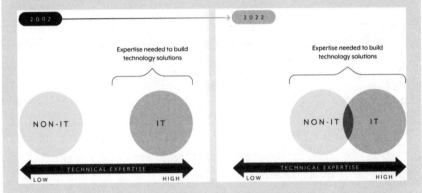

The technical gap between IT and non-IT is shrinking, yet our perception is still rooted in the world of 20 years ago. At the same time, IT and business alignment still need improvement. The "us vs. them" mentality between IT and the business may be part of the problem.

When thinking about technical expertise with this different perspective, it becomes clear that we may have a bigger pool of resources than we thought. This doesn't mean that Steve in accounting is going to be expected to start writing Python code tomorrow. But Steve will be able to use applications and AI to do his job better and faster. It means when we look at the work to be done and the types of expertise needed, we don't need deep technology specialists for every job. Yet, at some basic level, many business and technology leaders still believe we need to continue operating the way we did 20 years ago.

It is human nature to develop a scarcity mindset when critical resources run low. It's a natural human response to having very little of something important; it dominates our thinking. Researchers compare it to tunnel vision, where satisfying our needs becomes all that matters.[5] It is at the root of bad decisions, from unhealthy fast food when we are hungry to payday loans when we need quick cash. Studies show that our IQ goes down when we have a scarcity mindset.[6]

(continued)

(*continued*)

> After 20 years of managing scarce technical knowledge, scarce technical experts, and scarce IT team availability, we have a scarcity mindset in the enterprise. We are treating our technical expertise as a rare resource, only to be applied to the most important processes. We don't want to spread it too thin for fear that we will waste it.

Embrace Scale, Empower the Company

Steve Jobs once said: "People shouldn't have to ask management permission to do something. Authority should be vested in the people doing the work to improve their own processes, to teach them how to measure them, to understand them, and to improve them. They should not have to ask for permission to improve their processes . . . . [They] are in the best position to decide what should happen."[7]

The opposite of the scarcity mindset is the abundance mindset. In a business context, we'll call it the scale mindset. *It means embracing a new operating model that taps into the latent potential of the company.*

In a recent survey, Gartner found that "67% of CEOs want more technology work done directly within business functions."[8] Granting teams the ability to improve their work is crucial to reaching a company's full potential. It also creates a sense of ownership and pride for these team members, which ultimately results in more job satisfaction.

Imagine a rushing river held back by a dam. The river wants to go the path of least resistance, the fastest and surest, but the dam makes that impossible. By removing the dam and providing guardrails to direct the way the water flows downstream, companies can unleash the fast, powerful current of innovation.

Some IT teams and CIOs worry that removing the dam is a loss of control and an embrace of chaos. Words such as "democratization" and "citizen developer" trigger pained looks and trepidation. But as we'll explain in the democratization chapter, there is a big gap between a healthy democracy and total anarchy.

A scale mindset does not disempower the IT team. It raises its profile within the organization. Someone must step into an oversight and guidance role for quality, safe, and compliant automation. Business teams need to be empowered by training, consulting, mentoring, support services, and the right combination of technologies. The IT team is ideal for this. Rethinking technical expertise is not designed to replace them but elevate them as a steward of company potential. For example, rather than take the approach of creating a dam and blocking the use of AI and automation technologies, it provides the guardrails and oversight and enables the broader organization to utilize these technologies so it can unleash the overall organization to automate the 99% automation projects that otherwise will not see the light of the day. Central IT becomes less of an automation factory for business teams and becomes more of a service provider aimed to empower them.

Adopting the scale mindset will do more than expand a company's technical capacity—it can focus it. For most companies, this idea sounds like a pipe dream. The truth, however, is that many companies have already embarked on this journey and are seeing amazing results.

A Democratization Revolution

We would be wrong to assume that a scarcity mindset only affects traditional companies. Younger companies born in the cloud era also deal with these same challenges.

A large and successful marketing SaaS company recently experienced the tension of a classic IT and business falling out. Several major company-wide projects that IT had managed went poorly. There were cost overruns, long delays, and solutions that completely missed the mark. Trust between teams was low; IT and the business were barely on speaking terms. "We got to the point where the business was completely frustrated with the output," said one analyst. When IT built a project, support would be unavailable for months because of their deep backlog. The business teams felt like going to IT was a waste of time.

It seemed like the IT team chose their own priorities completely out of step with the company goals. Once, to the surprise of the company, the IT team announced that they built a new classroom training portal for customers. In the eyes of the business, not only was this a low priority, but it also didn't even make the list. It was a project no one had asked for. Within months, the new portal had issues that needed support, but the IT team had moved on to other projects.

When the business needed something done, they often worked around IT and purchased shadow IT tools. They felt it was justified, and after all, out-of-the-box native integrations and their shadow IT integration tools seemed to be getting the job done. This approach blew up in their faces when, at some point, someone connected a database with sensitive customer data to an external-facing spreadsheet. Customer names, email addresses, phone numbers, and addresses started pouring out in public for the world to see. It was a technical blunder— one that the IT team would have never made.

Leadership recognized the problem. In response, they formed a completely new automation team. The team's short-term goal was to ease the pressure for automation projects around the company. Their medium-term goal was to restore the broken relationship between the IT and business teams. Their ultimate goal was to help the company reach a new level of overall performance.

The new automation team's first order of business was to find an automation platform. They chose a low-code/no-code option that was easy to use regardless of technical knowledge. But the new team resisted the urge to open a service queue and start taking automation requests right away. Instead, they began by offering a class. They invited people from around the business and members of the IT team. Everyone who graduated received a license to automate.

Over time, this class became a cornerstone of the company culture. This team of only a few people created a path to automate hundreds of processes around the company. They did this by opening a path for employees to automate their processes. With a little education and guidance, hundreds of team members began building their ideas.

The automation team also created the infrastructure that an automation program at scale would need. The infrastructure included error handling, use of AI technologies through custom-built connectors for approved AI applications, and operations frameworks. To avoid catastrophes, they developed a process called the automation review pipeline. Every automation created by the business had to be reviewed and approved before it went live.

Eventually, the automation team grew into a center of excellence with two sub-teams. One supported internal, business-facing teams, such as HR, finance, IT, and security. The other supported revenue-facing teams, such as sales, services, and marketing. The teams were relentless in finding ways to empower the organization, whether through training, infrastructure, governance, or other means.

Without automating a single process, the automation team made a big impact. A few months into the program, they were receiving up to 20 automation review requests *per day*. Between 70% and 80% of the projects in the company were being automated by teams who weren't made up of deep technical specialists. The company's growth during this time also improved from a recent plateau.

The leadership noted the relationship between IT and the business was improving. Morale seemed to be picking up. The IT team even asked the business for help on certain automation projects.

Imagine if this company had continued its original path. How much potential would have gone unused? This is not some edge case or strange exception. *Every company can reach a point where people outside the few technical specialists are automating 80% of the projects. It takes a different mindset—a scale mindset—to get started. Once it takes hold, even the most skeptical IT veterans see the future is not in asking for higher headcount.*

Democratization is a big idea. It is trendy and at times controversial, but it can work. What played out in the marketing SaaS company happens all the time in companies that embrace the new automation mindset. But we can't just give business teams access and hope things work out for the best. We need to enable democratization with the right technology. Only then can we bring everyone on board.

The New Automation Mindset: Making It Happen

We've reached the end of Part 1 of this book. For each concept you have learned about in Part 1, there is a matching architectural underpinning in Part 2. Here, we will recap the concepts of the last three chapters to set the stage for the next three chapters.

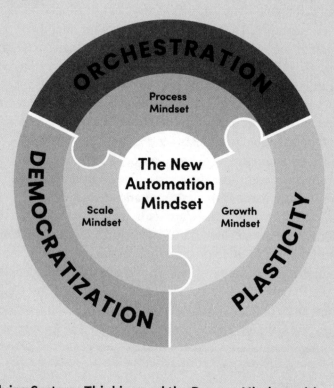

Applying Systems Thinking and the Process Mindset *with Orchestration*

In Chapter 2, we learned that many companies feel stuck because they use complex tools that automate tasks. To overcome the problems of automating tasks, we need a *process mindset*.

So how do we make sure we don't get stuck in task-centered thinking? In Chapter 5, we'll learn about *orchestration*. It is the technical underpinning of the process mindset, which enables our teams to use systems thinking to address the underlying business objectives of the process.

Like an orchestra needs a conductor, our businesses need an orchestration engine to bring end-to-end processes into harmony. With orchestration, we interweave the complex set of system actions, user experiences, and data that are the lifeblood of every process. The results multiply the existing investments we've made in both applications and even our existing automation tools.

Embracing Change with the Growth Mindset *via Plasticity*

In Chapter 3, we learned we need to embrace change in our processes with the *growth mindset*. It should be easy for our automated processes to change as fast as the market demands. In other words, our businesses should work like neuroplastic brains—wiring and rewiring processes all the time.

How do we support that dynamism? In Chapter 6, we'll learn about *plasticity*, the technological underpinning that allows us to continuously adapt, learn, and at times fundamentally rewire processes.

Achieving the Scale Mindset *with Democratization*

In Chapter 4, we learned that companies have people with all kinds of skills that can be directly applied to automating what we do. We need to apply the *scale mindset* to see the untapped potential and chart a path for business and IT teams to build the future.

There is a caveat, however: without a strong system of governance, scaling automation can quickly become anarchy instead of a democracy. We need guardrails to ensure security, scalability, change controls, compliance, and other such requirements are met. In Chapter 7, we talk about the technical underpinning for *democratization*.

If you have read this far, you have a solid grasp of the concepts that will guide unstoppable companies in the new era. Let's dive into Part 2 to understand how.

Accelerating Orchestration, Plasticity, and Democratization with AI

In Chapter 1, we talked about how important it is to refine the raw power of generative AI with governance and an execution engine. We'll touch on this execution engine in Part 2 and more in-depth in Part 4. But it is not a simple task—governance, for example, can take many forms. It needs security, access controls, privacy, and scalability to work. An execution platform should be versatile, powerful, and transparent.

Each key element of an enterprise AI platform aligns to the three architectural underpinnings of the new automation mindset.

(continued)

(continued)

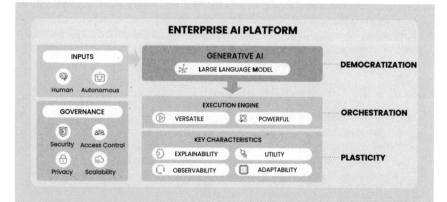

As shown above, generative AI is the best way to remove the "dam" that currently limits democratization, but it needs a way to control the rapid flow of innovation through strong governance and input mechanisms. Furthermore, it needs an orchestration engine that is as versatile and powerful as the AI itself, to keep up with the free form and limitless influx of blueprints coming out of generative AI. Lastly, this new generation of AI platforms will need to bring levels of plasticity never seen before at this scale, where people can not only understand what is being generated by AI but where there is a continuous feedback mechanism through which the AI is constantly evolving with the business needs.

We'll take a closer look at a model for AI in the enterprise in Chapter 7 and Chapter 15.

Notes

1. Torres, Roberto, 2021, "Enterprise app sprawl swells, with most apps outside of IT control," *CIODive*, **https://www.ciodive.com/news/app-sprawl-saas-data-shadow-it-productiv/606872/**.
2. Julio, Scott, 2020, "21 Shadow IT Management Statistics You Need to Know," G2, **https://track.g2.com/resources/shadow-it-statistics**.
3. Willett, Josh, 2022, "How big should my IT team be?" *Microbyte* (June 13), **https://www.microbyte.com/blog/how-big-should-my-it-team-be/**.
4. Marks, Gene, 2021, "Gen Z workers Are More Confident, Diverse and Tech-savvy but Still Lack Experience," *The Guardian* (December 5), **https://www.theguardian.com/business/2021/dec/05/gen-z-workers-confident-diverse-tech-savvy**.

5. Novotney, Amy, 2014, "The psychology of scarcity," American Psychological Association, *Monitor in Psychology* 45 (2), **https://www.apa .org/monitor/2014/02/scarcity**.

6. Vedantam, Shankar, 2017, "How The 'Scarcity Mindset' Can Make Problems Worse," *NPR: Hidden Brain*, **https://www.npr .org/2017/03/23/521195903/how-the-scarcity-mindset-can-make-problems-worse**.

7. American Society for Quality, 2014, "Steve Jobs on Joseph Juran and Quality," YouTube Video, **https://www.youtube.com/watch?v= XbkMcvnNq3g**.

8. Gartner, 2022, "The Future of the CIO as Technology Expands Beyond IT," Webinar, **https://www.gartner.com/en/webinar/451515/ 1064033**.

PART 2

Architectural Underpinnings

CHAPTER 5

Orchestration

"The conductor of an orchestra doesn't make a sound. They depend, for their power, on their ability to make other people powerful."

—Maestro Benjamin Zander

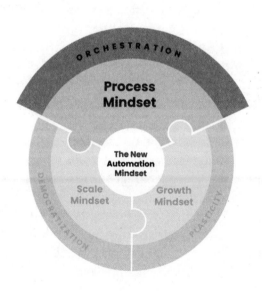

Health care is high stakes, and medical staffing firms deal with very complex processes. While their goals are like the average recruiting firm, clinician placement is more complicated. A company called Vituity makes it look easy. Their approach to physician onboarding and credentialing is a process automation masterclass we can all learn from, but it didn't start out that way.

"Our physicians see about seven million patients every year. Our core product is human—that is, clinicians providing care to people," says Vituity CIO, Amith Nair. "Our number one goal is that a physician is hired and staffed, ready to serve the community on day one." Clinician staffing involves hundreds of emails, actions, and data movements over four to six weeks. "Our rate-limiting factor was our legacy system and how we were not orchestrating any of our processes from end to end," said Nair. "So it would take anywhere between 700 to 1,500 hours to staff a single physician. We weren't looking at the process end to end, so we had to improvise."

It's enough to make any technology leader's head spin. It gets worse: Any delay means a hospital, emergency room, or ICU goes understaffed, which means patients either wait or receive inadequate care. "It's a life-or-death situation. Our product has to work on day one; there's no more testing. You cannot revert the code or anything to that effect. Our physicians have to be truly at the location, present, and providing care because the emergency room is one of the toughest areas in the hospitals."

The process is an automation opportunity. But there is something deeper at work. In Chapter 2, we talked about replacing task thinking with process thinking. That encourages us to look at the entire process and ask how to improve it from start to finish. For Vituity, applying the typical task-focused automation approach is not enough. Automating one or two steps out of hundreds may save some money, but it's not going to make a meaningful impact on the end goal. Additionally, if changes to a few tasks inadvertently break another part of the process, patients will be at risk. The stakes are too high. For these reasons, Vituity chose to apply process thinking to orchestrate everything. They unlocked their business when they chose to stop thinking about automation in the context of individual tasks and focused instead on how they could use automation to change how they do business.

Approaches to Automation

Automation is a broad term. In business processes, automation takes different forms. Each leads to different outcomes. In this section, we explore the task-based, straight-through, and orchestration approaches.

Task-based Automation

Task-based automation is where a company looks for single discrete tasks usually performed by a single role in the company and automates them. The goal is to free up employee time so they can focus on other activities.

If Vituity used a task-based approach, it would single out a few steps in its long staffing process and focus on automating those steps. They have plenty of opportunities: email attachment downloads, message templates, or spreadsheet uploads. The outcome would have been measured in hours saved on the task.

Task-based automation is great for quickly saving some time or removing a bottleneck from an existing process. The problem, however, is that it will never result in achieving the larger transformation potential we can achieve when rethinking an entire process through the lens of automation.

Straight-through Processing

For many years, straight-through processing (STP) was the pinnacle of automation. STP means processing records or transactions from start to finish with no human touch. The term has been around since the 1970s. In cases with thousands of transactions every minute, like payments, STP is a great fit. If task-based automation is microscale, straight-through processing is system scale. The technology takes over the entire process across systems and is designed to require no manual intervention.

Phrases such as "the autonomous enterprise" are popular, but STP is not the best approach for every process. Most business processes, when looked at end-to-end, still require people in some way to handle exceptions, make decisions, provide creative inputs, etc. Companies that embrace the "fully automated" (only STP) mantra sometimes tarnish their brands. In customer service, for example, people still prefer to work with other humans. We must recognize that people will always play a vital role in our processes. Our final destination as companies is not to become a vending machine. STP is best left for processes where speed is of the essence, but human expertise is not.

Orchestration

Orchestration coordinates people, software, and data in end-to-end processes to get jobs done. With orchestration, people—customers, employees, or partners—are still key components of the process where their strengths are needed most.

Orchestration is the pinnacle of automation. It allows our people and technology to maximize their respective strengths. Tech, especially AI, is able to interpret large sets of data across the entire process and even build a template for the ideal end-to-end orchestration, but people are best at creative tasks or nonstandard exception handling. Orchestration holds technology, human expertise, and automation in balance, maximizing outcomes for the company.

Incorporating orchestration into our automation strategy does not mean we throw away our task-automation tools or stop striving for STP where it makes sense. Orchestration helps us weave these approaches in where they make the most impact. It also helps to activate the process mindset in our teams. *By stepping back and thinking through how to orchestrate the end-to-end process, the appropriate uses of task-automation and STP will naturally fall into their ideal places.*

Orchestrating business processes means more than simply being great at the "happy path" of doing business when everything goes as planned. The military term "fog of war" seems appropriate for the unpredictable journey every company is navigating. Unexpected events are the norm in war. If we are not able to assess, respond, and adjust, we will lose the battle.

Southwest Airlines (SWA) employees probably felt like they were at war during the 2022 winter holidays. At that time, SWA experienced a complete meltdown, reaching over 80% of flight cancellations for more than a week.

This was shocking. SWA leads the industry in customer satisfaction and efficiency. Deploying a unique point-to-point operational strategy, SWA is known for friendly service and on-time flights while maintaining profit and record growth. They also run the fastest turnaround times in the business.

What happened? Their infrastructure was primarily optimized for the "happy path," where everything goes to plan, with minor disruptions. It wasn't set up to orchestrate an exception-handling process robust enough for the order of magnitude of disruptions the winter storm caused.

This is called IRregular OPerationS (IROPS), a standard term in the airline industry dealing with anything that impacts normal operations, including events like crew calling in sick, aircraft maintenance problems, and extreme weather conditions. To optimize recovery, SWA "Integrated Operations" needs lots of data points in one place. Orchestration can bring together that data from many different business systems silos:

- Flight;
- Passenger;
- Crew (pilot, flight attendant, airport staff, maintenance);
- Bags;
- Aircraft;
- Gates/stations etc.

Informed recovery decisions can then be made considering all possible impacts as well as ripple effects. Any decision (SWAP, DELAY, or CANCEL) has customer impacts, financial impacts, and compliance and regulatory impacts and has to take into consideration:

- Customer compensation cost;
- Aircraft utilization cost;
- DOT arrival penalty;
- Total customers impacted;
- Total customer delay minutes.

As visualized, ripple effects are especially complex for SWA, which operates with multi-leg routes. The trip from SFO-DAL-MEM has a problem in the SFO-DAL leg and is impacting the DAL-MEM leg needing a decision to be made to SWAP a new aircraft or DELAY the flight or even CANCEL the flight.

(continued)

(continued)

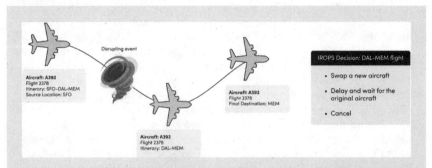

Making good recovery decisions will also benefit from orchestrating bidirectional communication with staff in the field to gather their local intelligence. Once an exception decision is made, orchestration is needed to populate the adjustments to all different business systems. This also includes orchestrated exception communication to pilots, crew, gate agents, and customers to make them aware of changes.

With robust exception process orchestration for a major disruption event, SWA would have had a much better chance to get back on track when bad weather caused havoc. However, while industry-leading at executing the "happy path," they lacked the orchestration approaches to handling a major exception event and thus lost the "winter storm battle."

The Jobs to Be Done

Good automation strategies consider outcomes for everyone involved. The late Harvard Business School professor Clayton Christensen said, "If you understand the experiences you need to provide customers, that tells you what you need to integrate and how you have to integrate it in order to provide experiences to get the job done."[1] We should start from the experience and work backward toward the technology. Task-based automation and STP look for ways to apply technology to a process. Orchestration asks how to get the job done best with every resource available.

Consumers don't buy a quarter-inch drill bit; they buy a quarter-inch hole. Similarly, they don't take Uber for the joy of riding but rather to reach their destination. Christensen's "jobs to be done" theory that we mentioned in the introduction is a helpful way to understand how this plays out in companies. Needs (or jobs) crop up in companies, and they hire a person or technology to fulfill those needs. Companies need to manage the sales process, so they buy a customer relationship management platform (CRM). They need to manage job candidates, so they buy recruiting software. These are all jobs, and the company is "hiring" software to get them done.

Christensen says doing a job "more easily, conveniently, or affordably" is the heart of disruptive innovation. It enables a disruptor to "imagine how to improve its product to appeal to more and more customers."[2] Orchestration is a means to that end: finding better ways to do jobs for your customers. Task automation and STP look inward to cut costs, but orchestration looks outward at business outcomes. Efficiency is still a natural side effect of orchestrating better ways to get jobs done. With orchestration, we get both improved business outcomes and greater efficiency.

The job Vituity does for customers is placing great physicians in critical locations to improve patient care. Improving the job means making hiring experiences as frictionless as possible. Vituity's disruptive innovation is being more efficient than their competitors in a complex, slow-moving market. To get this job done for their customers, they now orchestrate every process ingredient from start to finish. The ingredients fall into three categories: people, process, and data.

People	Processes	Data
Clinicians/doctors	Hiring	Contract masters
Employees	Credentialing	Employee masters
Hospital administrators	Negotiations	Site masters
	Site start-up	
	Back office	

Orchestration's Building Blocks

People, process, and data are orchestration's most basic building blocks. It's a subtle twist on the classic "people, process, and technology" IT model. End-to-end business processes—such as employee onboarding—always involve all three. These ingredients are intertwined and linked to one another. For employee onboarding you could break it down as follows:

- **People:** The new hire needs to review and sign their employment contract and tax documents. The manager needs to provide input on the apps they'll need. The HR team may need to handle questions or exceptions.

- **Process:** As a new employee is hired, there are many dependencies, and these form a process. For example, we don't want to order a laptop for the employee until we have confirmed their start date. Their payroll should not be activated until their first day. Setting their access and applications may be dependent on input from their manager. All these activities and business dependencies must be initiated at the right time, under the appropriate conditions, and only when the previous necessary steps have been completed.

- **Data:** The new employee will have an HR record, a payroll record, a system account, application accounts, equipment orders, contracts, and many other associated data. All this data needs to be created or updated as they progress through their onboarding journey.

By orchestrating the entire process, Vituity cut hiring time in half for new physicians, from four weeks down to two weeks. Employees take pride in placing 2,000 physicians in hospitals every year. More patients now have access to the care that they need. Vituity establishes a sustainable business advantage with a hiring process that is orders of magnitude more frictionless and efficient.

Amith Nair compares orchestration to the brain and a central nervous system in the human body: "It's the digital nervous system that's flowing data from one system to the other system so that we can actually get our physicians practicing medicine at the hospital in less than 60 days."

Technical Capabilities Required for Orchestration

The word "orchestration" is popular in the tech space. We see it used for microservices, infrastructure provisioning, devops, and more. When we discuss orchestration here, it is specifically in the context of business process automation. It encompasses another term related to process automation: workflows. While workflows are finite, orchestration is infinite. When we understand this, we see some of the key technical capabilities we need from an automation platform to act as an orchestration engine:

1. Event-driven workflows;
2. The ability to combine human and system actions;
3. Interoperability with other specialized automation tools;
4. AI to monitor, learn, and improve the workflows.

As we discuss later, event driven architecture (EDA) is a foundational element of orchestration. When we look at business processes, we see a complex web of different business events that result in a series of actions. An orchestration engine helps to remove this complexity by coordinating a set of event-driven workflows toward achieving the larger objective. These tools need a strong foundation built on events and the ability to interact with various event and messaging solutions (such as Kafka or SQS).

Simply coordinating event driven workflows would result in only straight-through processing (STP) solutions. Therefore, the orchestration engine also requires the ability to easily layer in:

- AI technologies to continuously read, interpret log data, detect anomalies and bottlenecks, and notify humans to take action;
- Human actions such as reviews, approvals, forms, make changes, and more.

While task automation is not the goal, it is required for steps in the process. Many orchestration platforms will also be able to automate tasks; however, there will always be cases where specialized automation tools will be required for specific steps in the process. An orchestration platform should not aim to be the one tool for everything (as this is unrealistic); it should instead provide the ability to interoperate with existing automation tools. By helping companies get more out of their existing tools, the new automation mindset allows us to maximize the investments we have already made in technology.

An Enterprise's Central Nervous System

Earlier in this book, we talked about neuroplasticity, the brain's ability to change its structure in response to new information and experiences. But the design of the brain is just the beginning. How our minds connect to our muscles to make our body move is amazing. It is also a great way to understand how orchestration should work. The brain triggers the process, sending a signal through the central nervous system. The body responds by moving. It operates on a constant feedback loop from body to brain, which adjusts based on feedback from the nerve endings around the body. With this simple flow, we accomplish incredible feats: think about cellist Yo-Yo Ma, or Olympic gymnast Simone Biles. Behind their greatness is a central nervous system trained to orchestrate their bodies with stunning precision.

Companies have countless software tools, but most make for better muscles than brains. Function-specific apps such as CRMs and ERPs play their designated roles. Some automation tools are built for task automation. Others are made for straight-through processing. Very few can orchestrate the entire people, process, and data ecosystem. A brain is required to bring it all together.

In the enterprise, some refer to the brain as their "orchestration layer." A proper orchestration layer has been the vision of middleware vendors for years. The idea was something like the motherboard we saw in computer hardware in the early days. That vision created the middleware market in the 1990s. Today, various integration and automation technologies have converged to make orchestration layers a reality. This new class of tool is called an enterprise automation platform, which we cover in more depth in Chapter 17.

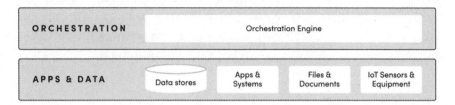

Grab, a ride-hailing service and the largest technology start-up in Southeast Asia, was no stranger to automation. Luiz Enriquez, their former CIO, shared his thoughts with me on the power of an orchestration layer:

"The whole concept of an orchestration layer is to empower a front end that everyone enjoys, like Slack. The orchestration layer is in the middle, and it talks to the back end. Today, the back end could be SAP, tomorrow it could be Oracle; it doesn't matter. Even if I decided to remove Slack and go to platform X, it is no big deal because I have my orchestration layer."

Usually, changing out ERPs, CRMs, and other core platforms is painful. Enriquez took an orchestration approach, leading to better outcomes. We should build all companies like this. It is an architecture where we orchestrate processes, ensure our data is up to date, and provides a seamless experience for employees. Everything working together to get customer jobs done. We expand on this in the next chapter.

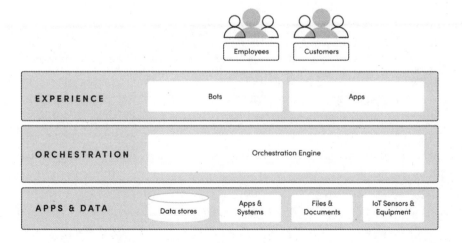

Perhaps we aren't all working with the same life-or-death gravity as Vituity, but all our work affects people's careers, lives, and well-being. Every employee is most satisfied when they are empowered and enabled to do their best work—the work they are most effective at. And when they're at their best, the customer experiences the very best of your business. That's exactly what orchestration can do.

Notes

1. Christensen, Clayton M., Taddy Hall, Karen Dillon, and David S. Duncan, 2016, "Know Your Customers' 'Jobs to Be Done,'" *Harvard Business Review* (September), **https://hbr.org/2016/09/know-your-customers-jobs-to-be-done**.
2. Ibid.

CHAPTER 6

Plasticity

"Evolve solutions; when you find a good one, don't stop."

—David Eagleman, neuroscientist

We want our companies to do better than survive tough times; we want them to thrive. Research suggests if a company is ever going to outpace a competitor, it is twice as likely to happen during a downturn.[1] Thus, we need to build antifragile systems that thrive under stress.

Strengthening muscles is a good example of this in action. When we hit the gym to lift weights, the fibers of our muscles tear and break down. They heal and rebuild, growing larger and stronger. Muscles are antifragile because stress, shock, and challenge makes them better.[2]

Neuroscientists found that our brains, like our muscles, are also antifragile. When challenged and trained, our brains tear down and rewire neural processes. For example, London cab drivers have to learn a very complex city road system in order to effectively do their job. Anders Ericsson, whose research inspired Malcolm Gladwell's book *Outliers*, scanned their brains before and after training. He found that parts of their brains grew larger after training, just like a muscle.[3] Other researchers discovered the same outcome in classical musicians.[4]

In the previous chapter, we explored the analogy of the brain and central nervous system with orchestration. The analogy extends to how our entire companies should work. Like brains, our companies should grow and rewire in response to challenges. Unfortunately, that's not typical. Market challenges are growing, but company processes can't keep up with the new rate of change. Processes are rigid. It takes eons to make even the smallest change. In this climate, a rigid company is a dying company. It will be hardest hit during tough times and go extinct at the first sign of disruptive innovation. Our brains use plasticity to thrive in challenges. Our companies need plasticity too.

"Plasticity is the capacity of cells or organisms to vary their properties or behavior when environmental conditions change."[5] What would happen if we built our company processes to operate like this? We would:

- Thrive despite external pressures from the economy or competition;
- Quickly refocus during times of internal organizational turmoil;
- Continuously improve to identify new and unique ways of meeting objectives;
- Enter new markets, maximize efficiency, create amazing customer experiences, develop innovative products and services, and more.

Unfortunately, companies with these traits—with plasticity— are rare.

The Rigid Company

I've encountered numerous companies over the years that all have a very similar story with regards to plasticity. In order to protect the innocent, I've combined a few of these true stories into this hypothetical tale.

Alice recently joined an energy trading company. She took over the role from another trader named Joe, who recently left the company. Part of the role is forecasting demand for energy across different regions. When demand spikes, they sell energy for a premium. It has a significant bottom-line impact, so Alice was excited to take it on.

She learned that the company's demand estimate processes were manual. For example, weather events were researched on forecast sites and pasted into spreadsheets for each region. Alice had a hunch that machine learning and public weather databases might be able to save some time. She figured they could automatically generate energy demand estimates, increasing efficiency. Better yet, they would be more accurate from a real-time weather data feed. It seemed like a great chance to make an impact.

Alice started by asking her boss if he would be supportive of the idea. He said her predecessor (Joe) tried the same thing but ran into problems with IT. He ended up building some scripts on his own to partially solve the problem, but when he left, no one else understood them. Alice found Joe's scripts, but she couldn't figure them out either. With no alternative, she continued with her plan to reach out to IT.

After the long process to submit an IT request with an attached business case, she waited. Eventually, after some more waiting, she got an update. Her request was routed to the architecture team. They were trying to decide whether to use RPA, the enterprise service bus, their ETL tools, or if they needed custom code. After three weeks, she was finally referred to the custom solutions team. The other automation tools either weren't the right fit or the teams that supported them had too many high priority projects. The custom solutions team quoted Alice a minimum of 18 months to deliver the project due to the complexity and limited resource availability.

Alice now understood why her predecessor avoided IT, built scripts, and eventually left. If she had to wait 18 months for a solution, the forecasting approach she was planning might be outdated. If she had to make changes later, it would mean updates to the custom code and likely another multi-month project. She wasn't even sure she would still be at the company in 18 months. Investing all this time and money into a rigid one-time solution made no sense. Discouraged, Alice continued her job, manually updating the forecasts.

IT is not the villain in this story. They are doing their best to deliver with the resources they have. Building automation solutions that can also harness the power of AI or machine learning tools, such as the example above, takes time and scarce expertise. IT is in constant demand, and they need to prioritize and manage their resources. They are put in the awkward position of telling Alice to wait for something valuable, simply because it is less valuable than other requests they are working on. Their arsenal of cutting-edge integration and automation tools made no difference. IT wants to help Alice, but their hands are tied.

Many IT teams will put a heavy emphasis on their integration or automation architecture. They value traits such as decoupling and reusability. While these are good values, reusability does not always lead to agility. Companies create libraries and ecosystems of reusable APIs, code, and event streams. Yet, simple changes to their processes and associated automations are still slow and difficult. While the APIs are reusable, the orchestration and underlying connectivity are cemented into place. These now become the bottleneck. An architecture view of the problem might look something like this:

RIGID WORKFLOW	Point-to-Point Solutions	Complex Middleware	Event Routing	Static Workflow Engines

DATA ARCHITECTURE	APIs & Microservices	Data Warehouses and Data Lakes	Business Event Streams

RIGID CONNECTIVITY	Custom API Clients	Ad-hoc Scripts	Custom Code	RPA Bots

APPS & DATA	Data Stores	Apps & Systems	Files & Documents	IoT Sensors & Equipment

MANUAL & REACTIVE USER ENGAGEMENT

Employees   Customers

So often, we explain how companies should work using analogies to machines. We should create "growth engines" or run like a "well-oiled machine." Yet that is the problem: We have designed our companies like rigid mechanical engines. One broken component brings the entire system down. Simple changes need months of planning and experts with specialized tools. This is the opposite of plasticity. This is rigidity.

Less Machine, More Brain

Alice's project is one example of thousands of impactful improvements waiting to be made in every company. If the company worked like a brain, it would quickly prototype the idea and continuously improve it over time. With each challenge, the process gets better. When done at scale, the company can grow stronger regardless of the circumstances.

Alice was not the CEO. She was not in a leadership role. This idea for change did not come from a central command center, it came from the rank and file. Alice and others in the business know the most about the "jobs to be done" in the company. They are in the best position to evolve and improve their processes. Plasticity requires ideas for improvement at all levels of the organization to be rapidly tested and integrated. *Plasticity isn't simply the ability of an organization to change; it is its ability to continuously change at all levels, all at once.*

Breaking the Mold

Plasticity needs an automation architecture. But it is not all about technology; it is about the people, too. Countless tech categories claim to be the silver bullet for automation. Yet the IT team in Alice's story had the latest tools, and the results were still unworkable. The automation strategy overemphasized technology at the expense of the people.

To adopt the new automation mindset, companies need both technical and organizational excellence. Seeing new technology as a cure-all is like wondering why frozen lasagna tastes the same when baked in a new oven. The chef, the recipe, and the tools all play an equal role in the results. Our automation technologies must operate in lockstep with the operating model, and this requires the right strategy. Enterprise automation is our recommended strategic approach to achieve plasticity. We cover enterprise automation in depth in Part 4; however, here we focus on the components of this strategy that specifically help the organization achieve plasticity.

The three key components organizations must include in their automation strategy are:

1. **Composable capabilities:** allowing teams to turn automations into the building blocks of our organization;
2. **AI-assisted orchestration:** the ability to rapidly connect our building blocks to achieve end-to-end outcomes either manually or through assisted AI;
3. **Flexible experiences:** enabling people to interact and participate in our workflows without requiring long development cycles.

While the concepts of plasticity extend beyond these areas, these components are where we recommend companies first look to eliminate rigidity. Most organizations will find that by focusing here, they will significantly improve business agility and plasticity.

Composable Capabilities

Readers of Gartner research will be familiar with composition, or the "composable enterprise." With composition, apps and data are like building blocks that can easily be combined to create different solutions. We reorder or reconnect them in different ways as our business and market changes. Gartner calls these building blocks packaged business capabilities (PBCs). A PBC typically relates to a specific function or capability in the company. For example, "contract management" could be a PBC that can track, store, and manage contracts. The sales, product, and support teams would each use it for different reasons. A PBC may be related to one application, many applications, or none. By focusing on capability over technology, we can design processes based on business objectives and outcomes rather than creating hard dependencies on specific applications.

The composable capabilities of enterprise automation extends beyond Gartner's definition but share many of the same outcomes. First, we group the automation components into three pillars:

- Process integration;
- Data integration;
- Experience integration.

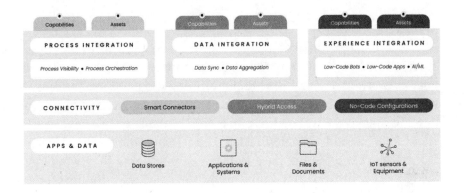

This separation accounts for differences in how we design and interact with automation components for each of these areas. For example, experiences are often delivered through chatbots, web apps, or mobile apps. Data may be exposed through APIs or transferred through files or databases. Processes, however, are often long running and may contain a combination of systems and experiences.

Focusing on enabling composable capabilities helps us achieve plasticity by making our data, processes, and experiences plug-and-play. By packaging and sharing capabilities or assets as building blocks, we allow the next automation to be created faster. For example, we might create an approval building block in the experiences pillar. Let's work through what that might look like.

This approval building block would allow any automation to request manager approval for any type of request. It would encapsulate the following logic:

- Look up the employee's manager;
- Determine if the employee's manager has delegated their approvals to someone else due to vacation or other reason;
- Send the approval request to the manager or delegate via Microsoft Teams;
- Send follow-up reminders as required and escalate to the next-level manager if no response is received in a certain time frame;
- Once approved or rejected, notify the original automation.

Once created, this component can now be used in every future automation that requires approval. For instance, during the pandemic, organizations had to scramble to put processes in place to control who was going into the office. If they wanted to secure manager approval for all employees entering the office, this reusable component would allow them to add that step faster. The person automating the new request process wouldn't have to think through how they would get the request approved; they would simply leverage the building block.

An optimal building block should be made up of at least one of the following three key technology components:

- **API services:** for rapid access to data in the building block;
- **Business event services:** granting the ability to respond to events in real time or notify other services of business events;
- **Modern data cloud:** for bulk data processing, analytics, and machine learning.

APIs and events enable other automations to quickly incorporate these capabilities into their flows. The modern data cloud allows for the storage and processing of data related to this capability. For example, if you were to create a "product recommendation" building block, you may need to store product data and historical purchase data in order to train and continuously retrain a machine learning model to accurately make these recommendations.

Each of these building blocks must be built upon a layer of rapid no-code connectivity. We differentiate low-code from no-code here as connectivity is now a commodity. Pre-built connectors to common applications and data sources are now widely available in most automation tools. Connecting to an application is not something our teams should have to spend days or even hours trying to figure out. If we are not using pre-built application connectors, our automations will require complex custom code and logic just to properly initiate a connection and authenticate. This means significant research and technical effort every time we want to connect to a new app. To make it worse, all this effort is required before even starting to automate the first step. This is slow and rigid.

Composition is not a new idea. This version is refined with learnings from years of integration and automation projects. Historically, companies separated APIs, event streaming, and data across different technologies and even different IT teams. These technologies would shine in their niche but fail when attempted to be used outside their designed purpose. For example, APIs are great at real-time data access but not so great at handling outbound events such as a contract being signed, a new order being placed, or the activation of a security alarm. Combining these technologies enables teams to create packages not limited by individual tools. Instead, they can focus on delivering full-featured business capabilities.

AI-assisted Orchestration

As discussed in the prior chapter, we need to move beyond simple task automation. To do that, we have to be able to orchestrate entire flows across people, processes, and data. Everything needs to be connected. The orchestration capability or our architecture enables this end-to-end automation. *The important aspect here, however, is that orchestration must be implemented with plasticity in mind. This means that the flows that we build should not be rigid or fixed. We should be able to easily change them.*

Furthermore, one of the most valuable areas in which generative AI can help organizations take a leap forward is precisely through an

AI-assisted orchestration layer. This layer should be able to understand the business need and act on it by combining a set of existing capabilities within the company. Going back to our "back to office" example, prompting our orchestration layer with something like "I need to automate the return to office process where any employee who wants to go to the office will need proof of vaccination and their direct manager approval."

Imagine if your AI-assisted orchestration layer would turn that into an automation that:

- Generates a low-code application form to receive employee request (while creating a new "return to office" *experience* capability);
- Upon request and based on employee location, it will use the relevant state's proof of vaccination API for validation (while creating a new "proof of vaccination" *data* capability);
- Send a Microsoft Teams notification to the direct manager for approval (reusing the "approvals" *experience* capability described above).

When you look at a typical integration or automation architecture diagram, you'll find that the orchestration layer is missing (not to mention any AI-assisted capabilities). Typical solutions today focus heavily on the services (APIs) and overlook what ties those APIs together. This leads to scripts, custom code, and other rigid ways of weaving systems and APIs together. Therefore, a flexible orchestration layer is critical to achieving plasticity.

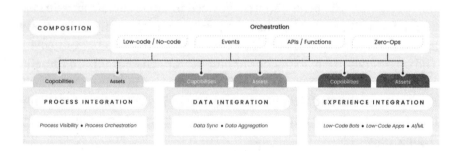

AI-assisted orchestration relies on two foundational elements:

- AI-powered dynamic workflows;
- Low-code components to support those dynamic workflows.

Low-code technologies have become more popular in the past few years. Without the complexity and operational overhead of code, building and managing solutions is faster. More importantly, these technologies have helped create an abstraction layer that facilitates "common understanding" from a broader set of personas within an organization. When applied to orchestration, it unlocks exactly the kind of flexibility we need to enable plasticity. We can quickly weave together the steps of an end-to-end process and make changes in a flash. If Alice's company had a low-code orchestration layer, the story would have been different. IT could have very quickly prototyped a solution, or perhaps Alice would have built her own solution with guidance from IT.

The other key enabler of orchestration is AI-powered dynamic workflows. Imagine a world where, instead of people constantly tweaking and tuning the process, a machine learning model could adjust the process. Orchestration tools are now capable of integrating with machine learning models to dynamically determine the next step of the process. Furthermore, with the help of generative AI and automation-centric LLMs (large language models), entire processes could be automated through an AI-assisted orchestration engine.

For example, a large hospitality company recently implemented an automation to process incoming customer emails to their hotel. The issue was that a customer email might initiate any one of 10 different processes. It might regard a room reservation, a banquet hall booking, a complaint, an inquiry about a bill, a lost and found request, or more. They leveraged machine learning to process incoming emails and identify the type of request. This allows them to immediately initiate the appropriate process and involve the appropriate teams. Instead of waiting hours or days for a response, the customer now gets an immediate automated reply sharing the availability and pricing of the ballroom they want to book for their wedding.

This technology can be taken even further to enable our processes to self-optimize. Machine learning incorporated with the right orchestration tools can automatically detect and make process changes. Let's take invoice automation as an example where invoice records are automatically created in the enterprise resource planning software (ERP) as they are received by email. Artificial intelligence could be used to monitor for changes made to the invoice records after they are loaded. This means that if an accounts payable clerk always adjusts invoices sent from ABC Co. to the parent company of ABC Global Co., the automation would automatically adjust to book further invoices to ABC Global Co. No intervention from IT, no changes to the automation, and the system automatically adapts.

Leveraging machine learning as part of the orchestration capability can result in the ultimate form of plasticity, where automated processes adjust and improve themselves.

Flexible Experiences

People are and will always be foundational to the success of any business. Automation is not a means to replace people, it simply maximizes our value and frees us up for creative, abstract, and strategic work. It allows us to do work that is satisfying and interesting rather than repetitive and dull.

Historically, the user experience has been a second-class citizen in automation projects. The priority is typically put on data movement and system actions. Little attention is paid to people's experience interacting with these newly automated flows. Customer experience (CX) and employee experience (EX) are popular buzzwords, but when automating processes, they are often ignored.

The dedicated experience integration pillar of enterprise automation is designed to make experience a focus point. It helps the right information, decisions, and alerts appear at the right time and place. For example, the method by which someone approves a request can mean the difference between a 30-minute process and a three-week process. People naturally avoid difficult tools and processes. Most will happily approve a request that pops up on their mobile phone, even though they would have put it off for weeks if it requires them to log in to a clunky app. We can't resign ourselves to whatever rigid methods our tools confine us to today. Crafting the user experience associated with your newly automated process needs thoughtful design and a flexible technology platform.

Flexible experiences require technologies that enable what we call just-in-time (JIT) experiences. Notifications, approvals, reviews, feedback, insights, decisions, and other activities are foundational building blocks to an automated flow. Flexible experiences require that our automation platform allows us to deliver these JIT experiences using the best-fit communication channel. It could be email, Slack, SMS text, Microsoft Teams, or a notification in their primary business application. Each experience has an ideal channel, and the automation platform should allow every process to flexibly connect with the right people, in the right way, at the right time.

Many tools and technologies today provide the ability to build notifications, forms, and a variety of different types of user interactions. The critical factor for creating plasticity within our organizations is the speed at which these experiences can be created and included in our automated flows. This area is often a source of bottlenecks. In most companies, new custom-created experiences will require application customizations and custom web forms, built by a developer or specialist. This is where delivery of the automation often slows to a snail's pace.

Ensuring your automation platform enables rapid delivery of these flexible experiences using low code or other means will unlock the third component of plasticity.

Putting It All Together

The T.E.A.M. acronym from middle school sports stands for "Together Everyone Achieves More." In basketball, baseball, or even enterprise IT, one great player is no guarantee of success. It might sound cliché, but it describes a basic truth in organizations. Aristotle said it better: "The whole is greater than the sum of its parts." When everything works in harmony, something greater than the individual parts can result.

When we put flexible experiences, dynamic orchestration, and composable capabilities together, we get a degree of business agility that is far better than we've seen in the past.

For the last 100 years, building companies like rigid machines was enough. In today's environment, this rigid approach is no longer viable. The new automation mindset builds companies with plasticity, like brains. They change, evolve, adapt, and improve in all corners of the company.

The rate of change in the world will only continue to grow. More system shocks, market downturns, and other unexpected events are always lurking right around the corner. If we want unstoppable companies unfazed by these challenges, plasticity is the key.

Notes

1. Sull, Donald, and Charles Sull, 2022, "Preparing Your Company for the Next Recession," *MIT Sloan Management Review* (December 6), **https://sloanreview.mit.edu/article/preparing-your-company-for-the-next-recession/**.
2. Taleb, Nassim, 2014, *Antifragile: Things That Gain from Disorder*. New York: Random House.
3. Ericsson, Anders, and Robert Pool, 2016, *Peak: Secrets from the New Science of Expertise*. New York: Harper One.
4. Münte, Thomas F., Eckart Altenmüller, and Lutz Jäncke, 2002, "The Musician's Brain as a Model of Neuroplasticity," *Nature Reviews. Neuroscience* 3 (6), **http://gottfriedschlaug.org/musicianbrain.test/papers/Muente_musician-plasticity.pdf**.
5. Skipper, Magdalena, Ursula Weiss, and Noah Gray, 2010, "Plasticity," *Nature* 465 (7299), **https://www.nature.com/collections/hvpvqqwvmy**.

CHAPTER 7

Democratization

"Authority should be vested in the people doing the work to improve their own processes."

—Steve Jobs

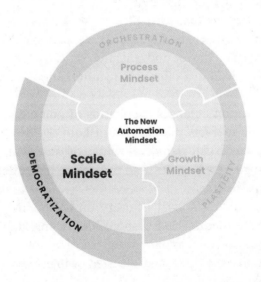

M any technologists don't see much difference between democratization and chaos. It echoes the rumored view of American statesman Thomas Jefferson: "Democracy is nothing more than mob rule, where 51% of the people may take away the rights of the other 49%."[1] Say the word "democratization" to a group of CIOs, and the reaction will be mixed. Some light up, describing it as "progress" and "the future." Others call it scary or concerning. I once heard a CIO say, "Sometimes the technical experts are there for a reason."

When IT leaders shudder at the mention of democratization, they really envision anarchy. At the most extreme, it probably looks something like the enterprise IT version of a *Mad Max* film. If we were to strip away anything resembling control, give powerful automation and AI technology to the masses, and let people loose, the company would probably explode and catch fire. All kidding aside, no one can blame a technologist for hesitating to embrace chaos. But if anarchy is our only alternative to the status quo, tech leaders are caught between a rock and a hard place. It is impossible for IT to bring about the automation revolution alone. But if the only other choice is to hand over the keys and pray for the best, the revolution is doomed from the start.

One could make the case that the anarchy we fear is already happening in companies today. In Chapter 4, we also talked about the perils of shadow and rogue IT—which are examples of anarchy. The choice between IT control and anarchy is a false choice. IT control does not, in fact, lead to a safer path to automation; it leads to shadow IT. Fortunately, there is a third option: democratization.

Democratization balances the worlds of anarchy and command-and-control and extracts the benefits of both. Despite what the naysayers think, successful democratization of automation is possible. With the right guardrails, roles, and controls in place, democratization can take companies far.

Competing interests exist in every organization—governance is how we manage them. Those responsible for maintaining the company's tech protect the company from risk. Line of business workers are trying to make their jobs faster, easier, or to achieve higher-quality outputs. These two objectives aren't always aligned. As leaders, our mandate is to embrace these as complementary strengths and build an operating model that supports both sides. In other words, our role is to build governance that allows a healthy "democracy" to thrive. We need to provide our "citizens" freedom while minimizing risk.

Balance Different Skill Sets for Success

As the old adage goes, with great power comes great responsibility. As discussed earlier, democratization is not saying we should blindly give great responsibility to every random "citizen." The popular terms "citizen developer" or "citizen automator" are imprecise and flawed for this reason. We'll use another angle of our government analogy one more time to explain.

In many countries, the process to construct a new building starts long before the first shovel hits the ground. Architects and designers make a layout that is safe, enjoyable, and useful. But even before architects begin their work, local governments set regulations and building codes in place for safety and security that fits the environment. For example, California building code requires structures to withstand large earthquakes. In cold states such as New York, regulations consider snow load on roofing. These laws ensure safety for new construction. When a natural disaster strikes that regulators did not account for, the regulations are revised.

Once it is time to build the structure, the laborers and designers bring their unique skill sets together. A construction crew might include tradespeople such as bricklayers, electricians, plumbers, and framers with the unique skills required to erect a new dwelling. Each member of the team knows their role and has special training and licensing. They also keep up with the latest products and techniques that might improve their work.

The electrician is a great analogy for integration and automation. Without regulations and training, someone wiring up a new building might find it easier to run a wire directly from one point to another in a straight line, perhaps through doorways and down the hall. But building codes and electrician training does not allow for this. Not only would it create a mess, but it would be an electrocution and fire hazard. Instead, the wires have specific ways they must be neatly run inside of the walls. Not only are these standards documented but also reviewed and enforced by building inspections. The standards set by trade groups and building codes are arguably more important than the wiring work itself.

In building construction, no tradesperson has to design the architecture from scratch. Blueprints guide how each piece of the project comes together. The architect may not have the same level of knowledge as the tradespeople, but they have a basic understanding. More importantly, they know how each piece of the project will work once it is complete. The design ensures that if the trades do their job right, the final structure will be sound.

Each of these roles—the architects, the governance, and the builders—must work in harmony for success. Without this symbiotic relationship, chaos would surely ensue. Imagine the bricklayer building a foundation with no direction. What would they build? Maybe whatever was easiest, such as a perfect square. Electricians and plumbers would run wires and pipes any which way without consideration for safety, let alone how the entire system needs to work. It sounds ridiculous, and yet this is the situation that we accept in the average enterprise today.

Find Balance

In the past, companies chose between security and speed. We need both. Success lies in the balance of democratization and governance. Like yin and yang, they create order by balancing opposing yet interconnected forces.

The yin and yang propose that life operates in a pattern of dualities with two opposing forces. Each side has different traits, but both need to coexist in a way that creates balance. Each force is the strongest when it has a piece of the opposing force on its own side. When technical experts empower business users to build, they are operating at their best. When business experts can build tech solutions within the guidelines from the technical teams, they are at their best.

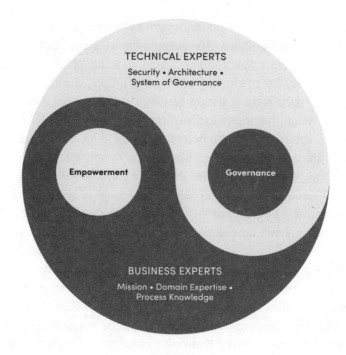

Democratizing automation allows people to automate workflows using their ideas of what is best for the company. Sometimes those ideas come from the business and other times from IT. As a result, IT's role is best described as a player-coach. Gartner calls it fusion teams, where technical experts join forces with functional experts with a shared goal.

This collaborative approach builds trust between the two teams and a healthy respect for the challenges that each team faces daily. While this may seem fluffy, it is critical, as without trust, many projects get bogged down in finger-pointing and disagreements. By putting IT and the business on the same team, they begin working together rather than against each other.

Bring Together IT and Business

Democratization of automation brings people together. This happens with shared, agreed-upon rules. Everyone has a role to play, and the result is magic.

Like trades, business line managers have specialized skills in their domain. They understand the vocabulary and the metrics of their domain. They also know the processes: in what order tasks must be completed, what to prioritize, and how markets are changing. Most importantly, they have a strong sense of mission and a clear understanding of what they need to do. Someone in sales ops will know how to improve the sales process better than any IT administrator. But to empower that person in sales operations to automate and improve their process, we need to enable them to automate safely.

The IT department has a complementary set of specialized skills to help the business operate smoothly. They have a unique understanding of governance, scale, and security. Technical professionals know how systems run efficiently. They also know how technical decisions can create tech debt, limit scale, or lead to security problems.

In this vision for democratization, IT needs to step into a more strategic leadership role. IT must enable people across the business to automate. Training, consulting, mentoring, and support are all needed. That includes providing the technology and means to do the work, but it also means establishing, communicating, and enforcing rules that protect the company.

Make Governance Your Friend

In the eyes of many businesspeople, IT governance is a bad word. They see it as bureaucracy that slows them down. Unfortunately, governance has given IT a reputation as the "department of no." Myths about IT rules persist:

- Governance does not adapt fast enough to changing environments.
- IT leaders don't understand how governance initiatives will affect business needs.
- IT sets rules and restrictions because it gives them a sense of power and control.

Behind every myth there is usually an element of truth. There are unfortunately many IT departments where all these statements are true. This, however, does not mean that these statements are always true. Governance can be either slow and painful or fast and effective. The difference is simply in how your governance processes are created.

Good governance is the only path to democratized automation. IT needs to act as a guide and mentor, and part of that mandate is overcoming the view that governance is bad.

One way to reframe governance is to put the rules in context of the opportunity. Celebrating certification graduates is one way to do this. A course for line of business folks would be all about governance, but elevating those who finish it as rock stars in the organization will make them feel as if they belong. We can build on that by sharing their success stories with their peers and the rest of the business. When we turn people who follow the rules into champions, we put a positive spin on a tough topic.

Lastly, we need to go beyond telling people that not all governance is bad; we need to show them. Putting in place governance processes that are fast, easy, and have a strong user experience will help the company see that governance can be simple. When governance feels too restrictive, it will confirm people's suspicions, and the business will go down the shadow IT path. A system of governance is good, but how IT communicates the governance and how people experience it will make the difference between successful and unsuccessful democratization.

How Atlassian Turned Democratization into Magic

Atlassian is a textbook case for a smart democratized automation program. Around 2019, the company leadership created an intelligent automation team to find new efficiencies. In the early days, the team would look for inefficient and time-consuming tasks in their processes to replicate human actions with software. After a year of automating tasks, they calculated that they had saved the company around 5,000 hours. The leadership team did the math, liked what they saw, and decided they wanted more. The CFO told the team to save the company 100,000 hours in the next year and multiply the output of their team.

(continued)

(*continued*)

The team kept automating as much as they could, but they quickly reached max capacity. In response, they reprioritized to focus on the top 1% of processes that could make the highest impact. Their team size made it impossible to reach the ambitious goal they had been given, and they were leaving work undone and lots of opportunities unrealized. "We had an automation team, and they used to build out all the automations. But their backlog filled up very quickly. So, there was a prioritization exercise, and they would just do the high-impact, high-value work, but there was a lot of work getting left undone," said Mohit Rao, head of intelligent automation at Atlassian. "So then, we built out a platform team, and their goal was to enable other teams to automate. Other teams were starting to use our automation platform to do their own work. I think you get better outcomes when we move the work closer to the business context."

This new platform team was initially asked to train a few of the other IT teams in automation. After training, each team began handling requests from around the company. But those teams all reached max capacity too, and a new backlog of unfinished work began to grow. Still, the company was not close to reaching the CFO's goal of 100,000 hours saved.

At this point, with everyone in IT at full capacity, the automation team thought they had run out of options. In a last-ditch effort to salvage their goal, the platform team created a program to equip automation champions in the business to automate their own processes. At the same time, they built out a governance system to ensure this work was done safely. Mohit describes it this way: "Now that we have enabled business users and IT users, the platform team can focus on creating guardrails and governance, environment segregation, automated deployments, testing, and more." Through democratization, they reached their impossible goal. 100,000 hours of effort were automated for the entire year.

Other parts of the company could automate for the first time with exciting results. The Atlassian Foundation is one example—a part of the company that works with nonprofits. They had a program called Engage for Good to connect nonprofits with Atlassian employees who wanted to volunteer. Manually matching hundreds of nonprofits with thousands of volunteers was getting out of hand. In the old paradigm, the Foundation had limited IT support. They wouldn't have gotten help from the automation team because they are not a core part of the business. But training the Foundation team empowered them to automate the matching process themselves. This saved enormous amounts of time for an already overloaded team. Hundreds more volunteers were matched with opportunities to do good around the world.

Governance in the Era of AI for All

Generative AI is only becoming more accessible every day. As generative AI systems become more sophisticated, they take on many repetitive tasks such as report writing, data analysis, and even parts of software development. Nontechnical users will create tools such as chatbots, emails, and more.

But what about going beyond tasks? While the potential to automate entire business processes is arguably one of the most exciting and rewarding areas, how do we make sure that the right people are doing the right thing? For example, HR teams probably want to limit access to employee data while finance teams want to do the same with the company financial information.

By democratizing access to these powerful tools, generative AI can help to level the playing field and empower employees to drive innovation and success within their organizations. But AI output is only as good as its input.

The need to define and standardize inputs, while also protecting the company from risks associated with sensitive data exposure or public AI models, creates a great opportunity for collaboration between IT and business experts. No doubt, generative AI is going to increase shadow IT in a business. Containing this, while harnessing the tools at scale, will take equal effort from both sides of an organization.

Enterprise AI platforms will aid this by providing the right levels of control, security, and accountability necessary to adopt AI at scale.

If an HR analyst wanted to generate a report on the company's ARR (annual recurring revenue) metrics or churn rates, the enterprise AI platform should be context-aware and potentially challenge why such a person would be accessing that type of data or trigger a human review process with their direct manager.

From a different perspective, what if a business analyst tries to automate the quote-to-cash process? Then again, the AI should not only be able to notify involved parties about the intent of this particular user but also have the necessary characteristics so that the person interacting with the AI can understand what is being generated.

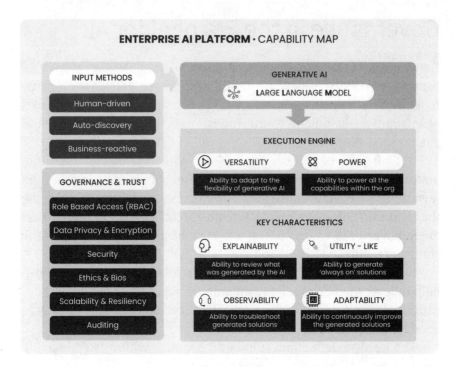

As we'll explore in Chapter 15 in much more detail, when thinking about the potential for generative AI beyond the task-automation mindset and into the broader (and more valuable) process mindset, we quickly realize the multiple dimensions an enterprise-grade AI platform will need to support to be successful:

- **Input methods:** will guide "the rules of engagement" between people and AI;
- **Governance:** will create accountability throughout every touch point;
- **Execution engine:** will turn the blueprints generated by AI into a reality by aligning with a set of core or key characteristics that are necessary to embrace AI at the enterprise level.

Find Common Ground

While car owners everywhere have the option to service their own vehicle, most choose not to. The complexity is too high for the average person to get their hands dirty under the hood. If the automation tools in your company have the complexity of a jet engine, everything in this chapter will sound like wishful thinking. The right technology approach is crucial to a strong democratization strategy.

We can't just open access to tools that are so complex they require computer science degrees to understand them. The impact would be negligible. To make anything happen, both the business and IT need a shared platform that enables both sides. *The technology needs to support the limited aptitude of the business users, the technical requirements of the IT users, and the governance capabilities mentioned earlier.* This means:

1. Business users need to be able to design their workflows in a way that is understandable to them. A low-code approach is a key requirement, with an easy-to-grasp, consumer-style user experience.

2. Successful collaboration needs a common language so both sides can interact and understand each other. Business users don't speak XML. IT does not always know all the business acronyms. But when they communicate about automated processes, both should be able to understand the flow.

3. Platforms need to be community-powered. New automations should not be built in a vacuum. Builders should have the ability to leverage templates and best practices from inside and outside the company. We want teams building on great ideas, not reinventing the wheel. Getting a head start from a great place only accelerates the pace of innovation.

Finding common ground in a shared technology also supports ways to rethink how teams operate. For example, Gartner, as part of their composable enterprise framework, proposes companies create fusion teams, which are multidisciplinary teams that include developers, users, and business leaders that are organized around a common goal.[2] Fusion teams typically pair technical pros with less technical business-people to solve complex business problems (for a detailed breakdown of the roles involved in automation, see Appendix A at the end of this book). A platform that brings experts together and supports collaboration between different skill sets is essential in implementing a fusion team and a broader democratization strategy.

Unlock the Untapped Potential

Democratization of IT, data, applications, and automated workflows supports a scale mindset that enables professionals across entire organizations to engage technology to do their job more effectively. By embracing democratization, a platform approach, and a flexible governance strategy, organizations can empower a much larger group of employees to scale their capabilities to unlock the potential of their workforce.

If we think back to the story of Atlassian, they started with challenges that affect most automation initiatives. But their success in scaling the capability of their workforce is born out of the sheer number of creators they have enabled and the resulting volume of app connections and workflows that they have built. Once the Atlassian strategy was fully implemented, the number of creators skyrocketed. They started with IT ops, and people ops, and then expanded to finance, marketing and sales ops, and customer success. As of this writing, they have empowered 425 creators. With this many automation builders, you no longer have a delivery bottleneck, and you can address the broader automation opportunity. This is where the rubber really meets the road. The number of processes or subprocesses automated at Atlassian grew exponentially. As of last count, 2,100 high-quality and well-governed process automations had been assembled. Metrics like these go far beyond hours saved for the company. They will pay dividends for years to come, and many have immeasurable impacts, such as connecting thousands of volunteers with nonprofits to do good in the world. Atlassian unfolding a democratized approach has changed the very DNA of the organization and what they can accomplish.

Notes

1. Thomas Jefferson Foundation, no date, "The Jefferson Monticello," last Accessed December 31, 2022, **https://www.monticello.org/research-education/thomas-jefferson-encyclopedia/democracy-nothing-more-mob-rulespurious-quotation/**.
2. Gartner, n.d., "Fusion Team," last accessed December 31, 2022, **https://www.gartner.com/en/information-technology/glossary/fusion-team**.

PART 3

A Practitioner's Guide to World Class Automation

CHAPTER 8

Mastering Your Automation Journey

"Ideas are the beginning points of all fortunes."
—Napoleon Hill

We all see automation through the lens of our personal or team goals. It is natural. Our minds work this way; new technology sparks ideas of all the exciting ways we can put it to good use. We'll commonly apply new technologies to the tasks in front of us, no matter where we sit in the organization.

Hopefully the first half of this book has inspired you to rethink your automation mindset. As a result, you have taken an important step in your automation journey by developing what Harish Ramani, CIO of Helen of Troy, calls the "helicopter view of the enterprise." From this vantage point, we rise above our immediate goals and projects to see the outcomes that need to be delivered across the company.

With the helicopter view, we can align our automation work to the business outcomes that make a company thrive. In other words, our new automation mindset makes us recognize the core outcomes that automation can:

- Drive revenue growth;
- Increase customer retention and expansion;
- Help retain employees and empower them to be productive;
- Improve supplier relations and efficiency;
- Encourage operational excellence.

Every automation initiative a company undertakes will impact one or more of these outcomes.

Take, for example, the Minnesota Mining & Manufacturing Company. That name might not ring a bell, but you certainly know them by their shortened name, 3M. They produce many products that we all interact with every day, from Scotch tape to phone cases. Even though they have hundreds of business lines producing over 55,000 products,[1] every automation in the company impacts revenue, customers, employees, suppliers, or operational excellence.

If 3M had a corporate goal of improving customer experience, they might replace a call center for a popular product line with an automated self-service portal for common requests combined with the ability to talk to an agent for unique cases.

They may also have a CEO mandate of improving the speed of their supply chain through better interactions with their suppliers. They could build an automated process that used computer vision and AI to scan inbound packages from a supplier for damage, automatically flag damaged materials, update inventory, and route a return proposal request for approval by the appropriate manager. This would dramatically reduce the time impact of damaged supplies on their production lines and directly support the CEO's mandate for improved supplier operations.

3M is a massive, one-of-a-kind company. All our companies are unique. However, we also share a lot in common. If you look back at your organization's top-level goals for last year, they probably include some derivative of revenue growth, customer retention, employee experience, improved partner operations, reduced costs, or improved efficiency. These outcomes are foundational to any business. *They should be foundational to any automation strategy, too.*

The Five Towers of Automation

Processes usually have a primary focus on one of these top-level goals. These core objectives, in turn, roll up to departments—for example, HR teams focus on employee experience. We call these the towers of automation, and each tower is named according to both the area of the business and the associated outcome. When we set out to execute an automation strategy, we advise that leaders organize their approach around these five towers.

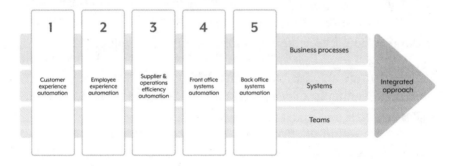

Towers of Automation

The five towers cut across departments, teams, systems, and even top-level processes. In each tower, there are core, basic processes that nearly every company will recognize. For example, you'll find the invoicing process in the back-office tower, or satisfaction scoring (NPS) processes in the customer experience tower.

Tower of Automation	Primary Organizational Objective
Customer experience	Customer retention and expansion
Employee experience	Employee retention and productivity
Supply chain efficiency	Supplier relations & efficiency
Front office	Revenue
Back office	Operational excellence

But we should be careful to say that this is not a call for homogeneous automation in every company. It is not even to say that every company should automate their processes in the same way. The whole point of the new automation mindset is to fuel ideas and creativity, ultimately leading to competitive differentiation. Every company will approach things uniquely, but we can use the five towers to examine what the best-known practices look like today.

At this point, we have also established that automation is not a checkbox on a list. It is best to think about automation as a journey. To map out this journey, a tool such as the maturity model in the following figure is a useful place to start. Every company starts somewhere. As the journey unfolds, they start taking on more cross-company processes. Eventually, they reach enough critical mass that they become unstoppable.

Working within the five towers is not about copying our peers; it is about striking a balance. *We need to promote creativity but with enough structure to direct our team's activities toward larger objectives.* Creativity also needs a starting point. We can all learn from each other. The best ideas are rarely all original. They are simply pushing the boundary of what has been done before. In other words, we should be able to implement our most creative ideas, but our ideas should "stand on the shoulders of giants."

The five towers of automation will help you to break down and organize your business into actionable automation initiatives. Each tower is also supported by a more detailed hierarchy of the common business processes. This hierarchy should illuminate ideas for automation not previously considered. It will also help you identify those processes and activities that make your organization unique. This will generate new and unique automation ideas. An example of a process hierarchy from back office looks like this (see figure in page 116).

Enterprise Automation Maturity Model

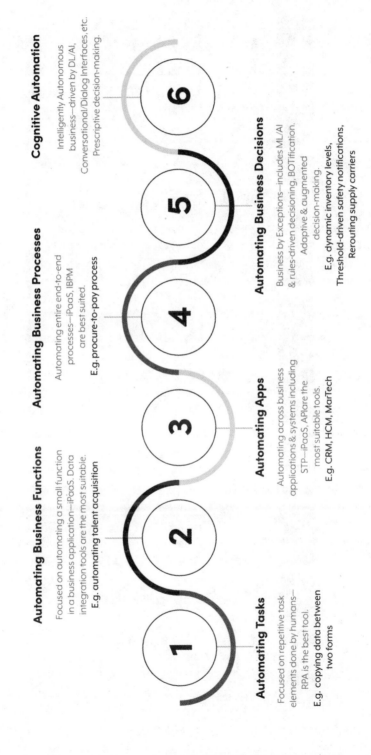

Automating Tasks

Focused on repetitive task elements done by humans—RPA is the best tool.
E.g. copying data between two forms

Automating Business Functions

Focused on automating a small function in a business application—iPaaS. Data integration tools are the most suitable.
E.g. automating talent acquisition

Automating Apps

Automating across business applications & systems including STP—iPaaS, API are the most suitable tools.
E.g. CRM, HCM, MarTech

Automating Business Processes

Automating entire end-to-end processes—iPaaS, IBPM are best suited.
E.g. procure-to-pay process

Automating Business Decisions

Business by Exceptions—includes ML/AI & rules-driven decisioning, BOTification. Adaptive & augmented decision-making.
E.g. dynamic inventory levels, Threshold-driven safety notifications, Rerouting supply carriers

Cognitive Automation

Intelligently Autonomous business—driven by DL/AI, Conversational/Dialog Interfaces, etc. Prescriptive decision-making.

Customer Experience Automation	Employee Experience Automation	Supplier & Operations Efficiency Automation	Back Office Systems Automation	Front Office Systems Automation
Customer Service & Contact	Talent Acquisition	Supplier Management Information	FinOps (AP, AR, Ledger Postings, Recon)	Sales Management
Measure and Share of Voice	Onboarding & Offboarding	Procurement and Payments	Quote to Cash	Customer Success & Operations
Customer 360 & KYC	Workplace Automation and Approvals	Manufacturing, Inventory and Material Management	Reporting and Compliance	Revenue Operations and Go-to Market
Product Led Growth & Content Marketing	Compensation, Benefits and Payroll	Returns Management	Finance and Accounts Management	Sales Order and Contract Management
Marketing Operations & Campaigns	HR Operations	Asset Operations and Management	IT Service and Security Operations	Demand Generation
Commerce & Digital Channels	HR – Learning and Development	Supply Chain and Logistics Automation	IT Operations and Infrastructure Management	Other Front Office Operations
	Employee Information Management		Legal, Compliance, Risk and Other Back Office Operations	

→ **High Automation Potential**

→ **Low Automation Potential**

Automation Discovery

Finding the right opportunities for automation in our companies does take some effort. Given the uniqueness of each company, there is no standard playbook that applies to every business. The unique dynamics of every company will make certain processes more attractive options than others over time.

In order to get started with your automation journey, we recommend investing in discovery workshops for the tower of automation you are most interested in automating first. These discovery workshops are typically run with both technical and nontechnical stakeholders for a given business area. They will often focus on one or two core processes where the organization knows there are issues. Using the process mindset, these workshops should reimagine the processes from end to end with an eye on the core business objectives of the process. We would recommend the workshop cover the following high-level topics:

1. Agree on the objectives and metrics for the current business process;
2. Outline how the process operates today;
3. Identify the points in the process where automation could:

    3.1. Positively impact the target outcomes (e.g. faster, easier, better experience);

    3.2. Eliminate steps in the process;

4. Flag any compliance and approval steps required for the process;
5. Estimate the impact of implementing all the automations identified. This allows you to estimate the corresponding business impact in terms of time/cost saved, risk reduced, improved experience, or revenue increase.

A workshop like this can be run by your internal team or a third party. Many consulting firms and automation providers have experts trained to run discovery workshops much like this.

An automation discovery workshop can help teams to adopt the process mindset in a structured way and help generate support and buy-in for automation from the business owners of these processes. They are a great approach for assessing the large and more complex processes in your organization to find big and high-impact automation opportunities. While big and high-impact automations are obvious candidates, they are by no means the only place to reap big rewards from automation.

The iceberg of untapped opportunity we referenced in the first half of the book means there are many ideas that go untried. These overlooked sparks of creativity are what we call innovative automations.

Innovative Automations

A structured and coordinated approach to the processes listed in the five towers of automation is a great way to start. But these processes only represent the tip of the iceberg. The new automation mindset is all about eliminating the barrier between those spur-of-the-moment strokes of genius and the ability to put them into action. When a culture of automation ignites in a company, incredible things start to happen. The real potential lies in putting the power in the hands of the people with great ideas. And often, those ideas are completely unexpected—they aren't on any lists.

There are thousands of mini-processes that execute all over the company and consume enormous amounts of time. Some examples might be:

- Sending invites and tracking responses to a company event;
- Retrieving market data from external sources;
- Incorporating team metrics into the company newsletter;
- Making approvals available on a mobile device.

Companies with the old automation mindset might look at these as low value and not worthwhile. As the mindset shifts, that view changes. When enough accumulate, the aggregate impact of thousands of overlooked automations can outpace the impact of automating our traditional processes.

It is a matter of reaching scale over time. Think of Walmart, for example. Someone may realize that store managers across the United States are forgetting to turn off all the lights after closing. Someone might think it would be cool to use computer vision on security camera video feeds to trigger a text message reminder to the manager five minutes before closing. It might save Walmart a few hundred dollars per store per year. Over time, they install Wi-Fi-enabled switches in every store and can automatically turn the lights off when the security cameras no longer detect motion in the store. Another employee thinks it is a great idea to hook the same automation up to their Wi-Fi-enabled thermostats, to save on heating and cooling costs. As time goes on, the value of the innovative automation ideas snowballs, quickly outpacing whatever would have been described in the business proposal for the original idea.

At first glance, the ROI may not appear meaningful for an individual automation. Building these innovative automations at scale can result in some of the most impressive business transformations due to their combined impact.

Inspiration for Automation

In the following chapters, we hope you will find inspiration that you can apply to your own processes. Each tower of automation has its own chapter, and in each chapter, there is a description of the domain, a list of the top processes in each, along with a handful of stories from real companies who have automated processes in each area. We also include a handful of "innovative automation" ideas in each chapter that we have seen over the years. While every automation may not be relevant to your company or industry, you'll surely find ideas and concepts that will spark a new perspective as you evaluate automation in your own organization. *If one of the towers closely aligns with your domain, we recommend you turn directly to that chapter and from there skip directly to Part 4.*

Note

1. Trefis Team, 2020, "Which of 3M's 26 Business Lines Makes The Most Money?" *Forbes* (January 27), **https://www.forbes.com/sites/ greatspeculations/2020/01/27/which-of-3ms-26-business-lines- makes-the-most-money/.**

CHAPTER 9

The Back Office

"Quality means doing it right when no one is looking."
—Henry Ford

In the first era of digital business, customer-facing roles were a top focus. Many now realize customer-facing roles are only as good as the back-office processes supporting them. A great omnichannel customer experience, for example, will not overcome operational breakdowns. Any goodwill created by customer experience investments will dissolve with poorly executed back-office processes. Therefore, operational excellence is a priority.

Of any department in a company, few have seen more change than the pillars of the back office: IT and finance. The functions reporting to finance have increased by 50% over the past few years.[1] CFOs are being asked to resolve issues in areas that are relatively new to them. CIOs have been elevated to business strategists as technology has become central.[2] Collectively, these evolving and critical parts of the organization are known as the back office.

While the back office is still "in the back," with minimal customer interaction, their perception is changing. No longer can we say the back office is an administrative cost center. Performance management, corporate strategy, digital transformation, and others belong to the back office. They are now vectors for competitive advantage. Back-office functions are crucial for a company with the new automation mindset.

Despite evolving mandates, the traditional responsibilities still matter. Back-office work enables the entire company to run efficiently. Procurement, finance, IT, HR, and others involve core processes that keep the lights on. But the expectations and consequences for the traditional responsibilities have skyrocketed. Traditional financial processes, for example, need to work faster in the digital age. A single mistake in a compliance report or customer interaction could cost a business millions of dollars or worse.

In a company with the new automation mindset, back-office roles cannot be siloed. While we differentiate between the two in this book, the back office has to be interconnected to the rest of the company.

Today's back-office operations are typically repetitive, manual, and data intensive. The opportunity for automating back-office work is enormous.

Unlocking Business Value for Back Office Functions

Many companies have worked hard to make back-office functions more efficient. Robotic process automation, cloud-based ERP (enterprise resource planning), and BPO (business process outsourcing) have been popular approaches. These programs produced some added efficiency, but there is still a lot of room for improvement with automation. Back-office processes still struggle with inefficiencies, long cycle times, and siloed data. There are immense opportunities for faster end-to-end processing, greater agility, and improved experiences.

Our process hierarchy view of the back office is a great way to break down your functions and identify the opportunities for automation. Use this as a guide for finding low-hanging automation fruit, but don't limit yourself to these processes as most companies have far more back-end processes and therefore far more opportunities for automation.

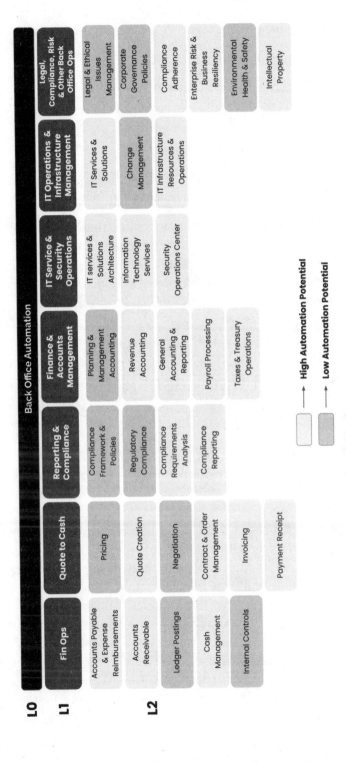

Back Office Automation

L0

L1

| Fin Ops | Quote to Cash | Reporting & Compliance | Finance & Accounts Management | IT Service & Security Operations | IT Operations & Infrastructure Management | Legal, Compliance, Risk & Other Back Office Ops |

L2

- Fin Ops: Accounts Payable & Expense Reimbursements, Accounts Receivable, Ledger Postings, Cash Management, Internal Controls
- Quote to Cash: Pricing, Quote Creation, Negotiation, Contract & Order Management, Invoicing, Payment Receipt
- Reporting & Compliance: Compliance Framework & Policies, Regulatory Compliance, Compliance Requirements Analysis, Compliance Reporting
- Finance & Accounts Management: Planning & Management Accounting, Revenue Accounting, General Accounting & Reporting, Payroll Processing, Taxes & Treasury Operations
- IT Service & Security Operations: IT services & Solutions Architecture, Information Technology Services, Security Operations Center
- IT Operations & Infrastructure Management: IT Services & Solutions, Change Management, IT Infrastructure Resources & Operations
- Legal, Compliance, Risk & Other Back Office Ops: Legal & Ethical Issues Management, Corporate Governance Policies, Compliance Adherence, Enterprise Risk & Business Resiliency, Environmental Health & Safety, Intellectual Property

→ **High Automation Potential**

→ **Low Automation Potential**

The typical back-office tasks can be categorized into seven areas:

- Finance operations (FinOps);
- Quote to cash;
- Reporting & compliance;
- Finance & accounts management;
- IT service & security operations;
- IT operations & infrastructure management;
- Legal, compliance, risk, and other back-office ops.

On paper, it is helpful to group tasks into these functional areas to reduce complexity. It can be hard to fit the real business processes into discrete functional areas. The root cause is often misalignment with the outcomes that matter to the company. One of the key outcomes of automation is bringing the back-office functions further into alignment with our business goals.

Automation Use Case: IT Service Management

A leader in hybrid cloud services had trouble brewing on the horizon, as cloud and hardware consumption models were rapidly changing. While they were navigating this change, they decided to hire their first CIO in 2017.

Wendy Pfeiffer's arrival as CIO found a company at a turning point. Over the next few years, they needed to pivot from a hardware to a software company. In its current condition, the IT organization could not support the intensity of this transformation. Challenges were persistent: the IT department had low approval ratings due to slow project delivery, and they were an inefficient cost center, drawing over 8% of the annual budget.

Dozens of back-office processes needed to be transformed to support the company's new direction. Wendy brought in a low-code enterprise automation platform so work could begin right away. She had the entire IT team trained on the tool. Then they began documenting, scoping, and reworking processes from the ground up. "Good enough is not okay at this point in time," says Wendy. "We're dealing with a time of unprecedented change, unprecedented challenges and complexity is ahead of us. So, we can't be satisfied with good enough, we can't be satisfied with what we did last round to deal with the complexity."

To start, they simplified the service ticket process.

The company implemented ServiceNow to help manage service requests. Unfortunately, buying an IT service management (ITSM) platform doesn't result in managed service requests; you still need people actively checking and using the tool for it to be effective. This wasn't happening. As a result, many requests sat in queues for too long. Employees grew frustrated.

This was a great opportunity for automation. They started by connecting all the workflows to Slack. Any assignment, escalation, approval, creation, and update of any tickets now happened in Slack. This resulted in several benefits including:

- **Proactive notifications:** Instead of a team member having to remember to log into ServiceNow every day to check on the work they need to get done, they are instead proactively notified. For example, when a business user responds to one of their questions, they see it pop up immediately, and they can take fast action.

- **Faster responses:** Previously, it may have been a few hours or even a few days before they noticed that the business user had responded. Now they could immediately respond directly from Slack, further reducing the delays for the business stakeholders.

- **Unblocking the business:** Once implemented, projects finished faster due to reduced IT request times. Projects no longer ground to a halt waiting on IT help.

Next, they tackled the delays in provisioning virtual machines (VMs).

Developers used to submit a request and wait a week for someone to manually provision a VM. This waiting time was often directly impacting how quickly their developers could build new products or features. For a software company, this means directly impacting their ability to get new revenue from these new products or features. Frustrated with the wait, one team even set out to build their own VMs but quickly realized the process wasn't scalable.

They implemented automatic provisioning and deprovisioning of VMs. In the old world, the infrastructure team would need to:

- Read the ServiceNow request;
- Determine the VM requirements;
- Open the VM admin console;
- Fill in all the configuration;
- Create a new VM;
- Validate that the VM was created successfully;
- Send an email to the requestor to let them know it's done.

All of this is now done automatically. The automation platform monitors ServiceNow for VM request tickets, routes them for approval in Slack, and then initiates VM provisioning using the configuration in the ticket. It even notifies the person who requested the new VM.

This instant provisioning shrinks IT request time from weeks to hours. If you step back and look at the end-to-end process and the overall impact on the business, the outcomes are even more significant. The reduction of server provisioning time from weeks to hours means that the developers can now test new ideas faster and release products weeks earlier than before. Instead of IT spending their time navigating apps and typing in configuration, they can now manage exceptions, troubleshoot issues, and work on more value-added initiatives.

One of those value-added initiatives was looking into a new way to catch suspicious activity before it turned into real security threats.

As with any tech company, security was always top-of-mind for the company. Tools and apps were generating too many security alerts to filter the signal from the noise. The security operations team had thousands of emails, millions of log entries, and countless tools to monitor. Using their automation platform, they continuously monitored Splunk (their logging platform) for specific events and activities. Now they could surface the more critical security events by notifying more people and using communications mechanisms reserved for high-priority alerts such as text messaging.

Even more important than notifications, they could now rapidly action these events. One type of action came in the form of creating a follow-up for specific teams. For example, they might create a ServiceNow ticket for a server administrator to check and see why a server has abnormally high network traffic. Another type of action was a fully automated response for certain events. An example of a fully automated action might be to immediately disable network access for a device on which a malicious virus has been detected.

By automatically handling some alerts and flagging others, the security operations team could now better keep tabs on suspicious activity. More serious security threats now had a very rapid response, within minutes or even seconds. In the world of security where missing one threat could cost your organization millions of dollars, these automations are critical.

The company pushed this concept even further by driving automation across IT functions. Wendy saw that about 70% of the IT team's time was being spent simply doing the basics, or "keeping the lights on," reactionary work that you can't plan for. This unplanned work was critical to the operations of the company but also a huge time drain for the team. Wendy and her team have been able to both detect when something requires maintenance and autonomously address 85% of these unplanned work activities.

Through these initiatives, automation became second nature. Within a year of adopting the new automation mindset, the company increased its IT service capacity by 30%. This means they could handle 30% more work without hiring any additional people. Consequently, their approval ratings shot up with an NPS score of 90+ for the last 18+ months. The IT department went from occupying 8% of the organization's annual budget to 1.8%.

In Wendy's own words, "It's this combination of using automation for the most delightful uses and using people for the most delightful uses and those two that the people and the automation being in harmony with each other, as we deliver service and capability to the company. It sounds kind of magical but it's really just a lot of small pieces of work that lead up to eventually these exponential improvements."

The company has successfully pivoted into a software company. Much of that work was supported by what Wendy's IT team has done as part of the back office. If IT simply remained a cost center and a bottleneck, the company wouldn't be able to work at the speed it needed. With a new mindset, their automation initiatives created real value for the organization, setting it up for success.

Automation Use Case: Streamlining Incident Management

One of the leading spend management solutions credits seamless back-office processes as crucial to their success. "We're responsible for performance and making sure the site is up and available, as well as how we manage and interact with the platform and services," says Hans, one of their engineers. "It's important to allow the engineers to focus on triage and resolution of issues instead of going back and forth between different tools to create tickets."

Coordinating the company's response to major incidents with their platform was critical to keeping the business moving and maintaining the trust of their customers. Before using automation, here's how things worked:

1. An issue with the platform would be detected by their monitoring tools and leverage VictorOps to page their engineering team.
2. One of the engineers on call would need to login to JIRA and create an incident.
3. The engineer would then need to go to HipChat to open a conferencing bridge, which would allow all the people working on the issue to discuss and coordinate their actions.
4. From there the engineer would post an announcement in Cachet to let their customers know they had identified an issue and were working on resolution.

That's a lot of logging into apps and performing administrative tasks. All of this being done by a critical engineering team member who would be much better off working on fixing the major issue that was just detected. Hans and team realized this was not the right approach and looked to automation for a solution.

The team leveraged a low-code enterprise automation platform to weave this process together. The resulting automation waited for acknowledgment from the engineering team that the monitoring tool alert was in fact a real issue and then took over from there. It leveraged the information from VictorOps to create a ticket in JIRA and assign the appropriate team. A HipChat room was automatically created with the appropriate team members, and they were notified to join. Finally, an update was posted to Cachet to alert customers to the incident.

The engineering team could now immediately start working on solving the problem instead of having to worry about logistics. Their time to resolution for major incidents was improved as a result.

This process was fine, but the team knew it could be even better: "We realized we needed to make this process less burdensome to the engineer. We wanted to make it simpler and invisible." They took the automation one step further and connected JIRA's incident management workflow with Cachet. This means that as they updated their JIRA ticket and moved it through the steps (from open, investigating, identified, fixed, watching, and eventually resolved), those updates were automatically reflected in the Cachet status dashboard. Customers receive timely updates on the incident without slowing down the engineers. It was a win-win.

The end result? Prized engineering talent does not go wasted on busywork. Incidents are resolved sooner. And customers are happier.

While the tasks are handled by back-office functions, the impact reverberates throughout the company.

Automation Use Case: Fine Payment Reporting

In the case of a leading car rental company, the company mission was to become the #1 mobility solutions provider. For that, it not only had to focus on generating revenue but also on managing their costs. They focused on reducing one of their major costs, traffic fines, using automation.

As you might expect, when people rent cars, they don't always perfectly follow the rules of the road. This results in fines and other liabilities being charged to the rental company. Normally these fines would simply be passed on to the customers; however, due to some regional regulations, the rental company had to report the driver's information to the authorities before a predetermined deadline. These deadlines varied from 7 to 30 days. Due to their slow internal processes, the rental company ended up being liable for thousands of customer fines when they failed to report them to the authorities by the deadline. This equated to hundreds of thousands of dollars in fines and penalties that the company could easily avoid.

Without the ability to quickly process and report these violations, the backlog just continued to grow, and fines continued to add up. They incurred heavy costs that ate into the bottom line of the company. Thus, they needed a solution to reduce the bleed of recurring costs by enabling them to quickly report these customer liabilities before deadlines.

For this company it's not only about cars; it's about tapping into different markets, managing the fleet, and scaling up hundreds of locations for thousands of drivers. The inability to keep up with standard operating requirements because of these antiquated paper-based processes was holding their growth hostage. The company had to process hundreds of fines from customers every week. The peak tally was more than 3,000 cases/month, equating to thousands of dollars in fines. Managing the load was unbearable without automation.

The company implemented an automation solution to retrieve the key information from the notifications received from authorities. They leveraged optical character recognition (OCR) to extract the information they would need to identify the vehicle and driver responsible. This included the license plate, the violation, and the time and date. They were then able to correlate the violation with a specific customer from their CRM. The combined violation and customer information was then automatically reported to the authorities well within the required timeline.

The solution ended up removing the manual process altogether, resulting in significant time saved for their teams. It also addressed the core objective of reporting customer liabilities (i.e. speeding) to authorities in a timely manner. This helped alleviate the heavy fines that they previously had to pay due to the missed deadlines, and they could refocus on growing in new markets.

Automation Use Case: Automated Cash Reconciliation

Finance teams work with large volumes of data on a daily basis and must do so with perfect accuracy. Many processes exist to check and cross-check the numbers to ensure accuracy of financial reports and monitor for fraud or other irregularities. One of those processes is cash reconciliation.

One of the world's largest event ticketing companies was no different. However, they found that their cash reconciliation process was taking far more of their team's time than it should. The finance team was spending over 20 hours weekly to simply get the data into Netsuite (their finance system), which took time away from more important activities.

The company had multiple accounts across two different banks, and therefore it required the team to log in to each bank's website, download the transactions into a spreadsheet, manually reformat and filter these transactions to prepare them to be loaded, load them into Netsuite, and then post the transactions. Beyond being time consuming, this was not a good use of their finance team's skills.

The team automated these processes with less than a week of effort. The new automated process worked as follows:

1. Download the transaction records from each of the banks using a secure file transfer service;

2. Load the bank files as-is to Netsuite for posterity and future audit requirements;

3. Initiate a process to iterate through each transaction in the bank records and apply predefined business rules in order to filter and map transactions to a format ready to be posted in Netsuite;

4. Post each of the analyzed and enriched transactions in Netsuite.

A very simple automation with significant efficiency gains. Twenty hours weekly equates to half of a full-time employee. This meant the finance team was now able to spend time on significantly more strategic and more rewarding work. This automation was only one small part of a much larger set of month-end, quarter-end, and year-end activities. Companies like this one are stepping back and looking at these larger finance processes and choosing to modernize rather than simply continuing to add more headcount.

The Power of Back-office Automation

Back-office automation is linked to other functions, such as front office or employee experience. Some key benefits that can be realized across the organizations are listed below.

Benefit	Overview
Top-line growth	As automation eliminates the need for paper-based processes and reduces the number of manual touchpoints, employees can focus on more valuable tasks that can positively impact the top-line growth of the company. This can have a cascading effect of improving customer experiences and even act as a competitive differentiator for the business.
Reduced cycle times	Automating end-to-end processes can reduce the cycle time through reduction in manual touchpoints and reduction in approval times. It can also improve adherence to service level agreements (SLAs) due to reduced variability in the process.
Improved data analytics	As automation records all the steps during the process, the data can be better used to carry out process and data analytics, which can provide valuable insights of the process.
Reduced errors	With reduced manual intervention along the process, chances of human errors are drastically reduced, so your clients can count on your systems to run efficiently.

Innovative Automations in the Back Office

So far in this chapter, we have talked through some examples of major processes that can benefit greatly from automation in our companies. But sometimes the best processes are outside of the obvious. While the mission-critical processes in every company should be infused with automation from end to end, the magic, delight, and intrigue can often spark from one individual with an innovative thought. Let's take a look at a few examples of innovative back-office ideas we have seen in recent years:

- **Connected light bulbs and security operations:** One company was automating notifications and incident response in their security operations, and they felt that the notification structure they had in place (email alerts and Slack notifications) was still not enough for the most mission-critical alarms from their security software. An example of a mission-critical alarm might be when unusual activity is detected with one of their core administrator accounts. For alarms like this, they worried that when people were away from their computers, they still might not see and respond to an incident message fast enough. In response, they set up an integration with a cloud SMS service (like Twilio) to send text messages to the security team only for these most critical situations. They made this even more impactful by linking this automation to Wi-Fi-connected Philips Hue lightbulbs in their office. The automation programmed the light bulbs to all turn red in response to a red alert message, ensuring that anyone in the room would immediately return to their computer to see what was going on. This specific automation was credited with saving the company from a major breach.

- **Helping new employees migrate from PC to Mac for the first time:** One BT team at a company that only issued Apple laptops to employees realized they were receiving many service tickets that were simply a result of new employees who had never used a Mac before. For example, the case of an app with important work randomly disappearing. Eventually, this was found to be caused by the user inadvertently switching to a new desktop. The team was able to dramatically reduce the number of these time-consuming service tickets by incorporating a small survey at the beginning of new employee onboarding that asked employees if this job was the first time they had ever used a Mac device. If they answered yes, they were directed to take a short training session that the BT team put together that addressed the most common issues that they had received over the past year. Not only did the BT team free up some of their time, but new employee productivity also increased.

- **No-touch provisioning and de-provisioning of apps with seat-based pricing:** The IT team is often asked to maintain the list of licenses for seat-based apps, such as Salesforce CRM and other similar tools that require

(continued)

(continued)

expensive monthly individual licenses. One company decided to eliminate the friction around provisioning new licenses and revoking idle licenses. Before, users had to walk up to a genius bar in the office to request a login, which would take several days to work through the IT queue. Today, the company allows any employee in the company to request a license for any application using an easy-to-use Slack bot. This is routed to their manager for approval and, once approved, the automation provisions access for the user. Taking this even further, another automation will trigger if, at any time, the user has not logged in to the application in a 90-day period. At that point, a message will appear in Slack asking the user if they still need access to the software. If they select the "yes" button, it is routed back to their manager for approval. In this way, the company saves the IT team from a common, rote task while ensuring their SaaS license costs stay as lean as possible.

- **Conversational answers to company-wide knowledge search with AI:** Employees have questions every day, and answering them usually involves asking around or sifting through files and document search results. Linking up Slack, generative AI, and an enterprise-wide search tool such as Glean, companies can deliver knowledge to employees in Slack conversations. For example, when an employee wants to know when the next company holiday is happening, they would typically go find the company holiday calendar. But with this automation, they can simply ask a Slackbot, "When is the next company holiday?" The automation would search through company files, knowledge bases, and document storage, and generative AI would serve up an answer that is sent back in Slack: "The next company holiday is August 12 - do you have any other questions?" Not only would this improve the employee experience, but it would lighten the load for people around the company who are "hubs" of knowledge.

Back Office Is the Foundation of Every Company

While some people downplay the importance of back-office functions due to them not being direct revenue-generating services, they are in fact the foundation of every company. Much like plumbing or electrical systems in your house, they aren't important until they don't work, and then it's the end of the world. Automating these foundational processes can have a direct impact on all aspects of customer experience, employee experience, and front-office operations and helps ensure the rest of your business does not grind to a halt. All of this results in real competitive differentiation for the business. It's for this reason that many companies start with the back-office functions when embarking on their automation journey.

Notes

1. Agrawal, Ankur, Kapil Chandra, Priyanka Prakash, and Ishaan Seth, 2018, "The New CFO Mandate: Prioritize, Transform, Repeat," *McKinsey* (December 3), **https://www.mckinsey.com/business-functions/ strategy-and-corporate-finance/our-insights/the-new-cfo-mandate-prioritize-transform-repeat**.
2. Protocol, 2022, "The Changing Role of the CIO" (February 8), **https:// www.protocol.com/events/changing-role-of-the-cio**.

CHAPTER 10

The Front Office

"Growth is never by mere chance; it is the result of forces working together."

—James Cash Penney

As the first era of digital transformation unfolded, marketing and sales leaders suddenly became major technology buyers. Customer relationship management (CRM), marketing automation platforms (MAPs), and an ecosystem of revenue-focused software applications transformed these functions.

Buyers of front-office apps are unlike any other buyers. When every app claims direct revenue impact, budget becomes less of an issue. As a result, marketing technology (or martech) is one of the largest technology landscapes in business today.[1]

The front-office tower of automation includes parts of the company that are customer-facing or revenue-driving. Sales and marketing are the largest functions of the front office. Based on industry, it might include other roles, such as a hotel front desk, analysts in a consulting firm, or wealth management advisors. Regardless of what you call them in your industry, the revenue-generating teams and functions often have very similar underlying processes. The good news is that these areas are all jackpots of automation opportunities.

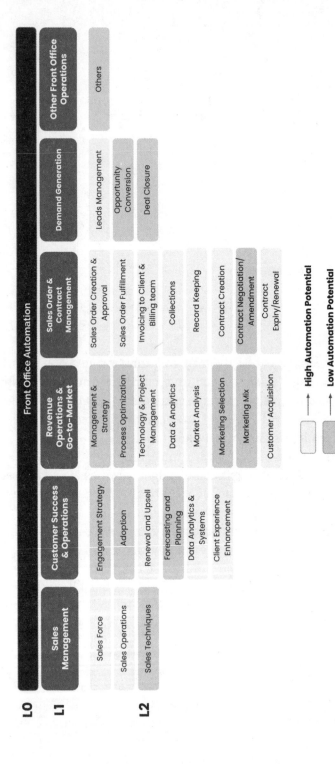

As part of our process hierarchy, we see that the front office activities can be grouped into six key areas:

- Sales management;
- Customer success and operations;
- Revenue operations and go-to-market;
- Sales order and contract management;
- Awareness and demand generation.

The front office is one of the most valuable automation opportunities because of its direct connection to revenue; however, it is also the most volatile. The average tenure for a chief marketing officer is 40 months, and it decreases every year.[2] Time is even shorter for a VP of sales, at 18 months.[3] Even the most successful leaders deal with rising demands and ever-increasing lead, pipeline, and revenue quotas.

Short tenures pressure front-office leaders to drive immediate impact with their initiatives. In the first era of digital business, the resulting action was often just buying new applications. Companies are now seeing the short-lived and rapidly diminishing returns of simply adding software. In the past we added an app to bring dozens of new capabilities to life, such as a new digital lead management approach. Now, a new app might slightly enhance one of those capabilities—perhaps it enhances the lead routing abilities within the lead management process. One of the biggest challenges for the front office in the next era is shaking that "buy new software" mentality and instead pursuing approaches that continue to generate long-term value from the apps they own.

Company Impact Begins in the Front Office

What are the automation goals for the front office? In short, they are the same as the business goals. Fundamentally we want to increase revenue. This is achieved by helping sales teams to sell more products or services, marketing to increase awareness, and customer support or delivery teams to retain and upsell more customers. But the outcomes do not stop there. A well-automated front office results in:

- **Enhanced customer experiences:** Front-office automations can have a major impact on the timeline for addressing customer requests, without the need to make deep customizations or changes to your applications. It can also help to create more personalized interactions with prospects and customers by giving customer-facing teams the just-in-time context they need.

- **Elevated employee experience:** Customer-facing employees get frustrated with administrative and redundant tasks that add little to no value to the customer experience. Automation eliminates this and thereby removes the excess stress, which often causes burnout.

- **Improve bottom line and top line:** By providing experiences that create "WOW" moments for the customers, the organizations are more likely to keep them engaged and have a longer relationship—this results in positive bottom-line and top-line financial outcomes.

The reverberating impact of these moments with customers are not just to make us feel good inside, they can dictate the ultimate fate of the organization.

The Rise of RevOps

Several front-office models have become popular in parts of the business landscape, especially tech companies. In the early days of digital transformation, it started with the introduction of marketing automation platforms (MAPs). Soon after MAPs were put on the map (pun intended), the creation of marketing operations roles quickly followed. These roles were needed to manage the huge number of new marketing systems and associated processes. Sales operations came quickly after, to manage the processes operating in the CRM and across other sales technologies (opportunity management, forecasting, quoting, deal approval, etc.).

More recently, specifically in the tech industry, we've seen sales operations and other revenue and marketing-focused operational roles redefined into "revenue operations" (RevOps). This new team is tasked with implementing, managing, and integrating the front-office apps that drive growth. These roles usually report directly into the sales or marketing teams. These teams are hyper-focused on enabling and evolving the end-to-end sales and marketing processes; technology is simply how they do it. This evolution we are seeing in tech companies, which are often at the forefront of new technology trends, gives us a hint as to how our front-office teams will need to evolve as we move toward increasingly automated sales and marketing functions.

Automation Use Case: Lead Management

Leads can come from many sources: virtual and physical events, web forms, chat solutions, and more. This results in a mess of different formats and at varying levels of detail and quality. The automation platform solves this first problem by either integrating directly to the source systems or providing mechanisms for teams to load lists of leads received from events or other sources.

If a company is driving growth with a lead generation strategy, automation is a must. Lead response times are a crucial metric to maximize value. A marketing process involving leads can include dozens of apps. Many steps are required to move a lead record throughout its life cycle. Each one needs to be imported, validated, cleansed, deduped, enriched, scored, routed, and attributed.

Even with all the dedicated apps to help, lead management is still very hard. Despite best efforts and tech spending, almost every company in the world struggles to contact new leads in less than the optimal five-minute benchmark. In addition, entire categories of software exist to help with this exact problem, yet companies still struggle.

Let's walk through an example of a fully automated lead management process.

The entire lead management process is dependent on the quality of the lead data, and therefore the first step is to ensure we have all the details about the prospect. Before this lead record can be entered into a MAP such as Marketo, Pardot, or HubSpot, it should be cleaned, enriched, and transformed with account/contact data services such as ZoomInfo, Clearbit, or Dun & Bradstreet. These vendors first validate the record by letting us know things such as whether the lead's email is valid or not. Assuming the record is valid, they then return an array of additional information on the company and contact for this lead. The automation platform routes the lead records one by one to these lead enrichment services and uses the resulting data to create a high-quality lead record in the MAP.

Once the incoming lead is validated and standardized in a consistent format, it must be checked by other systems including CRMs such as Salesforce to see if the lead already exists to effectively manage duplicates and then matched to an account.

Next comes services such as MadKudu and 6sense to execute advanced lead and account-scoring processes. In many cases, this "super score" is based on several disparate data sources including intent data, firmographics, and prior company engagements.

The lead score is then used to prioritize and route the lead to the appropriate sales rep (sometimes through complex routing logic using services such as LeanData and RingLead, or built directly into the automated process). The automation platform will notify and continue to remind sales team members in the systems they use most to ensure the leads aren't missed. Some companies may use Microsoft Teams, a sales dialer, email, or even SMS messaging to accomplish this.

Ensuring sales not only follows up but does so in a timely manner with messaging consistent with the nature of the lead is itself a multibillion-dollar industry with sales engagement platforms such as Outreach, Revenue.io, and SalesLoft defining the category. Measuring attribution is another massive headache, with solutions such as Bizible (acquired by Adobe) created to help marketers prove their impact on revenue generation. The automation platform engages these additional tools automatically.

The outcome of a basic automated lead management process looks like the figure on the following page:

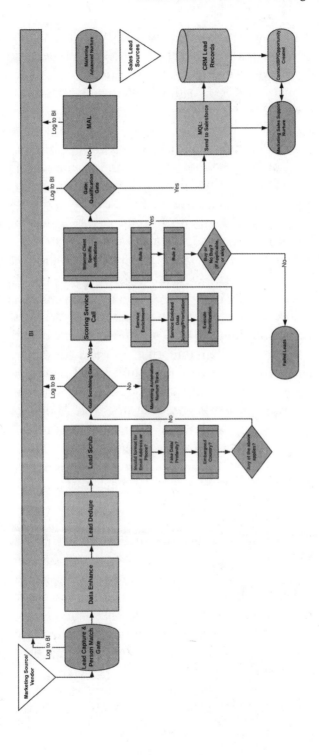

This process, with upwards of nine distinct applications involved, is typically bolted together using native integrations between the apps. The average company assumes sales reps are following up on leads in a specific view in the CRM. Without automated alerts to reps, average lead response times with this approach are usually within a day. In egregious cases, they can extend weeks, or sometimes they are missed entirely. Using the automated version of this process we outlined above, a lead can easily be contacted within five minutes of being captured. The automation can keep tabs on rep response times, and if a lead is assigned and ignored, then the lead can be rerouted to the next best rep to ensure rapid response. In addition, reps can be notified in a variety of ways to ensure leads are top of mind.

Imagine a potential customer is looking to buy a product or service from you and they are also evaluating your competitors. They fill out the form to be contacted on both your website and your competitor's website. Your team phones them in five minutes, catching them when they are actively thinking about this problem. Your competitor, whose strategy is hoping reps are monitoring their lead view, reaches out to the customer two days later. The customer will naturally feel more valued by your organization, and therefore you immediately have the advantage before even saying your first word about your product or service.

These lead automation processes do not need to be built overnight. For a major enterprise technology vendor, they began with simply building out sophisticated lead intake mechanisms. Over time they expanded to automating work that reached into sales, customer support, and even finance processes. At the beginning, their focus was on the quality of the data and ensuring the processes executed reliably end-to-end. But over time, they evolved their processes and began introducing machine learning (ML) to make advanced lead routing and prioritization decisions, which resulted in even faster and more personalized reach-outs to their most promising leads.

In lead management, if we can get the fundamentals down, the sophisticated work will follow naturally. Many companies have been able to achieve as low as 30-second lead response times using this approach. As a result, they also see conversion rates on leads double. With reliable and effective lead management, the company can now have confidence that every lead generated through marketing activities will be handled in a timely fashion. From there, it's all about letting the sales reps do what they do best: sell!

Automation Use Case: Food Delivery and Loyalty Rewards

For those of us in B2B tech, it's easy to forget that the front office involves far more than leads and prospects. In industries such as retail, the priorities look much different.

A large gas and convenience store chain has 800 retail locations, and they had a unique experience during the initial pandemic surges in 2020. Although foot traffic didn't completely collapse as people were still buying gas for their cars, revenue certainly went down for some time.

Shortly before the pandemic struck, they had added a loyalty program to drive return customers and compete with other gas and convenience chains. The idea was that customers could earn rewards such as discounts after a certain number of purchases. The problem was, the loyalty program was only useful for in-person purchases, and foot traffic had all but evaporated during the pandemic. On the other hand, revenue was not dropping as much as they expected because they were partnered with DoorDash, which allowed people to purchase snacks and candy from home.

The company was pleased that retail sales were being propped up to make up for the dwindling foot traffic, but at the same time they still wanted to encourage repeat customers with their loyalty program, which was being managed in a SaaS solution called Punchh. After all, this was the entire point of the rewards program that they had established.

Thankfully, the company already had an automation approach as a supplier of goods since they sold bulk gas to transportation and fleet companies, so working with supplier APIs was a standard process for them.

Using their integration and automation platform, they were able to string together the real-time purchase data from the DoorDash API and pull it over into Punchh. They combined this DoorDash data with the details from other parts of the retail experience, such as in-store purchase data and gas pump purchase data.

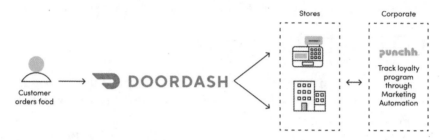

Once this program was up and running, the company was able to gain further insights into how the loyalty program was impacting customer purchasing habits across all 800 stores by streaming the data through big data analytics and AI/ML on Azure.

The company was able to successfully pivot their loyalty program to operate effectively during the pandemic and in doing so unlocked even more insights into their customers. This example shows how supplier data can sometimes significantly augment your processes, and when properly integrated, these suppliers can sometimes extend or even replace entire revenue streams.

Automation Use Case: Deal Desk

For sales teams in many B2B industries, end of quarter can be stressful. If a deal desk—the contract approval process for a sales team—is poorly constructed, it only adds to the frustration for everyone. It affects sales, leadership, finance, and most importantly, customers.

A poor deal desk process will have a lack of visibility on the opportunity across stakeholders. It creates a poor customer experience in managing time-sensitive processes. When the process is siloed and the finance team has little visibility into the opportunity, it is even harder to approve requests. Depending on nonstandard requests or contract changes, lots of stakeholders (finance, legal, immediate manager, skip-level manager, the chief revenue officer [CRO], product team, etc.) may need to review and approve the deal. With all the relevant info rarely well organized, each stakeholder must hunt it down before approval, slowing down the whole process. Some variations of these problems play out for many companies. Deal desk becomes a cost center rather than a tool to recognize revenue faster and reduce contract risk.

When this happens, customers don't receive prompt answers, and sales teams rely on heroics to try to salvage deals. Sales reps miss quota or big incentives, and the company misses quarterly revenue targets. Even worse, there are some completed deals that never should have been approved in the first place. The long-term impact of this might be a string of unprofitable deals, or worse, it could result in lost/frustrated customers who go on to damage a company brand through word of mouth.

The good news is that we can fix this with automation. If we reduce friction in the deal desk process, we'll start off on the right foot with our new customers, making it far easier for us to work with their procurement teams when we look to expand in the future.

To move the opportunity forward in our CRM, the sales rep must submit the deal for review. Reviewers should not have to check an inbox in a siloed application or wait for an email. Most companies commonly use a collaboration tool such as Slack or Microsoft Teams. The automation platform enables the alerts, approvals, and updates to appear in these tools that are always open for the users. This means reviewers shouldn't have to log into the CRM at all!

In the collaboration tool our approvers have what they need at their fingertips and in one click, can either dig deeper using included links or simply approve the deal. Once everyone has given their approval, the opportunity will automatically move to the next stage in the CRM. If and/or when a particular deal gets called into question, we now have a clear audit trail showing the approval of each reviewer along with an explanation of why an approval decision was made.

A large collaboration software company implemented a deal desk process much like this one and then tied it to their larger quote-to-cash process with automation. Now, 98% of their orders are processed in less than five minutes—90% of which aren't touched by any human. Automating their deal desk saved their sales and finance team 5,000 hours/month and sped their approval process up by 4x.

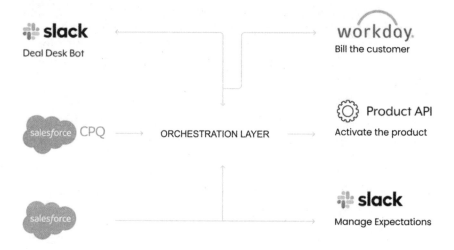

The opportunity for every front-office leader today is to not simply use integration and automation to fix the occasional manual process but to create a culture of automation that elevates the customer experience. As with any other defining attribute of your culture, this attitude and bias toward automation should bleed through into every department. Leadership across the organization must then partner to drive true business transformation through automation.

Innovative Automations in the Front Office

There are fundamental processes that every front office will want to automate, from campaign management to lead routing. Often, the front-office teams are some of the most creative and motivated to test new ideas. As we've mentioned throughout this book, it is critical to empower these creative minds to put their ideas into action. Some of the most exciting ideas in the company can come from these moments of inspiration that are not directly related to the core processes in the company. Often, it is these ideas that have the largest impact on customers and revenue. Here are a few examples:

- **Finding new sources of customer intent data:** In the early days of the pandemic, in-person meetings, events, and other ways to interact face-to-face with prospects evaporated overnight. For a scaling start-up who relied heavily on these interactions for growth, this change had the potential to be catastrophic. Fortunately, someone in their company had the idea for an automation using intent signals coming from third-party websites. Any time a customer or prospect began searching on these industry-specific sites, related sales and marketing reps would be instantly alerted in Slack so they could prioritize their outreach. The end result was that the company made up for the loss of in-person interactions in a dramatic way, reaching 110% of their targets in back-to-back quarters.

- **Using AI call analysis to automate leave-behind suggestions:** Tools such as Gong.io, Chorus by Zoominfo, or Revenue.io use natural language processing (NLP) to generate data on sales calls. This data can be harnessed in many ways. One company created an automation that triggered when Gong caught certain keywords pertaining to new products the company was rolling out. They figured sales reps may still be getting up to speed on new products, so when keyword mentions from

(continued)

(*continued*)

customers and prospects corresponded to the new solutions, sales reps would receive a Slack message with links to suggested follow-up content that was stored in the company's sales enablement platform. In that way, even if the rep missed the opportunity to mention a solution on the call, they could quickly course-correct in their follow-up emails. Sales reps appreciated the help, and it resulted in no missed opportunities for the company.

- **AI-generated call summarization and field updates:** Logging calls and updating the CRM platform has come a long way—generative AI has the potential to take that to a new level. Generative AI can take a call transcript from a tool such as Gong.io and summarize it down to key Salesforce fields that would be useful data for later. These might include: What were the next steps? What was the use case discussed? Were any competitors mentioned? While many platforms may offer some version of this functionality, generative AI gives companies far more power. You can put guardrails up that will define the worldview for the AI. You can also submit partial data to protect sensitive information if you are using a public model. Generative AI can also use that data to create follow-up emails and write templates, and the automation can send the email to a sales rep in Slack for approval before it is sent out.

- **Closed-lost reactivation emails:** Closed-lost deals often hold value for sales reps, but it is rarely valuable enough to justify a rep diverting attention from active pipeline unless they are desperate. An automation can feed closed-lost opportunity and account data into generative AI, which can draft reactivation emails. These emails can be sent to the sales rep who owns the deal in Slack or Teams for approval and then sent out to the right contacts in Outreach. In this way, the automation is supplementing work that might otherwise go untouched in a sales rep's day to day.

- **Auto-categorizing job titles by buyer persona:** Job titles can be diverse; for example, different people with chief marketing officer, CMO, SVP of marketing, or head of marketing titles might all have the same responsibilities. For marketing purposes, a company might want to group all of these titles under the buyer persona of "marketing leader." In the past, that would have been manual work in a spreadsheet or marketing automation platform. With generative AI, it can be as easy as telling the solution to "update all contact and lead records with a marketing leader title to the marketing leader buyer persona" and letting the AI do the work.

All over the world, front-office teams envision how to make the processes efficient and drive automation to supercharge their entire marketing, sales, and customer support efforts—from capturing new leads to growing the customer base—and everything in between. The real opportunity for the front office is to look beyond its boundaries into other parts of the business. As processes within the front office become more automated, connecting them to the rest of the company will unlock great potential.

Notes

1. Brinker, Scott, 2022, "Marketing Technology Landscape 2022: search 9,932 solutions on **martechmap.com**," *ChiefMartec*, **https://chief martec.com/2022/05/marketing-technology-landscape-2022-search-9932-solutions-on-martechmap-com/**.
2. Graham, Megan, 2022, "Average CMO Tenure Holds Steady at Lowest Level in Decade," *Wall Street Journal* (May 5), **https://www.wsj.com/articles/average-cmo-tenure-holds-steady-at-lowest-level-in-decade-11651744800**.
3. Lemkin, Jason 2022, "If Your VP Sales Isn't Going to Work Out—You'll Know in 30 Days," *SaaStr* (June 19), **https://www.saastr.com/if-your-vp-sales-isnt-going-to-work-out-youll-know-in-30-days/**.

CHAPTER 11

The Employee Experience

"Employee experience is the new battleground for talent."

—Jacob Morgan

Diane Gherson, former CHRO at IBM, once said that if people felt great about working with us, our clients will too.[1] She went on to explain that nearly two-thirds of client experiences were directly correlated with employee engagement scores. Happy employees lead to happier customers, more productive people, and better companies.

In recent years, the plight of employees has made headlines. Trends such as the Great Resignation, Quiet Quitting, and remote vs. in-office work have fueled debate. At one point in 2021, nearly 40% of all employees were thinking of leaving their jobs for greener pastures. Surprisingly, compensation ranked 16th on the list of reasons why.[2] Ahead of that were a litany of reasons that revolved around the employee experience. How people experience work, day in and day out, is a key driver for how well we can retain and motivate them.

What processes make up the employee experience tower? It is everything that involves how an employee engages with their employer. It starts from recruitment and goes through onboarding, learning and development, all the way to off-boarding when it comes time to leave.

There is an enormous amount of potential to delight our people and drive more productivity with automation.

It is necessary to build seamless processes to support the entire employee journey and create the moments that matter. Not only will we have happy employees, but we'll find efficiencies along the way.

No matter where a person lives in the world, they all want a fulfilling work life. Automating aspects of this experience has great potential, but it is not without risks. We do not want people to feel like they work for a cold, soulless vending machine. It's important not to lose the human touch that makes people feel valued and important. A Gartner analyst recently told HBR that "employees today want to be treated as people, not just workers."[3]

As the name suggests, this tower of automation is all about experiences. This can make leaders feel that this area is less important because the concept of experience seems nebulous and difficult to measure. However, it is one of the greatest differentiators for companies. Employees who work in empowering cultures and enjoy their jobs will go an extra 10 miles for the companies they work for. This means every single aspect of everything the company does will be done better. There are few things in a company that have such a broad impact.

Removing the ambiguity from employee experience is important. Drawing on employee feedback to identify the areas of improvement for their day-to-day experiences is by far the best approach. This takes a subjective feeling such as "I'm unhappy with my job" and turns it into an actionable and measurable outcome such as "My vacation requests never get approved on time, and therefore, I can't confidently make vacation plans." We've now gone from something vague and unfixable to something we can address with automation! Leveraging employee feedback to turn employee experiences and feelings into actionable improvements is critical to automating the employee experience.

Automating Delightful Experiences

Our recommended strategy for improved employee experience has three components: culture, technology, and processes. If we want to create delightful employee experiences, all three have to come together. As an example, let's take a look at how these play out in the talent acquisition process:

Culture: In talent acquisition, company culture can be communicated in many ways. It can come across in shared values, the special things done for prospective employees, or the way interviewers are coached. We can use automation to enhance the culture of the talent acquisition process by, say, sending automated, handwritten thank-you notes (that's a real thing!) to all candidates as they enter the hiring process, or ensuring interviewers receive a quick reminder of the top five values to communicate before heading into an interview. The example of a handwritten note might make you pause; it doesn't seem a natural fit with automation. Remember that automated processes don't mean they lack personalization, and it doesn't mean people are not involved in those processes. It simply means they execute consistently and automatically loop-in-human actions at the right place and the right time.

Technology: Recruiting tech has grown in the past few years. Candidate management solutions have gotten more sophisticated, but asking executives and managers to log into yet another tool to fill out post-interview scorecards, submit hiring requests, or approve positions is a recipe for a poor experience. We can abstract this work away from the specialized technology into something like Microsoft Teams or Slack so the engagement is quick and satisfying rather than frustrating and eye-rolling.

Processes: The steps that we take throughout the negotiation and signed offer letter process are critical to securing high-impact talent. To ensure less candidates slip through the cracks and accept competing offers, we can work to reduce the time it takes to complete the approvals process for offer letter amendments. Consistently executed processes can also help with eliminating some of the unconscious biases or preferential treatment, which often plague hiring. This results in bigger outcomes like a more diverse workforce and getting the best candidates for the role.

Every process in the employee experience tower can be broken down into these three component parts. By thinking through processes in this way, we often find automation opportunities hiding in plain sight.

Below is the process hierarchy view of the employee experience tower of automation. There are several high-impact and far-reaching processes. This combination of high business value and high visibility makes the employee experience space a great source of use cases, which can be used to help you demonstrate the value of automation.

Let's take a closer look at a few examples from this tower.

Automation Use Case: New Employee Onboarding

Starting a new job off on the right foot is an important ingredient for a quality employee experience. New employees are eager to hit the ground running and make an impact. Equipping them from day one with the tools they need is the least we can do. It goes a long way in setting them up for success, reducing churn, and cultivating the desired work culture.

For many companies, new employee onboarding is done by a handful of employees each week. The semiconductor company Broadcom, on the other hand, onboards thousands of employees at once. Since the company operates by mergers and acquisitions, at times they need to find ways to onboard up to 15,000 new hires in a matter of days. Getting that many new hires up and ready to work with provisioned laptops, app licenses, and single sign-on is no easy feat.

Although not every firm has the same kind of mass onboarding needs, everyone can learn from the process that Broadcom has refined over the years. The company has graduated from cumbersome spreadsheets to a fully automated approach. They can operate at scale.

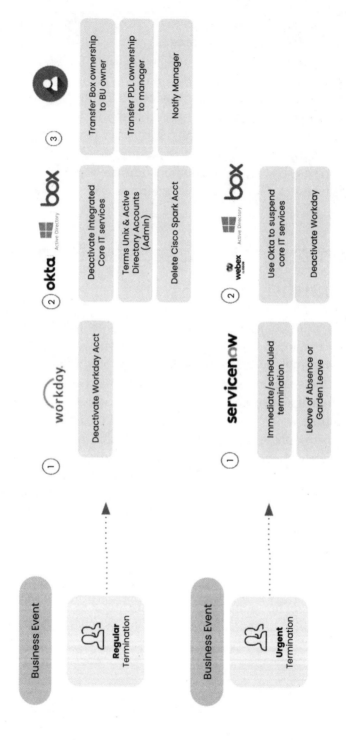

It all starts with a business event, or trigger. The importance of this element in the process cannot be understated. Some automation approaches use listeners, which check for certain characteristics on a regular interval. Others are manually triggered, with an extra step added to the process for a person to turn on a bot or other process. For Broadcom, the action sequence is set off immediately via API once a new employee record is created in Workday. The provisioning that follows happens within minutes. Since Broadcom is dealing with thousands of records at one time, extra steps, especially manual steps, are out of the question.

HR either uploads a large spreadsheet of names or enters them one by one. From there, a new account is created in the identity management platform Okta for single sign-on. While this process happens as soon as the employee data is entered in Workday, the access in Okta is automatically restricted until seven days before the start date. This allows the team to work ahead as much as they need without concern that new employees are receiving access to information inappropriately early. Sometimes, new hires don't end up coming onboard, and names that HR had originally provided are no longer needed.

The team built alternate paths into the process automation to accommodate for these instances as well:

- **Rescind/no-show:** if an offer is pulled back or someone doesn't show up for work, they need to be able to undo all the access provisioning in short order;
- **Rehires:** resurfacing old employee records for returning employees;
- **VIP:** white-glove processes for executive-level employees or other high-touch hires.

Once a new hire is within the seven-day window of joining the company, the basic necessities required for every employee are set up. These include an active directory login, Google Workspace, Webex, Box, office softphone login, and support access. In addition, a new laptop is automatically ordered and either shipped to their local office or their home depending on if they are a remote employee or in-office hire. At this point in the process, their manager is notified, but nothing is sent out to the new employee.

Since managers are left with the discretion to determine the exact start time, they are given the option to finally turn on a new hire's access. The manager sees none of the orchestration that is happening behind the scenes—all they see is a simple portal with their new employee's name and a few dropdowns and buttons. The form includes inputs for special requirements, such as role-specific software applications or additional hardware. Once the manager approves by tapping the "provision" button on the screen, a welcome email is automatically sent to the new hire's personal email with instructions for how to log on and begin their journey.

In the average company, it is a common experience for new employees to feel dazed and confused in the first two weeks. Typically, IT will provision them access to the very basics, such as email and other workspace necessities. But gaining access to specialized apps requires emails from managers to operations colleagues in other departments, which can take several days to get sorted out. Sometimes apps are forgotten and are only noticed later. The inefficiencies in onboarding are so common we don't realize how much lost productivity it really creates.

Broadcom doesn't have these problems. New employees experience a seamless and speedy onboarding experience that is powered by automation. Without delay, they can focus on their mission from day one. At scale, when the company onboards thousands of employees at one time, that gain in productivity is substantial.

Since Broadcom operates chip fabrication and R&D that requires in-person work, they had to send thousands of employees back to the offices in the height of the pandemic in 2020. Having this foundation of automation allowed the team to easily purchase, provision, and ship over 11,000 iPhones with custom contact tracing software to keep their employees safe. Without automation, CTO Andy Nallappan points out that the company would have suffered. "The purpose of automation is more than cost savings, more than scaling, it is just to keep the business running. If we did not have that automation when the pandemic hit, we would have suffered. It would have impacted our customers."

Broadcom is now averaging 30+ new automation additions per quarter, which equates to 105,000 jobs run per month and 6,500 hours saved per month. Complaints dropped from one every single day to just about zero. New employees are more productive and faster than ever.

Positive initial experiences such as the one Broadcom created can help set the trajectory for the rest of someone's career with the company. These kinds of automated processes that make the employees feel welcomed, accommodated, and empowered create a culture of performance that impacts every facet of the company.

Automation Use Case: Overcoming Context Shifting Fatigue

This showcase focuses on a leader in the data center and digital infrastructure space who we will call ConnectCo. Like many companies, ConnectCo recognized that the employee experience in daily operations could be greatly improved by reducing their team's involvement in low-value and repetitive activities.

ConnectCo saw opportunities for reducing manual effort in processes such as:

- Performing background checks in the onboarding process;
- Ensuring employee compliance with post-pandemic, return-to-work protocols.

Saving hours in the workday by automating these manual processes is great, but they wanted to take automation beyond simple efficiency gains by automating rule-based processes.

The head of product management for data & analytics at ConnectCo knew of several examples of hard tasks that were crushing employee morale. The problem was that these were not just simple data entry tasks, they were higher-order functions that involved analysis and decision-making. This challenge was not for the faint of heart—yet the executive wanted to see how far automation could go.

The first project ConnectCo focused on was service ticket automation. They receive an average of 30,000 service emails a day. Each of these emails could require the assistance of a different team and therefore need to be triaged for the type of work that is being requested and for priority handling. Multiple team members, therefore, had to read each email as it came in and create the corresponding work order with the correct priority and team assignment. This was a highly repetitive task that was not only using up precious employee time but was also leaving employees exhausted and unsatisfied with their jobs. High turnover in these kinds of roles can be an often-underestimated cost of poor employee experience.

Rather than relying on human analysis and routing of each request, ConnectCo leveraged machine learning models to catalog or tag the type of work being requested, the priority, and the name of the internal team who needed to handle this type of request. The automation was as follows:

- Execute immediately when a new email was received to the customer support mailbox;
- Lookup the customer record from the CRM using the domain of the sender's email;
- Send the text from the body of the email to the machine learning models;
- Retrieve the classifications (work type and priority) from the machine learning model;
- If the confidence rating of the machine learning models is high, create a work order in the service management system. If confidence is not high, route the request for manual classification by the team.

Any requests that required manual routing to the team for classification were automatically "learned" by the machine learning models. This means that over time, the accuracy of the models continued to improve, and a larger portion of the requests were fully automated.

With the team able to move away from the highly repetitive nature of this work and instead only handle occasional exceptions, they were able to take on new and meaningful projects.

The next automation they investigated was even more interesting. ConnectCo manages data centers all over the world, and their enterprise customers often come on-site to install their own servers. Sometimes, these customers will leave boxes or other packaging on the data center floor. This may seem minor, but in a data center running mission-critical servers this can pose a security risk, safety risk, and most importantly, a fire risk. Historically, the surveillance cameras act as the conduit through which an employee of ConnectCo monitors the customers and if they identify debris left behind, they are required to notify the offenders and ask that they remove materials.

You may wonder what this automation has to do with employee experience. The fact is that employees who are constantly put in the position of having to be the "bad guy" experience significantly more stress and are generally unhappier in their roles. System generated messages sent through automations can often offload these types of activities viewed as negative social interactions off staff. This ultimately removes the social embarrassment from the scenario and improves the experience of both the employee and the customer.

ConnectCo did exactly this. They leveraged automated image analysis of the security feeds to trigger a workflow. The automation first notified the customer that they had left debris on the floor so that if it was a simple mistake, they could simply turn around and clean it up. If the customer chose to ignore the notification, after a set period, the automation would automatically add a line-item for the "clean-up charge" to the customer's next invoice. The security guards no longer felt like nagging parents constantly having to tell their children to clean their rooms. As a result, job satisfaction increased. The customers didn't experience the embarrassment of a person pointing out their mistakes and instead received a simple system notification thereby removing the personal nature of the interaction (in a good way).

The automations ConnectCo created confirm what we already know about the value of relieving employees of mindless, manual tasks. They also reveal that the same benefits exist when automating more complex tasks. These benefits include freeing time for other activities, offloading jobs that nobody wants to do, increasing employee retention, and creating faster and better outcomes for customers and coworkers.

Automation Use Case: Onboarding in the Gig Economy

Multinational organizations have a large workforce and many office locations, and some of their most critical workflows/functions are happening in the human resources (HR) department. This includes elements such as payroll, employee onboarding including contractors, and resource planning that touches critical aspects of the employee experience.

A global ride-hailing company was no different. The onboarding of the new drivers on its global transportation management platform required time-consuming manual data input across four different systems, which created inconsistencies and posed a huge problem for the company's ability to scale. This was creating major roadblocks to the enterprise's desire to drive global expansion. The company understood the value of relieving employees of mindless, manual tasks—saving time, reducing costs, and optimizing workflows. They also saw it was fundamentally impeding their ability to grow revenue.

However, the company not only had these business problems, but they were also facing underlying technical problems with their data. The drive data was spread across spreadsheets and multiple back-end systems, which created a nightmare when trying to gain insights from their driver data. Drivers were the backbone of the company's revenue stream, and therefore they needed high-quality data in order to be able to identify potential problems and course-correct quickly. Thus, the company centralized driver onboarding using Salesforce as the system of record. They leveraged a low-code enterprise automation platform to quickly synchronize data to the remaining systems and further automate the end-to-end driver onboarding process. Within the following year, the company recruited about 6,000 drivers. Automation reduced the manual effort associated with onboarding drivers by 97% or the equivalent of 160.5 working days per year. Moreover, this reduction in effort virtually eliminated their backlog. No more delays in activating drivers. The team could now onboard significantly more drivers, and the company could aggressively scale its business.

The impact of this automation affected multiple parts of the employee experience. The bandwidth that the team got back allowed them to focus on solving drivers' problems and servicing their requests faster, thus greatly improving the drivers' experience with the company.

The company replicated the overall success of the driver onboarding automation for the bigger and more complex use case of onboarding end customers. With operations streamlined and an amazing employee experience, they are now pursuing a successful launch into new global markets.

Innovative Automations in Employee Experience

It is so easy to focus on the essentials in our HR and people orgs—so many of our processes are fundamental to keeping the company running and the doors open. But often, little ideas about culture come from the most unlikely places, and these end up defining our company in the minds of our employees. While the fundamental processes can sometimes be overlooked as table stakes, these magical touches are what make the difference.

- **Automating gift delivery for milestones:** One company set up integrations with gift vendor Snappy Gifts to automatically send a gift to every employee on important milestones including birthdays, work anniversaries, and family additions. If, for example, an employee was marked to be planning parental leave for the first time in a calendar year, they would receive an appropriately priced thoughtful list of gift options. To ensure the gift-giving did not feel impersonal, the team also automated notifications to each employee's manager to remind them to wish their team member well and offer that they relax on their birthdays and other special occasions.

- **Matching employees with volunteering opportunities:** The Atlassian Foundation had a large list of volunteering opportunities that needed help from volunteers. They were seeing that most company employees were willing and even enthusiastic about taking time off to give back, but volunteer opportunities were still vacant. The company built out a survey to capture data on volunteers around the company, their availability, and their skill sets. They then automated the matching process, to find a list of available, willing volunteers for each opportunity the foundation had cataloged. The result was thousands of more volunteers could now contribute in a meaningful way. Not only did this improve employee morale and raise their perception of the company, but it also made a real difference in accomplishing something meaningful in the world.

(continued)

(*continued*)

- **Facilitating new employee mentorship:** New and even seasoned employees are often looking for mentors to learn from. This company built a mentor-bot to match employees who were willing and skilled enough to mentor new employees with those who wanted mentorship. This included new employees in their first 90 days as a sort of buddy program, and it also extended to existing employees. A Slack bot served as a mechanism for employees to request mentors and to send reminders throughout the new employee journey to ensure the mentor:
  - Remembered to schedule regular one-on-one meetings with the new hires;
  - Covered core topics that the company wanted every employee to hear about;
  - Introduced the team member to other key people in the company.
- **Automated learning and development:** Machine learning algorithms can analyze employee data to shape personalized training paths. For example, sales reps are one of the most measured roles in the company—this provides fertile ground for tying training to real behavior. For instance, if a sales rep has consistently short sales calls, generative AI can assemble a learning path for them in the company training platform, or if a customer success manager is receiving below-average NPS feedback from customers, they can be directed to a training path specific to customer service. These can improve employee skills in areas where they most need help and ultimately drive greater job satisfaction.

The Future of Work

What does the future of office work look like? If we peer into the crystal ball, the image is unclear. Whether we will be in offices, working from home, or working from coworking spaces has yet to be seen. Coming off the pandemic, the future of the office is uncertain at best.

But some things are clear. The future of work will involve dozens of software applications for each employee. That list is only going to grow. As we craft more intentional ways of working with the dozens of applications that our people interact with every day, they will begin to find more satisfaction in their work. As we discussed earlier, context switching has a chilling effect on our productivity. While app stacks continue to grow, we have an obligation to find ways to cut back on the daily context shifting employees do. Not only will it improve their experience, but it will also improve the outcomes for the company.

Outside of all the processes and automations that we could undertake to improve the employee experience directly, the very act of implementing the new automation mindset in our companies will make our people happier. Democratization, as an example, has an amazing effect on the team morale and the creativity and joy they bring to their work. Giving teams the liberty to change and improve the way they get work done can lead to significantly higher job satisfaction.

Notes

1. Burrell, Lisa, 2018, "Co-Creating the Employee Experience," *Harvard Business Review* (March), **https://hbr.org/2018/03/co-creating-the-employee-experience**.
2. Sull, Donald, Charles Sull, and Ben Zweig, 2022, "Toxic Culture Is Driving the Great Resignation," *MIT Sloan Management Review* (January 11), **https://sloanreview.mit.edu/article/toxic-culture-is-driving-the-great-resignation/**.
3. *Harvard Business Review*, 2022, "Rethinking Your Approach to the Employee Experience," (March), **https://hbr.org/2022/03/rethinking-your-approach-to-the-employee-experience**.

CHAPTER 12

The Customer Experience

"Even when they don't yet know it, customers want something better, and your desire to delight customers will drive you to invent on their behalf."

—Jeff Bezos

W e all say customers are our top priority. It is a claim everyone can agree on. After all, the customer experience leaves a lasting impression. It is the difference between whether people become promoters or detractors of our brands. The way companies think about customer experience is key to how the customer journey plays out. Thus, creating and obsessing over a great customer experience is a smart approach.

It has been said that the companies that can drive the best customer satisfaction will be the ones that end up on top. Yet, in 2022, Gartner published research that found most customer experience programs are not delivering on the promise of improving differentiation or helping brands compete.[1] The reality is, most CX (customer experience) programs are mired in metric optimization and may have lost sight of the real goal, which is crafting moments that matter between people. A recent Deloitte article, titled "Customer Experience Is Dead," observed: "It sounds so obvious, yet somewhere amidst the myriad of changing business models, commercial rhetoric, and fast-paced technology, the customer became just another term—faceless, nameless and less-human."[2]

Being a trusted partner to our customers is easy to say but much harder to do. Because so many customer interactions happen in the digital space, customer expectations have shifted to match. This means that customers want their experiences to be faster, self-service, app-driven, and more. On the other hand, they don't want the impersonal or restrictive experiences that are over-automated and impersonal. Have you ever phoned a customer service line with a specific question and the menu of choices you are presented with does not include anything related to what you need? Your immediate thought is: "Seriously, just let me talk to a person." Customers wanting digital experiences does not mean they want experiences with all people removed. There are times when we all prefer to speak to a human rather than a machine. Brands that don't have this balance risk causing long-term damage.

It's incredible to think about how far CX has come. We've all experienced the Amazon effect, where we all want things faster. Shipments in six to eight weeks used to be normal for items ordered online. People went from expecting shipments in months, to weeks, to days, and now hours. As comedian Ronny Chieng states: "No item too trivial, no quantity too small, to be hand-delivered into your home like an emperor. Anything in the world that comes to your mind. . . Prime Now [is] two-hour delivery . . . How much further can we go as a civilization? How much more convenience can we get? . . . Let's get 'Prime before.' Send it to me before I want it. . . . Use artificial intelligence to substitute my own intelligence to send me what I want before I know I want it."[3]

Ronnie's idea of "Prime before" isn't that far-fetched. AI and machine learning are more accessible than ever. Customers are becoming increasingly interested in creative uses of AI technology to automate recurring purchases, personalize offers, and more. Anticipating what your customers might want is by no means out of reach—it is here today. We now have services such as Stitchfix, which chooses clothes for us before we know we want them, and TikTok, which chooses videos for us before we know we want them based on an algorithm.

With markets becoming increasingly winner-take-all, the customer experience is one of the primary battlefields of competitive differentiation.

Design CX Automations with People in Mind

Customer work happens at the level of individual customer relationships. In choosing what to automate and how, we must keep the people that matter, customers and employees, at the core of the automation design. It's critical that automations operate based on how customers and employees want to interact. If we understand how they want to interact, we can design automations that best align with those needs and in a way your organization can support.

The customer experience tower of automation is made up of the key touch points between organizations and their customers. This includes customer service functions, managing customer data, marketing, and commerce. As with all of our towers of automation, this represents a subset of customer-related functions and touchpoints but is a great starting point for thinking through your CX automations.

Automation Use Case: Customer Portal

If you have a simple product, getting all your employees up to speed is a simple matter of training them on the message. The challenge is, most companies do not have a simple product. Most companies have complex products, or in the case of larger multinational companies, hundreds or thousands of products.

The complexity of product lines grows when you consider companies whose business model involves growth by acquisition. If sales teams are constantly having to learn and understand new product lines, supplying the right data to customers can be a challenge.

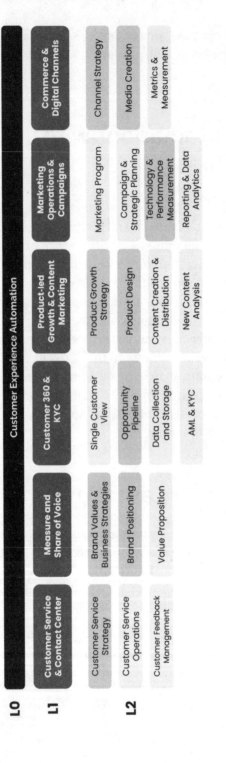

Data about the product or service is crucial to the customer experience. No matter where a customer is in their buying journey, accurate product data is important to their decision. Someone in the awareness stage might wonder if the dimensions of the widget fit their space. Someone in the consideration stage may wonder about processing speed benchmarks to help make their business case.

For this example, we will be sharing the experiences of a large, global company who supplies many of the world's food processors with machinery. In a large, complex organization like this, master product data can live in multiple sources. In their case, it was spread across dozens of systems.

Throughout the various stages of product design, the data about the products lived in various computer-aided design (CAD), simulation, and software development systems. The list of these tools was already enough to make anyone's head spin. To add to the complexity, the solutions are custom-fit to customer requirements—because we are talking about machinery that is large enough to fill rooms. Therefore, configuration files and customer dimensions are also stored in different custom software. On top of this, the assembly instructions for when the machinery was delivered lives in yet another software application.

Only once these custom elements are completed does the data become relevant to the application stack most of us are familiar with. But the vendor in question is operated by acquisition, and so they worked with multiple ERPs, CRMs, and service management tools across divisions.

The company envisioned a "product highway" that would capture the data as it moved through the product life cycle, ending in a final data record that could live in a master data hub. The end goal was to have a master product record for each product that contained all the data. If they could build this kind of record, they could create a central data hub that contained everything. And once an API layer was constructed around the master data hub, it could keep all of the disparate ERP, CRM, and other systems up to date.

Perhaps more importantly, from this master data hub, the company could create a customer portal. That single touchpoint—a simple portal—was the most important element of their sales process. Behind the portal, an enormously complex mix of tools and databases needed to be stitched together. But there was no reason a customer needed to know any of this complexity existed. All they care about is accessing the data they need to make decisions about buying new food-processing products.

In this case, a fully automated experience made the most sense. Having a customer speak to a representative—who would have to go hunting around the dozens of tools with data spread all around the company, only to provide potentially inaccurate information—was not a viable approach. Additionally, in this industry buyers likely don't want to have to call in to sales to find out mundane product details.

The product hub was a hit. Customer engagement was up significantly. The portal provided customers with the ability to look up and ultimately receive new product parts faster, keeping their operations running smoothly. It was also a competitive differentiator as other food equipment manufacturers were not providing this kind of information-rich self-service experience. The likelihood of a customer moving to a competitor for their equipment was now almost nonexistent.

Even though the project was undertaken to improve the customer experience, it ended up elevating the entire company. Now, people from product managers to engineering to design can rely on consistent, quality data no matter where they look. With a master data hub, the entire organization benefits from data accuracy—and the potential exists for the customer experience to be elevated in more ways than one.

Automation Use Case: Frictionless Customer Check-in

For a leading car rental company, a seamless customer experience was an integral part of the growth journey. Reducing friction was the foundation for a better customer experience. However, the reality was very different. The customers usually booked the rentals through third-party providers who fail to pass along relevant pre-rental information, so the company had to duplicate requests to customers. As a result, customers typically had to wait up to an hour at the counter for check-in.

The company wanted to expedite the car rental process by capturing pre-rental information ahead of time (via email and SMS), thus creating a better employee experience by streamlining complexity of back-end processes between disparate systems such as ERP, CRM, business analytics, and the customer service ticketing system.

The solution was to use automation to streamline the end-to-end customer experience without interruption. It removed the noise in the process altogether, resulting in significant time saved for the customer and their team. Customer retention increased. Employees gained latitude to focus on delivering great service, not just collecting information. This helped enhance the overall customer experience with a touchless check-in, reducing the wait time from one hour to only seconds.

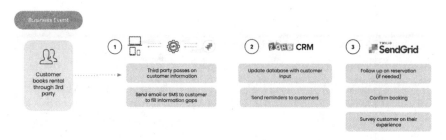

Innovative Automations Throughout the Customer Journey

The customer journey is subject to constant optimization in every company. For that reason, every stage of the customer journey can be improved with automation. Let's look at each one.

Awareness stage: From the time someone visits your website, there are many ways to optimize the experience of potential customers. For example, a well-planned website with content that speaks to potential buyers (which is critical for products that involve long sales cycles) that blends with easy-to-use chatbots can help pinpoint the needs of your audience. Marketing automation can help nurture these leads over time by systematically linking the users with specific owners or content in the organization that can then drive personalized communication and get the brand firmly entrenched in the customer's mind. Some other automations might include:

- **Dynamic content:** Dynamic web content to adapt to the interests and needs of your customers. We can't always have a generic set of web content that appeals to every person. Tailoring your website to dynamically adjust and surface content or ideas based on the individual can drastically improve their experience.

- **Self-service:** Self-service mechanisms to schedule follow-up calls, demos, or information sessions. Filling out forms and sending them into a black hole is not a great feeling. Being able to take immediate action to schedule a next step is a much better experience.

Consideration stage: When someone moves to the consideration stage, their needs usually become clearer. Thanks to analysis of communications sent to the customer and their interactions (including emails opened, links on the website studied, etc.), usage of tools on the website (calculators/sentiment polls), and responses to "easy answer" questions over time, your communications with the customer can become more specific and tailored to their needs. The more data we have, the more creative automations become. A few examples during the consideration stage:

- **Instant answers:** Instant answers for customer questions using tools such as chat bots or automated mechanisms for rapidly connecting potential questions with the right subject-matter expert internally. When customers have a question, they want an immediate high-quality answer.

- **Forming connections:** Every customer wants to hear what other customers are saying. Leveraging automation to connect customers with prior customer reviews, case studies, or even with the ability to directly speak to other customers can rapidly increase their confidence.

Purchase stage: The right automation technology can make the actual purchase process frictionless for the customer. Automating steps such as multi-level approval workflow, communicating role-specific benefits, and terms and conditions for individual users can be helpful for the buying organizations. Here are a few others for the purchase stage:

- **Automated promotions:** It is frustrating to buy something only to learn that if you had entered a certain code or clicked a different link, you could have saved money. Automatically surfacing promotional codes, offers, or other benefits increases customer trust and improves experience.

- **Redline management:** B2B companies often have to deal with contracts, legal terms, and redlines. This process can sometimes take months. Leveraging automation can facilitate the reminders, the formal review hand-offs between teams, the meeting scheduling, and the final signatures.

- **Automated fulfillment:** After a purchase, the customer is excited to get their new product or service. Automating the fulfillment of their purchase can be achieved through instant notifications, immediate welcome messages/meetings, rapid access to the product/service (where possible), and sharing additional information to help them get started.

Retention and loyalty stages: Acquiring customers is hard work. Therefore, keeping them is a top priority. Integrating customized communication across various channels for the user can ensure ongoing engagement. You can use this multichannel communication to offer sneak peeks into new and upcoming offers or target specific customers with offers that are relevant to them based on their profiles. This level of personalized engagement allows you to boost your cross-selling ability and build customer loyalty. Some possible automations:

- **Personalized recommendations:** We can alert customers to new products, services, or more value from their existing purchases. Recommendations can come based on data from the customer's prior interactions with the company and simple machine learning models.

- **ID struggling customers:** Monitoring support request data, customer communities, returns, support website visits, survey results, or even social media activity can provide indicators of customers who are not having good experiences with the company. Helping these customers can result in some of the most impactful customer experiences. Helping a struggling customer at the time they need help the most can create lifelong promoters of your organization.

- **Automated identification and VIP treatment for loyal and high-value customers:** Customers know when they are loyal and provide a company with significant gain. They also want to be recognized for this. Automation can help you identify these customers and automatically

(continued)

(*continued*)

inject VIP treatment across their journey. This may be less wait time for support, automated gifts, personalized thank-you notes, discounts, etc. Proactively recognizing these customers encourages continued loyalty and growth.

Reputation and advocacy stages: Customer experience defines the way customers perceive the organization. A meaningful experience forges loyalty, cultivating advocacy and improving brand reputation. Automations enable consistent and timely omni-channel communications, streamlining processes that have direct impact on how customers interact with and experience your brand. Advocates are loyal customers and repeat buyers. They hold the unique position to amplify your brand reputation, encourage their peers to drive higher adoption, and emerge as influencers in the market. At this stage, there are options for customers to share their feedback with external stakeholders. Some automations to think about:

- **Automated company or product reviews:** Streamline the process for customers to share their feedback about the product or company. As an example, I would never review an app in Apple's app store; however, once the box popped up in the app and I simply had to click a star rating, I was more than happy to provide my feedback. The process was simplified and therefore now helps to spread the word of the customers.

- **Automated monitoring of social media to identify promoters and detractors of your company, product, or service:** Proactively engaging with these people can show that your company hears people's positive feedback, concerns, or questions. It can change the perception of the company from a nameless entity to a group of people who care.

The Future of CX

Is automation the panacea to all CX problems? Absolutely not! Typically, automation works best in scenarios where business insights pertaining to the customer and their needs are well understood across all departments. Automations that bring your company's different teams, different systems, and disconnected data together to provide customers what they need and when they need it are often the most effective. Starting with your customer's journey and identifying where they are encountering less than desirable experiences is usually a great place to start. If they are looking for faster, more personalized, more modern, or more connected experiences, automation is often the answer.

Notes

1. *Gartner*, 2022, "Gartner Says Most Customer Experience Programs Are Not Delivering on the Promise of Improving Differentiation and Helping Brands Better Compete," (May 10), **https://www.gartner.com/en/newsroom/press-releases/gartner-says-most-customer-experience-programs-are-not-deliverin**.
2. *Deloitte*, n.d., "Customer Experience Is Dead," last accessed January 10, 2023, **https://www2.deloitte.com/mt/en/pages/strategy-operations/articles/mt-consulting-article-customer-experience-is-dead.html**.
3. Chieng, Ronny, 2019, "Ronny Chieng, Asian Comedian Destroys America!" *Netflix*, **https://www.netflix.com/title/81070659**.

CHAPTER 13

Supplier Operations

"Alone we can do so little; together we can do so much."

—Helen Keller

The global supply chain has experienced some of the most painful system shocks in recent business history. We all remember seeing empty department store shelves as the COVID-19 pandemic set in. And the supply chain seems to have struggled to recover ever since. Workers have been demanding higher wages and better working conditions. Overwhelmed ports, labor shortages, factory shutdowns, and empty retail shelves are all common challenges.

As consumers, the empty shelves are only the tip of the iceberg of a complex, difficult-to-manage supply chain. Nearly every company has to work with suppliers. Companies may be sourcing raw materials for manufacturing, leveraging external service providers, or relying on partners to support other parts of their business. The interactions between a company and its suppliers/partners are ripe opportunities for automation.

The supplier and operations efficiency tower encompasses procurement, logistics, material management, and manufacturing. What these processes look like varies greatly from industry to industry.

However, in most organizations the key functional areas can be grouped as follows:

- Supplier management information;
- Procurement and payments;
- Manufacturing, inventory, and material management;
- Returns management;
- Supply chain and logistics.

The pandemic drove large swaths of the supply chain to modernize and digitize. We are seeing continuous change in business operating models, geopolitics, and regional regulations. Business conditions are also fluctuating with supply chain disruptions and new players entering the market. This volatile environment results in the need for enterprises to evolve their business process and constantly adapt to new trends to gain and retain a competitive edge.

One example of a recent transformation is the Internet of Things (IoT) and connected devices. Many major shipping companies are beginning to overhaul their shipping containers with IoT tracking; the result is a much better sense of where cargo is in real time. Although track-and-trace processes used to be laborious and time consuming, these modernizations are changing that. The reduction in labor is not the only benefit: these new technologies also produced an immense amount of data about the movement of cargo. In the future, this data can be used to create an even more efficient and environmentally sustainable supply chain.

With increased focus on agility and responsiveness, many leading companies are looking to run their businesses on cloud-based apps and technologies. While switching to the cloud in itself isn't a bad thing, many companies have been left with many unintegrated point solutions to manage supplier data. This fragmentation of internal tools combined with the increasing need to have suppliers directly tied into core processes has resulted in increased investment in automation in this space. In a recent survey conducted by *Harvard Business Review*, companies plan to accelerate automation adoption in supplier and operations processes in the next two years.[1]

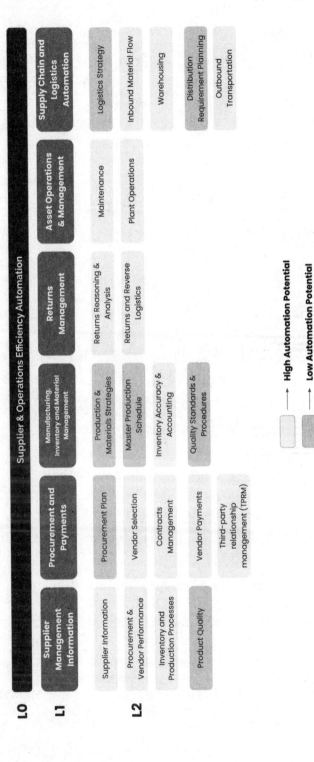

- 43% will digitize more supplier information;
- 37% will expand data analysis capabilities of their supplier base;
- 35% will introduce technologies to improve collaboration with internal procurement stakeholders;
- 33% will introduce technologies to improve collaboration with suppliers.

Supply Chain Process Automation Opportunities

Every supply chain has two flows—goods and materials flow in one direction and data, and information flow back in the other direction. As goods are sent from the sender to the receiver, information from each step along the journey is relayed back to the sender.

Typical challenges that need to be addressed in the supply chain are:

- Real-time end-to-end supply chain visibility;
- Risk management of the supply chain;
- Removal of inaccurate data and reporting;
- Integration of disjointed systems and processes.

Typical processes that are part of this supplier operations tower include order to cash, procure to pay, source to contract, plan to product, and more. All these challenges and all of these processes have opportunities to apply automation to significantly streamline operations. Let's talk through a few examples.

Automation Use Case: Seamless, Self-service Returns

Today, an enormous part of the customer experience revolves around a quality e-commerce experience. As Amazon continues to set the standard for customer expectations in this area, other brands are need-ing to keep up and find creative ways to differentiate. Customers want to receive their purchases quickly and expect quality support and pain-free returns processes.

Companies have many choices when it comes to platforms for payments, listings, storefronts, returns, and other key processes. But in many cases, e-commerce business grows over time, and the apps a company chose early in the process are no longer suited for the scale at which the company is operating.

One of the world's largest direct-to-consumer computer periph-erals brands found themselves in such a situation when they realized that their return process was in bad shape. The company sold key-boards, mice, webcams, and other computer accessories to consumers and businesses all over the world. Customers were growing frustrated with the hoops that they had to jump through. Phoning a service request line with long waits and frustrating prompts did not start the engagement well. This problematic experience only continued for the customer as they went on to talk to an employee who was struggling to navigate a poorly designed RMA (return merchandise authorization) solution that had been built many years ago.

Unlike the food-processing company in the previous chapter, this vendor did not have hundreds of products that were individually complex. Rather, they had thousands of products, each of which was relatively simple. The problem, however, was very similar—disparate databases, large amounts of data records, and a high rate of data evo-lution in a short amount of time. This resulted in customer returns getting lost in their enormous collection of apps and databases that made up their back end.

Customers want digital experiences. They do not want to dial an 800 number, wait on hold for a person to come on the line, only to spend 15 minutes trying to list the product name, date of purchase, serial number, transaction ID, and more. The company needed to give the customers what they were expecting, which was an easy-to-use online portal where they could file their return in minutes.

Making foundational changes to a critical process such as this has massive implications for the customer experience. A vendor of this scale is processing thousands of sales transactions every day.

A disruption of one day or even three days is something that would begin trending on social media, make news headlines, and lead to a significant revenue loss. The stakes are high.

Their current RMA solution was built with custom code in Salesforce Service Cloud. They couldn't quite drive the kind of solution that they needed with this technology, so they looked elsewhere. Zendesk sounded like a better fit. It aligned well with their RMA goals for improved customer experience, and it was able to handle their enormous product inventory. Additionally, they were expecting to save millions of dollars in licensing fees as a result of the change in SaaS providers.

They had to keep in mind that their RMA process was not handled solely by Zendesk, it was spread across many systems. The process was also backed by some very large data sets. For example, their Oracle business suite of databases contained north of one billion records.

The systems supporting their end-to-end RMA process included:

- Zendesk: the main e-commerce platform;
- Product registration management: tools where customers can register their device;
- RMA management: for tracking and handling customer returns;
- Service management: call center solutions and others for support employees;
- Product databases: rich product details on every SKU;
- Oracle e-business suite: customer records, inventory management;
- UPS: partner for labels, shipping, and tracking;
- TransferWise: partner for money transfers, quotes, and refunds.

Many of these solutions were built with custom code from the ground up, and others were heavily customized to fit the unique needs of the business. There definitely would not be an "out of the box" solution to solve this complex problem.

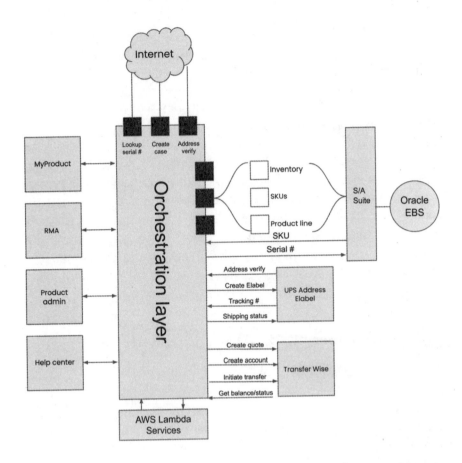

They implemented an automation platform to orchestrate this process end-to-end. This enabled customers to submit their RMA requests through the website, and all the rest of the steps were executed automatically. This included looking up the product, validating warranty, generating shipping requests, tracking status, and routing exceptions.

The migration to this new automated solution went off without a hitch. What originally was planned to take nine months only took nine weeks. In large part this was because the company selected an orchestration layer that was low-code, so the ability to democratize development and rapidly iterate on the solution shortened the implementation time dramatically.

But more importantly—there was no interruption for customers. Customers seamlessly began leveraging the new portal for RMAs and were none the wiser that the process was completely overhauled and replaced overnight.

What customers did notice, however, was that the RMA process was now easy and simple. Those who wanted to return or exchange a product could simply submit a return request online through a simple form. The return shipment info is then automatically emailed to them, and the customer can send back the defective product and will receive a replacement in the mail. No phone calls, no lost requests, no frustrating waits. The next time one of these customers wants to buy a keyboard or a mouse, they are much more likely to buy one from this manufacturer. They know if something goes wrong, the company is there to help with a frustration-free experience.

Automation Use Case: Digital Supply Chain

When we think of a supply chain, our minds immediately go to physical supply chains: freight, shipping containers, trains, and the movement of goods and services. But today, many companies in the content business (think: movies, music, and TV) are operating digital supply chains (DSC). There are many stakeholders to consider in a content-driven business, and the process automation is not all that different between the two.

As consumers of movies and TV shows, we rarely think about the technical and process work behind the scenes. But there are many elements that viewers have no idea are happening: digital rights, royalty payments, file transfers, and other processes. Many of these happen between two or more entities—whether they are individuals or companies. A team that is thinking about a digital supply chain might look at their process with a perspective like the illustration on the following page:

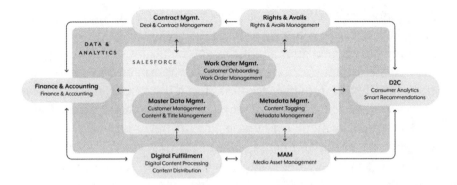

What do actual digital supply chains look like? They are extraordinarily complex, with various internal and external processes that execute over the course of several months (and in some cases years) as content moves from idea through to final product.

For example, the following diagram shows the production process for a large content company that makes feature films for streaming, theater, and TV:

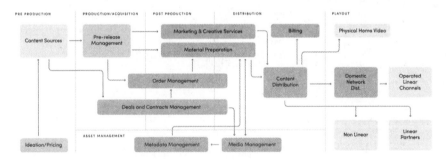

For this company, the entire supply chain for a new movie kicks off based on a single data point, known as the "first photography date"—the first date that the movie will begin filming. Once that date is known, the company knows that the movie is not just an idea, but it is a real project.

Once the automation initiates, it begins collecting additional data about the movie such as the release date, plot, actors, director, and producers. Much of these early points of communication are either happening in a custom external-facing portal or via email. The company has created automations to automatically process and parse these emails to capture assets and other key information from the messages. Email is an imperfect medium, but it is still mission critical for dealing with external stakeholders, especially smaller suppliers.

The media content containing the full recording of the movie typically arrives via an email containing a link to a file-sharing service. Most commonly these large media files are hosted in Amazon S3 or studio-specific tools such as Ateliere. At this point, the content company begins their prerelease management process. This is where the screening copies are made. The movie content is watermarked, subtitles are added, and so on. Many steps in the process are automatically sent to third-party suppliers—such as content localization for different regions around the world.

Several notifications throughout this process are automatically triggered for different teams who need to get involved at just the right time in the process. For example:

- Once the visual assets arrive from the external graphic design agency, an email with links to the marketing visuals is automatically sent to the marketing department;
- Once the watermarked, subtitled, and translated content arrives, an internal memo automatically goes to the distribution team;
- Once a contract is signed, an internal notification is automatically sent to the contracts team.

The company historically struggled with teams failing to do their part in the process because someone forgot to tell them or because they hadn't noticed the new movie in their system. With notifications through their preferred channels and the necessary reminders, this problem vanished.

Once the prerelease processes are all done, the content needs to be distributed to consumers. In the case of players such as Disney or Netflix, the distribution is internal—it lands on their own streaming platforms. But in the case of other studios, they need to get the content out using partners all over the world. They still sell physical copies, so content needs to go to DVD and Blu-Ray manufacturers. It also needs to go to TV channels, movie theater distributors, and streaming platforms. Why rely on phone calls or manual emails when the automation can automatically share the content and place orders with these manufacturers instantly?

We've all seen movies and shows disappear from streaming platforms; that is because a contract between two companies ended. As a studio makes money from the licensing deals, they are motivated to ensure streaming platforms comply with the terms of the deal, and automation enables them to do this quickly and efficiently. In order to do this, they need a mechanism to capture the data on how many times the content is viewed or played and send it back to their internal tracking systems. Someone can download and upload the details via spreadsheet, but when legal ramifications are involved if a stakeholder isn't properly paid, this company chose to automate it entirely.

The automation of this end-to-end digital supply chain process is one that we can all learn from. Surprisingly, most of them are not automated. In fact, the company we are describing here is the first in the world to fully automate this process from end to end. Even if your company does not have a digital supply chain, you can likely see commonalities with your own processes in the form of the problems they faced. What's stopping you from becoming the first in your industry to automate a core end-to-end process?

Automation Use Case: Robots Roaming the Aisles

Shoppers at some retail convenience stores might be surprised to notice that robots are roaming the aisles along with them as they browse. Several start-ups and established companies are producing robots that resemble tall Roombas, specifically designed for stock monitoring. Using computer vision, these robots roll around the store, confirm that prices are correct, see how many items have sold or disappeared, and report back to a central database. It's a futuristic notion that can allow companies to ensure items stay in stock, keep tabs on shoplifting losses, and eliminate price discrepancies. One interesting use case is the last mile of ensuring inventory is actually on the shelf. A store may have lots of inventory on hand, but that inventory may be sitting in boxes in a back storage room. If the item is not on the shelf, it won't sell.

It is also a way to ensure that the supply chain keeps up with demand. While human workers may not realize that an item is experiencing a surge in demand or may not feel empowered to alert the right person in the chain of command, a store-strolling bot can instantly catch demand surges.

Once the master database is updated, an API connection to key suppliers can trigger larger orders for regions that are experiencing higher needs. For example, if a winter storm blows through an area and hand warmers and umbrellas are suddenly flying off the shelves, the store-roaming robots can ensure that the convenience store can capitalize on the surge in demand and take market share from competitors who may have been slower to react.

It sounds futuristic, but many stores are already purchasing these exact robots. Badger technologies, for example, a firm owned by Jabil, is rapidly building out infrastructure for firms to capitalize on the data from always-on in-store bots. They note that companies can lose up to 4% of their potential revenue from out-of-stock items.[2]

Innovative Automation in Partner and Supplier Relationships

How we interact with our partners and suppliers varies greatly for every company. The major processes we have covered here are a look at some of the common threads that weave through each company. But we would be remiss to not talk about the unique ideas and sparks of inspiration that come from our people who are closest to the processes. In many cases, some of the most transformative and differentiating ideas come from automations that step outside of the boundaries of common processes.

- **Automating partner marketing to drive growth:** One company who relied heavily on partner/channel sales to drive revenue was looking for ways to ensure their products were top of mind with partners over other vendors. The marketing team realized that partners would engage more and promote the company's products more often if they were marketed to just as often as the company's customers. Therefore, they set up an automation to pull partner contacts into the marketing automation platform. Once this was done, they began to realize that they could automate and personalize the messages to the partners based on partner performance and other data, which was captured in the CRM. Through this simple automation they drove partner revenue up by 33% in one year.

- **Replacement sourcing for end-of-life parts:** A point-of-sale vendor noticed that a credit card reader, which they sourced from a third-party vendor, had a lifespan of about two years. Once it began approaching end of life, it would begin misreading credit cards requiring a handful of swipes before the customer could complete a purchase. Thankfully, it would produce a read error alert, and the company could use this to trigger a new part order with their supplier, followed by an automatic UPS label generation to ship the part directly to the customer. The end result was that customers would receive replacement parts before they even realized they had a problem (enhancing customer experience), and the supplier relationship was streamlined in such a way that only the most serious exceptions needed to be addressed by the team.

- **Supply chain route optimization:** Generative AI can be given data on supply chain routes and be asked to deliver useful insights. These include: analyzing data from suppliers, logistics providers, and other sources to optimize shipping routes, reduce lead times, and improve overall supply chain efficiency. As IoT sweeps supply chain routes and becomes more common on containers, transportation, and sites, AI algorithms can help companies optimize inventory management, including forecasting demand, tracking inventory levels, and automatically reordering supplies.

The Supply Chain of the Future

Supply chains will continue to be overhauled and rebuilt for the foreseeable future. Companies are under pressure to localize their supplier relationships in response to geopolitical uncertainty and deglobalization. This will result in even more complex hybrid supply chains, and the need for automation will simply increase.

While our experience of the supply chain in the early 2020s has been a painful one, it has resulted in a significant shift and push for modernization. Today, the technology exists to deliver these modern automation-powered supply chains—modern automation tools, AI/ML technology, warehouse robotics, and more. The ingredients are all there. It simply needs a chef with the right mindset.

From Partnerships to Platforms

Our interactions with partners and suppliers are often simply one element of our company's external interactions. The way in which our company interacts with customers, partners, suppliers, employees, regulators, investors, and other stakeholders is not simply an opportunity for optimization or improved experience. Bringing the right stakeholders together, providing them with the right information at the right time, or supporting the growth of their businesses are all extremely high-value services for these stakeholders. In fact, more than half of the 10 most valuable companies in the world are companies that derive a significant part of their revenue by delivering these services. These businesses are called platform businesses.

Now that we have concluded with the last tower of automation, we wanted to take a detour into platform businesses and the exciting opportunity for modernization that it presents to all businesses. The last chapter of this section will look at what makes a platform business and how your company can leverage automation to become platform driven.

Notes

1. *Harvard Business Review Analytic Services*, n.d., "Managing Procurement Risk: Enterprise Agility for a Changing World," last accessed January 10, 2023, **https://forms.workday.com/en-us/reports/managing-procurement-risk/form.html?step=step1_default**.
2. *Badger Technologies*, n.d., "Actionable Data for Retail," last accessed January 10, 2023, **https://www.badger-technologies.com/**.

CHAPTER 14

The Platform-Driven Business

"Innovation comes from the ability to see the world in new ways, to find patterns where others see chaos, and to see opportunity where others see threat."

—Rosabeth Moss Kanter

The concept of platform businesses became popular in the first few years of the 2020s due to the overwhelming success of several platform businesses in a short period. In 2021, 6 of the 10 most valuable companies in the world were considered platform businesses.[1]

The unfortunate truth is that the concept of a "platform business" has become somewhat overused and twisted in definition over time. The original definition of a platform company was a company whose service was to connect producers and consumers of various kinds. A few examples are:

1. **Uber**, which connects those who want a ride with those who can provide a ride;
2. **Google**, which connects advertisers with those interested in their products;
3. **Facebook**, which connects friends and family with one another.
4. **Apple**, which connects app buyers with app sellers.

Not every company can—or even should—make its primary business a platform business. However, every company can benefit greatly from the ideas behind them. We can all apply the concepts that made these organizations wildly successful.

Becoming a platform-driven business does not mean becoming another tech company. Instead, it means reimagining how to do business in the digital age. These companies are rethinking how they are operating in a world where their customers, partners, and even their employees are expecting more of them.

You may be wondering what this has to do with automation. If you look back to our definition of a platform company, it's all about connecting people and companies together to help them better get a job done. As you've seen throughout this book, that's also what automation is all about. You want to make people's lives easier by looping them into a process at just the right times, automating the things they don't want to worry about, and providing a great digital user experience along the way. Thinking through how to transform your company into a platform-driven business is just a great way of thinking outside the box about automation. As I've gone through this exercise with different companies, I find that it unearths new ideas. It also makes concepts such as "digital transformation" meaningful and actionable.

Becoming Platform Driven

We could spend much time discussing the theory behind platform companies, but I find actions are much more valuable. As you read through this chapter, think about your business today and how you might become platform driven. In order to do that, let's start with the four primary methods that a traditional company can leverage to become a platform company.

1. **Method #1: Data Platform:** Leverage your proprietary data or services to help other businesses, your partners, or your customers achieve their goals.
2. **Method #2: GTM Platform:** Create a platform that leverages your existing go-to-market (GTM) investments to connect customers with partners or with other products.
3. **Method #3: Services Platform:** Make your services available via your platform to the ecosystem and be a digital building block for others to leverage in their automations.

4. **Method #4: Operations Platform:** Build an internal platform to break down silos and foster operational excellence.

As you might imagine, these are not the only ways to become a platform company. We find that by looking at your business through each one of these lenses, you will often come up with unique ideas for how your company can be platform driven. Therefore, use these methods to structure your thinking or use them as part of a brainstorming workshop with your team.

Let's talk through each of these methods in a little more detail and review some examples of companies implementing these platform-driven strategies.

Method #1: The Data Platform

Businesses create endless streams of data. The total data volume across the globe is now estimated in zettabytes (2 to the 70th power bytes) and continuously growing. But with all the talk about data being so valuable and people stating, "Data is the new oil," why aren't we all rich? The reason is that most of this data is untapped. It is stored inside a company database, spreadsheets, documents, or other hidden places.

For any data, beauty is in the eye of the beholder. In other words, it only has value if it relates to the right people at the right time. A dataset on the economic growth of countries vs. a dataset on the top TikTok videos in each country will have different value to different audiences. (How do you think these pieces of data would resonate if you asked a teenager and an investment manager about each of them? You're right, the teenager loves analyzing economic data and the investment manager is addicted to TikTok.) All jokes aside, the key to turning untapped data into value is simply about connecting it with the right audience to help them get a job done.

Let's now step back to our platform-driven business. If every company has data that is valuable to someone, every company could theoretically create a value-generating data platform. The hard part is figuring out what data you have, who may want to pay for it, or how it could be used to drive alternative revenue streams. Here are a few quick examples of traditional companies who have created data platforms.

Kelley Blue Book (KBB) started in the 1920s as a book offering people the ability to find independent prices for used cars. Think back before the internet and before computers, how do you figure out what your car is worth? How much should you sell it for? This is the problem Kelley Blue Book solved. With one hundred years in business, they clearly have a product people want. The heart of what they are selling is in fact data, and therefore if KBB simply made this available online (which they did), it wouldn't be as impressive of a story. KBB took it one step further by understanding what their customers were really trying to do.

In KBB's case, their customers usually wanted to sell their car. Instead of simply providing their data, they now combined their trusted pricing data with a service to connect you to a used car dealership willing to pay top dollar for your car. They help the customer by keeping the offers from the dealerships honest, and they help the dealerships by connecting them with a steady stream of used car inventory. KBB benefits from increased website traffic and a new revenue stream from dealership referrals.

Kelley Blue Book went from book sales to a platform-driven business. They leveraged their data as their core asset and built both an ecosystem and a seamless automated process for used car sales around it. KBB aren't the only ones to do this; we are seeing this across industries.

Some companies may not have multiple stakeholders to connect to one another and instead may simply sell their data as a new revenue stream. A few examples:

1. Nasdaq offers their "Data Link" platform to sell their market data to both companies and individuals who may want to use it. This could be to build an app, power advanced analysis, or enable investment firms.

2. FedEx has launched Dataworks to monetize their immense logistics data. By combining the data with weather, traffic, and other relevant data, they can drive immense insights for companies looking to understand global logistics down to the last mile. This may help

their customers ship more reliably, help large logistics operations such as the COVID vaccine deliveries, or even help detect package fraud or other crimes being carried out through delivery services.

Companies like these typically make their data or the insights derived from this data available through APIs once access has been purchased. A technology once reserved for Silicon Valley companies, exposing data via APIs is now possible with only a few clicks.

The third step in *Harvard Business Review*'s "4 steps to monetizing your business data" is "Buy, don't build."[2] Automation technologies can easily be embedded into your data platform. This means you don't need to hire a team of developers to build a big fancy platform, you simply leverage a third-party solution. These embedded automation solutions allow you to create a data platform, share your data via APIs, and even provide your partners with low-code tools to integrate your data with their systems.

Remember, you do not need to be a data company to create a data platform. You saw from the FedEx example that in some cases, the data produced from your normal business operations may be of very high value to your customers, partners, or even companies in completely different industries.

Method #2: The GTM Platform

It is estimated that in 2021 businesses spent $781 billion globally on advertising. This is only a fraction of the total go-to-market (GTM) spend that businesses invest in their sales and marketing functions. Getting connected with potential customers is one of the most important functions of any business and therefore justifies the immense investment. With such a focus, many companies create themselves a platform to share their message with the world. However, creating a standard sales and marketing platform is not what we are discussing in this chapter. We are looking at how traditional companies leverage their existing sales and marketing investment to create a new revenue stream using the concepts from platform businesses.

In very simple terms, imagine your company invests millions of dollars in getting the attention of a specific set of potential customers. Now that you have their attention, besides selling them your product or service, can you leverage the attention you've gained to provide that customer with additional value? And maybe provide value to another company too? This is the foundation of creating a GTM platform-driven business.

Walmart has created an amazing example of GTM platform. As the largest retail company (by revenue) in the world, their total advertising investment in 2021 was more than the GDP of Greenland. Some of that advertising was used to direct people to **Walmart.com** in order to have people purchase whatever they need with a few clicks. A traditional company would stop here. Customer visits website, customer browses, customer possibly makes a purchase. However, Walmart saw the potential of this captive audience and decided to offer more than simply the products that they sold.

Walmart saw that if a customer visited their website and looked for a product that they didn't carry, the customer would simply leave. All the marketing effort to bring that customer to the website was effectively lost. Not to mention the customer experience. By not finding a product, the customer may start to believe that Walmart's website isn't a reliable place to find the things they need. How would they solve this problem? You guessed it: they needed to become platform driven.

Walmart created a third-party sellers' market where small, specialized retailers could list their products to be shown to anyone browsing the Walmart website. Their platform simply connects online retailers with customers. Now, when a customer comes and searches for a product on **walmart.com**, they are significantly more likely to find exactly what they want. Walmart can charge a service fee to the retailer for processing the transaction through their website. The retailer can harness the power of Walmart's marketing power to get visibility for their products. Everybody wins.

You don't need the marketing budget of Walmart to create a GTM platform. Even a small coffee shop with no marketing budget could create a GTM platform. The coffee shop naturally brings in customers based on their store location, and those customers may be highly coveted by other businesses. As an example, a coffee shop located in a financial district would have many customers working for banks and investment firms. The coffee shop could easily set up a platform to connect advertisers with these customers. They could allow these companies to purchase pastries in a branded package that would be given away to everyone who buys a coffee. Now the advertiser is getting their name out to their target audience, the customer is getting a free pastry, and the coffee shop is getting the revenue from an additional pastry with every coffee. Platforms can be Walmart-sized or coffee shop-sized but still follow the same foundational business principle of leveraging your captive audience to connect buyers with sellers.

Method #3: The Services Platform

Throughout this book we have discussed the concept of creating building blocks, reusable services, or a composable enterprise. The idea is to allow you to quickly weave together digital services from across your company into an end-to-end process. But what if part of that process was handled by another company? This happens all the time. Now let's imagine that this other company, we'll call them ServCo, required you to phone them in order to have them do their step in the process. Ugh. Our beautiful end-to-end automated process now requires a manual phone call because ServCo needs us to call them.

Is this step necessary? Or is that simply how they've always operated? If ServCo offered an API, email, or other digital approach to requesting their service, we could simply weave that step into our automated flow. Which means, if a competitor to ServCo offered a digital approach to engagement, you may be looking to switch vendors.

A services platform enables your customers or partners to digitally integrate with your service offerings. This might be to order your product or services or possibly simply to interact with these services. In this increasingly automated world, cross-company automations will be the norm, and therefore providing a service platform will eventually be a requirement for all B2B interactions. Let's look at a few examples.

Every new employee hired at most companies requires some degree of a background check. Determining if the person has a criminal record and validating their education and experience ensures that we are hiring who we think we're hiring, an important step in the hiring process and something that quite a few companies provide as a service. One of these companies was a Canadian company called Backcheck (later acquired by Sterling).

Backcheck was founded in 1997. During their early days they allowed customers to call them up or submit a request by email to perform a background check. Over time, more modern HR solutions, such as Workday, became available. Recruiting and onboarding processes were increasingly becoming more automated. Backcheck took note. They likely realized that some of their larger customers didn't want to have to call them or email them for every new hire. As a result, they created a service platform to allow customers to request their service and retrieve the results of this process, all without manual effort by HR.

Backcheck invested in creating a service platform made up of APIs and corresponding integrations with common HR and applicant tracking systems (ATS). This capability made it such that a company could effectively initiate a background check for a candidate and receive the results all without manual intervention. This results in less time required from HR and a faster hiring process for both the candidate and the company. It also means businesses will be consistently using the Backcheck services for every hire, which means more revenue for Backcheck. While this example shows a fully digital service, there's also a different way of thinking about services. For that, let's talk about Nest.

Nest unveiled their new smart thermostat in 2011. It was an amazing product created by Tony Fadell and his team. Fadell was one of the original creators of the iPod. After releasing their smart thermostat, which learned the habits of the homeowners, they moved on to create a service platform for their new device. This new service platform enabled the thermostat to be controlled with any technology the owner approved. While this sounds basic, it unlocked a world of new capabilities for the owners of these devices.

Nest may not have been making a significant revenue stream by offering this service platform, but they were benefiting. By enabling connectivity to an ecosystem of home automation tools, they inherently created hundreds of new capabilities for their product with minimal investment. As an example, someone might say, "Alexa, turn up the temperature in the house." With their platform service, integration with the Alexa home assistant now becomes possible. With capabilities like this, more people wanted to buy a Nest.

Beyond unlocking the ability to interact with other technologies, they also enabled another interesting capability. California often experiences strain on the power grid, and when the demand gets too high, it can sometimes result in rolling power outages. The utilities are forced to perform these outages to protect the power grid. With a service platform connected to thousands of Nest thermostats, another very powerful capability was brought to life. Nest partnered with the local utility company to create agreements between the power grid operator and the owners of Nest devices. The agreement provided the Nest owner with a gift card for participating and allowed the power grid operator to automatically adjust the temperature of their Nest device. At scale, this enabled the power grid operator to turn off thousands of air conditioning units during times of peak energy usage where problems were expected. This provided increased control over the power demand and reduced the need for power outages in the region. These are not capabilities that Nest originally planned for but a clear example of the amazing outcomes that can be created through a service platform.

Stop and think about the services, products, or technologies that your company provides today and ask a few questions:

- Which services are accessible by API today?
- How could your partners or other companies help enhance your service offering?
- Would your customers want to interact with your services via automation?

Answers to these questions will help you identify if a service platform makes sense for your business.

Method #4: The Operations Platform

In the first three methods, we discussed ways of creating a customer- or partner-facing platform business to unlock new revenue streams or opportunities. This last method turns the focus inside the organization.

As a company grows, the different organizational functions and teams get organized in groups under different leaders. Silos are unwanted, yet they naturally occur. Nearly every large organization struggles with silos and the difficulty in hand-offs and services provided between these silos. Many of us have experienced this when phoning a company for support and having our call forwarded in a circle between different teams in the same company. Everyone we speak with claims that our request is the responsibility of "someone else." These silos slow down processes, negatively impact customer experiences, and sometimes lead to teams moving in different directions with conflicting goals.

Using a platform business model to break down internal silos is a natural fit. Leveraging ideas from methods 1 and 3 (data platform and service platform), we can enable our teams to work more seamlessly together. It is called an operations platform. It is an extension of the big concepts we explored earlier in this book: democratization, plasticity, and orchestration.

Achieving these outcomes involves having teams create internal platforms that drive benefits for all their stakeholders. We discussed the concept of Gartner's composable enterprise and how teams can share data and services across the company. In simple terms, teams are removing barriers and making it easy for their services to be requested or initiated by other teams across the organization.

The following three steps are key to building a successful operations platform:

1. **Promote consumption:** Include goals for every team to create easy methods for other teams to access their data and services. This involves thinking about their team as miniature platform-driven businesses (methods 1 and 3).

2. **Measure adoption:** Success of each team and its corresponding platform should be measured by stakeholder adoption and ratings. Success is not simply building shared technology; it is about building services that are aligned with what the other teams need and are leveraged heavily.

3. **Share language:** Provide a common automation platform on which each team will create these shared services. This automation platform must facilitate orchestrating cross-functional business processes. Again, in order to be successful, this platform needs to support democratization, plasticity, and orchestration.

Platform companies connect people and help them jointly achieve success and reach previously unachievable new heights. Few people would argue with the fact that this is exactly what we want for our companies. The only thing left to do is to get started.

Bring Fresh Thinking to Traditional Business

Not every company can or should be a platform company, but the wildly successful combination of business and technology strategies that we find in these companies can certainly benefit everyone. They help us to think about our own companies with a new perspective and allow us to rethink how our businesses will operate in an automation-powered world.

Every company that was reinvented or moved in a new and more successful direction always started with an idea. Use this chapter to start brainstorming within your team or within your organization. Book a workshop. Share the methods outlined in this chapter to get people thinking. You could even crowdsource ideas across the entire business. You'll be amazed at the truly innovative ideas people come up with when given the liberty to think big. It's using these ideas that will enable you to become a platform-driven business.

Notes

1. Wiedeman, Reeves, 2021, "Why Does Every Company Now Want to Be a Platform?," *New York Times*, (Sept. 15), **https://www.nytimes.com/2021/09/15/books/review/jonathan-knee-platform-delusion.html**.
2. Marr, Bernard, 2022, "The 10 Best Platform Business Model Examples," *Bernard Marr & Co*, (March 18), **https://bernardmarr.com/the-10-best-platform-business-model-examples/**.

Additional Bibliography

Davenport, Thomas H., 2022, "How Legacy Companies Can Pivot to a Platform Model," *Harvard Business Review*, (March 9), **https://hbr.org/2022/03/how-legacy-companies-can-pivot-to-a-platform-model**.

FedEx, n.d. "Data Makes the World Work Better," last accessed January 11, 2023, **https://www.fedex.com/en-us/dataworks.html**.

Hansen, Ulrik Stig, and Eric Landau, 2022, "4 Steps to Start Monetizing Your Company's Data," *Harvard Business Review*, (September 27), **https://hbr.org/2022/09/4-steps-to-start-monetizing-your-companys-data**.

Cramer-Flood, Ethan, 2021, "Worldwide Ad Spending 2021: A Year for the Record Books," *Insider Intelligence*, (November 30), **https://www.insiderintelligence.com/content/worldwide-ad-spending-2021-year-record-books**.

PART 4

Making it Happen

CHAPTER 15

The Enterprise AI Platform

"The development of AI is as fundamental as the creation of the microprocessor, the personal computer, the Internet, and the mobile phone. . . . Entire industries will reorient around it. Businesses will distinguish themselves by how well they use it."

—Bill Gates

Generative AI has changed the way we see our tasks, jobs, and organizations. Where we used to see "status quo" now we see opportunities. But other than examples of how to generate code, create a project summary, or create a chatbot that provides Einstein-like answers with the personality of Snoop Dogg, how should organizations think about generative AI?

On one end, large language models (LLMs) have finally crossed the "democratization barrier." My eyes were opened the moment I saw my 14-year-old niece using ChatGPT as easily as she uses Instagram. Enabling entire organizations to improve and innovate with complete disregard for technical barriers has always been the holy grail of democratization.

More than text, code, or images, what generative AI can give you is the ability to add substance to your ideas. Looking at this from an enterprise lens, AI can rethink existing processes completely. But how?

Generative AI is versatile and expressive. But the output is raw and varies based on the input.

When generative AI burst onto the scene, the existing tools were too narrow in scope to keep up. Specialized, purpose-built software is out of step with the vibrancy of generative AI.

To harness generative AI at scale, there is a clear need for a partner. That partner will knit a company's existing resources together with AI. It takes two forms: orchestration and governance. Without those, a company will be fully exposed to the challenges of generative AI.

The Challenges of Generative AI in the Enterprise

While generative AI and LLMs are extremely knowledgeable, they are not very smart. LLMs are built on extreme amounts of data (think dozens of gigabytes). That makes them knowledgeable about data. However, LLMs are language models, not knowledge models. In simple terms, AI responses are just statistical approximations of what the user is inquiring about. They are good at what they do because they are based on so much data. But they do not "know" what they are saying.

In other words, until AI becomes smarter, humans will need to stay in the driver's seat. But for businesses that want to jump headfirst into AI at scale, they have to overcome some hurdles:

- **Skills impedance:** If people with low technical knowledge ask AI to generate a solution, they won't always know how to evaluate it. Especially if the output is code. If they turn to IT for help, the democratization value of AI drops. If they implement bad code, the risks increase. This points to the need for a level of abstraction that can validate generated content. But it also should not constrain the power and versatility of AI.

- **End-to-end simplicity:** The success of tools such as ChatGPT or Dall-E was due to their ease of use. Today, it's as simple as using any other consumer app such as Instagram (as proven by my niece). While AI is easy to use, implementing anything in a large company is complex. Once we have to start thinking about deployment and review cycles, we again risk losing the benefit of generative AI. In addition to being easy to use, AI has to be always available, almost like a utility; it is there when you need it.

- **Observe and take action:** Humans need to see and understand what is happening to troubleshoot when needed. That may include generating new prompts or providing feedback to the LLMs.

- **Continuous improvement:** When something does go wrong, how do we prevent that from happening for other solutions over time? Feedback is crucial for the LLM or the AI platform to improve over time.

- **From blueprint to execution:** Getting ideas from the wealth of data in LLMs is only the first step. Generative AI excels at creating these maps of what's possible. For those ideas to become a reality, there needs to be "something" that can take those blueprints and turn them into real solutions.

- **TRUST:** All of this needs to happen in an environment with trust and governance to be successful at the enterprise level. Proper guardrails, access controls, and security have to be front and center. No organization should compromise trust for innovation.

The bottom line is that the enterprise needs more than code and ideas generated by AI. With the wrong approach, the democratization potential of AI will be a mirage. If these solutions require an entire IT team to work, we are back to square one.

Without a doubt, ChatGPT and other models will help people automate daily tasks. But alone, it will not (in the foreseeable future) translate to transformational enterprise-wide solutions.

The Platform for Actionable Generative AI

As described in the challenges above, generative AI is almost constrained by the limits of text, code, images, or tasks. To take generative AI to the next level it needs a platform that can realize the limitless potential of LLMs. This platform not only should provide an impressive natural language understanding but move beyond generating text or images and focus on building complex solutions (e.g. apps, automations, or integrations).

An enterprise AI platform should be constructed around a purpose-specific LLM clearly aligned with the domain the platform is catering to (e.g. automation). However, in the context of an enterprise-grade platform, LLM alone is not enough to hit the mark.

Enterprise requirements are not just about technical capabilities. They need to be surrounded by enterprise-grade security and governance as well.

If we account for all these challenges and requirements, the following architecture diagram represents the must-have capabilities for a robust enterprise AI platform:

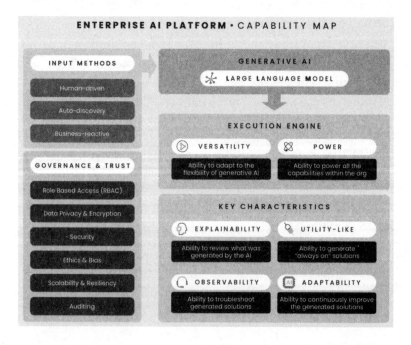

Input Method Capabilities

One of the most important capabilities of generative AI is the ability to receive human input, understand it, and output something in return. However, as we explore the potential for an enterprise AI platform, the following three types of input methods should be considered.

Human-driven

This is the most common way of interacting with today's generative AI technologies. Humans input certain data and expect a certain outcome. For an enterprise AI platform, human-driven refers to the ability to receive inputs in a natural language fashion and generate an expected output or solution.

For instance, in the context of automation use cases, one could provide the following prompt to the AI platform: "Automate the quote to cash process considering the systems involved are Salesforce, Net-suite, Docusign, and our Product system."

In this scenario, while the AI is going to do most of the heavy lifting on figuring out the right solution and implementing it, the human interaction was very intentional with a very specific goal in mind.

Auto-discovery

This other type of input is based on the potential for organizations to leverage industry LLMs that can suggest which automations would be relevant for any given organization based on their existing processes and software stack. Furthermore, the promise of "process mining" could finally be fulfilled, and these platforms could potentially create implementation roadmaps, creating a very effective process.

Business-reactive

Lastly, as briefly mentioned in the core capabilities section, generative AIs excel at pattern recognition. Thus, they could quickly identify exception patterns, correlate them with business metrics, and offer recommendations for new solutions or process optimization.

Execution Engine

The heart of an enterprise AI platform. This execution engine needs to be able to:

- Support the breadth of solution ideas that can come from generative AI;
- Orchestrate the different capabilities that exist within an organization.

Versatility and Power

Generative AI is not bound by any tool limitations as the potential outcomes are only limited by our imagination. However, in order to act on these ideas, this engine needs to be a multipurpose orchestration tool that can not only react to the dynamic nature of AI-generated solutions but at the same time, has to be powerful enough to leverage and integrate every other capability within the enterprise.

Key Characteristics

These capabilities refer to the core technical specifications that an enterprise AI platform should provide out of the box.

Explainability

Until AI technologies mature over time to develop real "smarts" and build enough trust, in the short and medium term there will be the need for a "human in the middle" who can verify that the solution delivered aligns with their needs.

If the solution is generated as code or complex components, it means an IT specialist would be the only type of persona qualified to validate the outcome from the AI, which would defeat the purpose of democratizing access to nontechnical personas.

In order for a nontechnical persona to validate a solution, it needs to be "understandable." Thus, explainability is the ability to generate solutions that can be accurately interpreted by any human.

Utility-like

As mentioned earlier, the main reason for the explosion in the popularity of generative AI technologies is owed to the fact that all technical knowledge barriers were removed and virtually anyone can work and interact with machines. Given the new types of personas within an organization that will benefit from an enterprise AI platform, the deployment models for the solutions generated by these tools need to be completely abstracted from the end users.

In the same way we are used to dealing with utility companies, where we buy a new lamp and just plug it into the power outlet and "turn it on," the experience should be similar for the solutions generated by AI where once validated, users should just be able to "plug or run" these solutions.

Observability

At this stage, we've been able to generate, validate, and run an AI-generated solution. However, given the breadth of complexity some of these solutions (e.g. process automations) will have, an enterprise AI platform should provide the necessary means for nontechnical personas to monitor and troubleshoot any issues that may arise during the lifetime of these solutions.

Moreover, as these issues arise and get solved, there should be a continuous feedback loop that helps the LLM driving the enterprise AI platform improve over time. This leads us to the fourth and last core capability.

Adaptability

At the center of every AI model, there is the concept of training. Whether it's supervised (human-driven) or unsupervised (autonomous), an enterprise AI platform should provide the ability to train and enhance its model based on issues discovered as part of the execution of AI-generated solutions.

For instance, imagine the enterprise AI platform being able to recognize and identify exception patterns such as an increased frequency of 429 error codes coming from Salesforce during peak loads. This continuous feedback would enhance the LLM to understand Salesforce API rate limitations and adjust execution frequency accordingly.

Enterprise-grade Capabilities

Enterprise-grade security and governance is a set of policies, procedures, and technologies that are used to protect an organization's information and systems. As such, an enterprise AI platform not only needs to abide by them but extend them in the context of AI.

New elements such as ethics, bias, and misinformation should be handled gracefully by these platforms. Even "traditional" capabilities (e.g. RBAC) need to be enhanced in order to support the different types of personas that may be onboarded on such platforms. Thus, for any given user, designating which processes can be automated, which systems can be accessed, and the level of interactions with those systems should be heavily monitored and governed by the enterprise AI platform.

While not directly callout, there are a number of capabilities that are expected from enterprise-grade platforms, such as scalability and reliability. Just like the previous example, these capabilities need to be exponentially enhanced to support the scale of new use cases in a way that is maintainable and cost-effective.

Lastly, what is important to notice is the fact that it's exactly these types of mandatory enterprise capabilities that the current iterations of generative AI are missing. Platforms such as ChatGPT are currently unable to guarantee data privacy and quality of input data, which has led to many organizations shutting down access completely to these tools.

Therefore, for the new generation of enterprise AI platforms, enterprise-grade capabilities should be front and center to ensure adoption at scale.

CHAPTER 16

The Automation Ecosystem

"You're making million dollar moves but taking nickel shots."
—Tara VanDerveer, Stanford Women's Basketball Head Coach

When packing for a flight, it used to be the norm to fill a carry-on bag with consumer electronics. I'd grab my PDA, GPS, digital camera, iPod, headphones, and flip phone. We'd toss in a few portable DVD players and Gameboys for the kids. On flights, I felt like my sole job was to locate the next device needed by the family. All these devices provided great value, but the combined list was overkill. Today, all these functions are handled by our smartphones.

Now, smartphones meet most needs as the foundation of our digital lives—but not for everything. There are still large markets for specialized, purpose-built cameras. Pro photographers like to use DSLR cameras that cost thousands of dollars. Thrill seekers prefer to take a rugged GoPro along for their adventures. Filmmakers will shoot their movies on big 8k cameras that capture the tiniest detail. While camera specialization is unimportant to the average person, it is still useful for specialists.

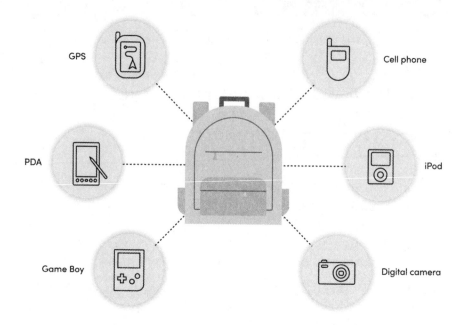

When I consider automation in most companies, it feels like my grab bag of early 2000s electronics. We have RPA, APIM, ETL, ELT, Reverse ETL, ESB, EDI, Event Streams, BPM, and the list goes on. There is no room for more tools in the pile. Most companies use many of these specialized tools but still struggle to get the value they were promised. The approach is broken and unsustainable.

The cost and effort of most automation tools is intense. It gets worse when a specialist tool tries to fit a generalist role. As we said earlier, orchestration needs both muscles and brains. Specialist automation tools are muscles. They solve specific problems well. To succeed in this new era, we don't need to throw out these integration and automation tools, we just have to apply them in the right way. And this requires orchestration.

In the case of automation, there will always be a need for specialized tooling. Much like pro photographers need more than a smartphone camera, some parts of our companies will always need specialized tools. But the main problem today is that specialized tools are being overused.

It comes down to problems with overspecialization or overgeneralization. Much like you don't want the family doctor performing your brain surgery, you also don't want the brain surgeon doing your annual physical. There is a time and place for specialization. It is a good rule of thumb to solve 90% of our problems with general tools, and only use specialized tools for the rest. Too much specialization clouds the big picture and slows us down.

The number of potential automation solutions is large. It seems that new acronyms are being added to the list every day. If your company currently leverages tools such as iPaaS, API platforms, or RPA, you may be wondering where these tools fit into the new automation mindset. In this chapter, we'll answer that question by taking a brief look at some of the most common tools.

Automation Tools

There are many integration and automation tools in the ecosystem, but here we will dive into some of the most common. We're going to cover robotic process automation (RPA), integration platform as a service (iPaaS), business process management (BPM), API management (APIM), and data pipeline (ETL/ELT) tools. Several of these software categories have been in use since the 1980s. We'll conclude this section of the book with a brief discussion of some of the shadow IT tools that are also breaking into the market.

Robotic Process Automation (RPA)

Origins: Software test automation, "green screen" scraping, and macros: a technique of recording a series of actions via graphical user interface (GUI) and playing them back on repeat to automate manual tasks.

Age: 40+ years old.

Aliases (other names and acronyms): Bots, process automation, robotic desktop automation (RDA), task automation.

Focus: Pure efficiency. Saving human work hours on manual tasks. "Better, faster, cheaper" is the mantra, with the goal of reducing headcount.

In depth:

RPA is a tool that mimics the actions of a human to automate the interactions with applications through the screens normally reserved for people to use. When we say RPA mimics the actions of humans, we mean this literally. For example, to create a new invoice record in your ERP, you might first click the "New Invoice" button, then fill in each field on the form, and then click the "Save" button. An RPA bot replicates exactly these steps by simulating mouse and keyboard strokes (or other techniques) to click the buttons and fill in the form.

Although some RPA tools offer cloud deployment, RPA is architected for an on-premise environment. Often RPA bots live on the desktops of individual employees or are deployed on servers to run on their own. It can be attended automation, which is triggered by a person, or unattended automation, which happens on a recurring schedule or using other triggers.

2021 was a big year for robotic process automation (RPA). A blockbuster IPO, mergers and acquisitions, and talks of upcoming events set the stage for an interesting future. Market growth for RPA is projected to expand from $1.7B in 2020 to $9B by 2025 according to IDC.

Despite the success, there are signs that something strange is happening with RPA. For instance, the Sapphire Ventures CIO index reported that RPA is one of the top technologies that companies are hoping to spend less on in 2022. Troubling data suggests the software is not living up to its transformational hype. Forrester thinks RPA market growth will flatten as soon as 2023. IDC reports that the automation market potential of $40B dwarfs the $9B projected for RPA.

RPA is most successful when used in situations where a system has no alternative ways to read or update the data stored within it. For example, a supplier webpage contains data you need for your process, but this supplier has no APIs or other mechanisms to get the data. RPA is a great choice for retrieving this data by interacting directly with the webpage. Additionally, RPA tools are often good for retrieving data from unstructured data sources such as a PDF file or Microsoft Word document. As you will see when we discuss gaps and limitations, RPA tools don't do as well automating processes end-to-end, scaling to large numbers of automations, or being used in a democratized way. If you think about it, mimicking human labor is just another form of outsourcing—"botsourcing." It is also the purest form of the task mindset in a sleek package.

Gaps and limitations:

- **Scale:** It does not scale well. Often companies struggle with broad automation initiatives based exclusively on RPA. It is a lot of work to maintain a large volume of bots due to their fragility and frequent support requirements. Even if a vendor bolts on API, OCR, AI, or process mining, the needed maintenance only grows.

- **Governance:** It is hard to govern. Democratization needs governance, but RPA platforms struggle with org-wide deployments. With the heavy dependency on server infrastructure and deep technical skills, the ability to have a broader set of people across the company building automations is rarely successful. If a company is successful at training a broader team of builders, governance quickly becomes a problem. What people are building, the systems they are connecting to, and the data they are handling is typically not feasible to monitor and manage when using RPA tools.

- **Maintenance:** It can turn into tech and economic debt. RPA is the best fit for quick tasks where something repetitive needs to be done fast. The collection of bots will grow, and so too will the maintenance needs. In essence, the army of bots demands another army of bot managers. While the bot was supposed to take a load off the humans, the humans end up needing to take a load off the bots. If operational overhead is not carefully considered, optimistic ROI calculations can quickly be eroded.

Although RPA often gets called low-code software, it doesn't always work out that way. It is typically not easy to learn, fast to deploy, or easy to maintain. The technology still needs specialists to build and maintain the automations. RPA may be easier to use than resorting to custom code, but it falls short of the ideal democratization canvas.

Business Process Management Suites (BPMS)

Origins: BPMS tools existed as early as the 1980s in tools such as FileNet; however, the category was defined by Gartner in the early 2000s. **Age:** 30+ years old.

Aliases (other names, acronyms, similar tools): Business process management (BPM), intelligent business process management (iBPM), business process automation (BPA), business rules management system (BRMS).

Focus: Business processes-centric modeling and workflow execution. This is done with task management and forms for human workflow steps. BPMS tools typically include process execution modeling, monitoring, and analytics.

In depth:

Business process management suites, or BPMS, is software designed for the practice of business process management (BPM). BPMS is a blanket term for several subcategories of tools related to the process discipline. The discipline takes many forms: drawing processes visually, responding to business events, connecting systems, or defining rules-based automations.

BPM platforms were developed to help organizations better understand and improve their processes. Business rules management systems (BRMS) are designed to manage complex business rules. These systems use rule sets created by business analysts to dictate business operations.

BPA platforms were designed to automate business processes. Over time, the same capabilities were built into function-specific applications. CRM and ERP systems are good examples. They streamline a group of processes related to a business function or department, like sales or finance.

Gaps and limitations:

- **Speed:** The outcomes achievable with BPM are powerful—but slow. Success is measured in years. After all, the goal is a total reimagining of major processes with a group of experts and developers. While BPM vendors see a positive outlook on their market growth, a huge percentage of the BPM consultant ecosystem has moved on to RPA. There they have found quicker wins, higher margins, and lower-hanging fruit. However, as discussed in the RPA section, these consultants are now seeing the problems with the narrow, task-focused view of RPA.

- **Size:** BPM tools are sometimes called "big iron" software, for the most mission-critical processes. It's like the engines of a big ship: huge, strong motors, and specialized experts to keep them running. While BPM can achieve powerful outcomes, it is being left behind. It is becoming a bygone era as companies turn to other less rigid categories for faster outcomes. That said, the fundamental concept BPM with its broader end-to-end view of processes is conceptually the right approach. We can think of BPM and RPA as two ends of a spectrum. BPM is too focused on process without a firm grounding in an easy ability to execute tasks and system actions. RPA is too focused on tasks without a bigger picture view of the process. The answer is somewhere in between.

Integration Platform as a Service

Origins: Middleware. The original player in this space was Teknekron Information Bus, followed by Tibco.

Age: "Integration platform" is 30+ years old. "As a Service," 15 years old.

Aliases (other names, acronyms, similar tools): Integration platform as a service (iPaaS), enterprise service bus (ESB), middleware, enterprise application integration (EAI).

Focus: Often referred to as "plumbing," integration technology is for moving data between platforms. This typically happens with APIs, files, or direct database connectivity.

In depth:

iPaaS platforms integrate multiple apps, syncing datasets, initiating actions in other tools based on data events. They enable data to move from one system to another at varying schedules. They offer the ability to perform batched integrations (hourly, nightly, weekly, etc.) and in near real-time where actions are processed within seconds as business events occur.

These platforms have evolved significantly over the last 30 years. It is important to note that modern iPaaS solutions are much different from the legacy ESB and middleware tools. The modern iPaaS solutions typically run in the cloud and are significantly less focused on complex message routing compared to historic ESB platforms.

The more modern tools include the "as a service" title, which means they run as cloud-native services rather than relying on on-premise servers. Typically, they have:

- Strong connectivity to many apps and services typically via APIs, events, files, or databases;

- Robust data transformation capabilities;

- The ability to manage and respond to business events and interact with event/message streaming services.

These capabilities make it possible to pull data from one application either in batches or one record at a time to update data in the appropriate downstream applications. For example, an iPaaS may be configured to monitor Salesforce, and every time a new customer record is created the iPaaS will automatically download the new customer record using the Salesforce API and then call the Netsuite API to create a matching customer record in the finance system. The resulting business outcome is that every time a new customer is added to Salesforce there will be a matching customer record in Netsuite within minutes. No manual data entry for the accounting team.

Gaps and limitations:
Integration is an important category because it forms the foundation of orchestration and enterprise automation platforms. However, traditional integration platforms have struggled to evolve from their legacy roots. In the iPaaS space, not all tools are alike.

- **Cloud claims:** While a key requirement of being an iPaaS is the ability to run in the cloud, there is a big difference between cloud-native platforms and historically on-prem platforms that have simply been ported to the cloud. Both are labeled as "cloud," but only cloud-native platforms truly make use of the auto-scaling, fault tolerance, and utility-like benefits of what cloud services should be. We will cover this in more detail later in the chapter.

- **Complexity:** The other major differentiator in this space is that traditional integration platforms are complex, technical tools. They require experts with computer science degrees and wizard hats to maintain them. Coding, development, and long wait times characterize the outcomes resulting from the use of traditional integration tools. More modern platforms have adopted the low-code movement as a foundation of how they operate and therefore become strong candidates for our architectural framework of democratization, plasticity, and orchestration. But buyer beware, not all iPaaS fit this mold.

API Management

Origins: As APIs have grown more common and valuable, systems designed to publish and manage them have evolved into existence.

Age: Formal APIM systems began coming onto the market circa 2009.

Aliases (other names, acronyms, similar tools): API gateway, API portal, API platform, API lifecycle.

Focus: API Management (APIM) solutions focus on the management of company APIs and the creation of new endpoints. The goal of most systems is to create an organized, standardized, and controlled set of APIs for use across the company.

In depth:

API management tools focus on two elements: API connectivity and API discoverability. Most API management tools offload the more technical requirements such as security and performance (connectivity) and try to make a company's APIs easy to find for developers (discoverability).

The connectivity element is provided using a configuration or code-based API gateway. The API gateway acts as a layer between the API caller and the downstream system. The gateway offers authentication, advanced security and encryption, rate limiting, caching, and other functions. This focus on managing the technical requirements allows the back-end systems to focus on providing data and the other functions. API consumers end up with a consistent and standard experience because they are all connecting through the API gateway.

APIM tools also enable companies to manage their vast set of APIs. Imagine a company with 500 different applications, each with an average of 50 API endpoints. This is 25,000 different API endpoints that a developer could leverage. Without a central way to document and manage APIs, it can be hard for a developer to know they exist, let alone connect to them. This is where the API catalog or developer portal capabilities of an API management platform come into play. These tools allow a company to document, organize, and make their APIs searchable by developers. This ensures that as APIs are created, they aren't lost in the abyss of other APIs.

Gaps and limitations:

- **Pure-play limits:** The focus of APIM is on connectivity and discoverability. The missing link with most APIM tools is the logic that makes up the API. If you already have a set of APIs, and you want to control and organize them, an APIM will likely fit that need. Yet this is rarely the only need. APIs provide the most value when they can be used as building blocks. When you can create an API to encapsulate a set of actions across several other APIs, we start to see automation. Most APIM platforms do not do this well. While they excel at creating and organizing, they typically leave the logic to manual code. The result is nearly the same level of work as custom-building the automation from scratch. This ultimately means an inability to democratize and a lot of work to make changes (no plasticity).

- **API "religion":** A frenzy of API-led architecture has led many companies down a false path. The theory of API-led architecture is that building a vast library of APIs is a smart strategy. The thinking goes that we build APIs as reusable components and then combine our APIs into more APIs that combine our combined APIs. So we've got a lot of APIs, but have we made any positive impact on our business? Leveraging APIs as building blocks is the right way to go. However, building APIs as the solution, rather than simply a component of the solution, results in a lack of focus on the ultimate outcome. Many IT teams have invested millions of dollars in creating these API-led architectures but unfortunately with only a focus on the technology. These companies often end up with scores of APIs but very little business value.

ETL (Extract, Transform, Load) and ELT (Extract, Load, Transform)

Origins: Originates from the very start of integration.
Age: 30+ years.
Aliases (other names, acronyms, similar tools): Data pipeline, data loader, data ingestion, extract transform load (ETL), extract load transform (ELT).
Focus: ETL/ELT load bulk data from applications and other data sources into a centralized repository such as a data lake or warehouse.
In depth:

ETL (extract, transform, load) and ELT (extract, load, transform) tools are usually part of a large-scale strategy to centralize company data. The end goal is to improve data reporting and data analytics. These tools move data in large volume from multiple sources into a common data model. At some point, the tool transforms the data to match the model.

It is important to note that historically ETL was sometimes used to refer to batch application to application integration; however, this definition is now rarely used. Therefore, for this section we use ETL and ELT to refer to the more modern definition of tooling used to load data marts, data warehouses, and data lakes.

The primary difference between ETL and ELT is where the transformation happens. With ETL the tool extracts data from the source, transforms it to match the data model, and loads it into the data warehouse. ELT focuses on the extract and load, leaving the transformation to the data warehouse. It extracts the data and loads it as-is into the data warehouse.

ELT is the more modern approach as it provides several benefits such as increased speed to load data, ability to retransform historical data, and reduced complexity. This is possible because of recent advancements in data warehousing platforms such as Snowflake.

Gaps and limitations:

- **High volume, only:** ETL and ELT tools are commonly lumped together with other integration and automation tools. They do perform many of the same functions. But the similarities end there. ETL and ELT tools work best for a very narrow use case of moving high volumes of data from edge applications to a data warehouse. This is both a pro and a con for these tools. When used as intended, they outperform other tools in the market.

- **Related use cases:** Limitations for these tools come when moving outside of the core use case. These tools struggle with app-to-app integration, event-based automation, or process orchestration. It may seem technically workable to use an ETL/ELT tool, but it will be clear the effort required to build them outweighs the benefits. It only gets worse when we look at how hard it is to troubleshoot and support these use cases. ETL/ELT tools are the ultimate definition of specialist tools. They should be used for your reporting and analytics project but not for automation.

Unmanaged Automation Tools

We talked in detail about the perils of shadow IT in Chapter 4. One of the main causes is a challenged relationship between the business and IT. When the business does not feel like they are getting what they need from IT to achieve their goals, they begin looking to solve the problem alone. That means buying their own tools, hiring their own people, and heading down a bad path to shadow IT.

Some vendors capitalize on this by offering easy-to-use no-code tools for integration and automation. From the outside, they look like a great fit for meeting many of the requirements we've outlined in this book. They are low-code and can sometimes orchestrate simple multistep processes. They are beloved by entrepreneurs and sometimes embraced by the business because they are easy, cheap, and fast. However, looks can be deceiving. No enterprise IT department worth their salt would condone the use of such tools, and for good reason. While these typically have a great user experience, they often lack more foundational capabilities such as security, governance, compliance, and monitoring. Building solutions while ignoring these foundational needs creates long-term problems in the form of technical debt, data quality issues, and security risks. Even for small companies, weighing the pros and major cons of these unmanaged automation tools is a wise decision.

A Primer on Cloud Platforms

Cloud computing is a concept that was arguably pioneered by Salesforce circa 1999. This means, the cloud on average is about 10+ years younger than most of the technologies described in this chapter. For this reason, not all tools claiming to be cloud are providing the larger benefits of cloud technologies.

By looking throughout the evolution of the cloud, we can define two distinct approaches to how organizations decided to adopt it:

- Cloud as a cost-saving mechanism (or cloud optimized / lift & shift approach);
- Cloud as an enabler for disruption (or cloud-native approach).

This is a key consideration as most vendors have adopted the cloud following the former approach. It should not come as a surprise since these organizations have invested heavily in their own tech stacks for years before the cloud emerged. Thus, it was orders of magnitude faster and cheaper to port their existing stack into the cloud than re-architecting, refactoring, or potentially starting from scratch, to fully leverage what the cloud had to offer. Let's dig further on why cloud native is so important nowadays.

(continued)

(continued)

Cloud Optimized vs. Cloud Native

The core value proposition of SaaS is the fact that the traditional burdens of on-prem software, namely installation, hardware provisioning, maintenance, versioning, etc., are no longer a customer concern but a SaaS concern. These benefits originate from the cloud-native principle that drives the SaaS architectural paradigm. With SaaS, customers can not only start small and grow over time, but they get to save money on capex (no infrastructure to maintain) and operational costs (less people to operate).

For instance, let's talk about Salesforce. When a customer adopts Salesforce, they don't have to worry about setting up their infrastructure, high availability, networking, prepare for peak loads, protect against DoS attacks, etc. A Salesforce customer is *buying peace of mind* by not dealing with security or scalability concerns, *efficiency* by having a full-blown robust application provisioned through the click of a button, and *future proof investment* by always running the latest and greatest technology. This is all because Salesforce decided to embrace the potential of the cloud to its fullest by following a cloud-native architecture.

While there is no standard definition of cloud native, there is consensus that it is the result of building modern applications for the cloud by following the principles of "microservices," "containerization," and "container orchestration."

On the other hand, moving to the cloud with a cloud-optimized mindset (e.g. lift & shift to run the same code base on the cloud) essentially focuses on the ability to run software on the cloud and not necessarily on improving the end user experience by removing the operational burden.

Now imagine if instead, Salesforce provided their application runtimes as a service, but it was up to the customer to decide where to run it (e.g. in which region), how to run it (e.g. high availability with multiple copies across different availability zones), and how to maintain it (e.g. handle version upgrades once or twice a year). One may argue the whole value proposition of SaaS would be diminished as all those concerns are like what organizations had to deal with during the on-prem ages.

Therefore, platforms that were not born in the cloud but ported to it will keep the same on-prem concerns such as peak load provisioning, high availability, observability, version upgrades, and traceability.

For organizations to fully grasp the value of the cloud and being able to focus on solving business problems, they should look for tools that were born in the cloud, that provide easier ways to handle complexity while lowering (or completely removing) the operational burdens from their platforms, and that scale hand in hand with your organization.

A Look at a Hypothetical Process

As we talked about, enterprises mix and match these tools to automate their processes. Analysts build frameworks to guide customers on their journey. Gartner calls their framework Hyperautomation. HFS research calls it OneOffice. Forrester calls it an automation fabric. The underlying idea is always that automation tools should be used where they fit best. However, doing this in practice is very difficult without orchestration. Very few companies, if any, have achieved the best practices that analysts propose.

What happens in reality is the decisions for applying each tool are made by the team that purchased the tool. Each team uses, and often overuses, their tool of choice to try to solve all the problems that come their way. Any resemblance of a macro, intentional strategy at that point is lost.

So far, we've looked at the various automation tool categories and gone over their strengths and weaknesses. Now, let's apply them through a hypothetical process in a midsized company. Let's assume that the company we are talking about is named FusionSoft, sells a SaaS product, has around 2,000 employees, and is trying to use a hyper-automation approach. The process in question is billing and fulfilling a customer purchase. It is being automated by the IT team with limited help from the business.

Nearly every company can relate in some way to a process like this. A purchase by a customer is a momentous event in a company, and the purchase order is often what initiates this. The process touches several teams, including sales, finance, customer success, support, and product.

Let's dig into FusionSoft's purchase order (PO) process.

Part 1: PO Processing

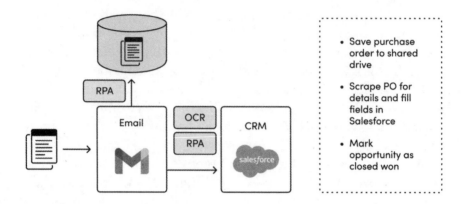

Tools Involved

- Optical Character Recognition (OCR)
- Robotic Process Automation (RPA)

When a PO is first received by FusionSoft, an email arrives in a shared inbox. This is the business event that starts the process. The sales operations team used to manually check this mailbox, but the busywork became overwhelming. They therefore built an RPA bot that saves the PO attachment and runs it through an optical character recognition (OCR) tool to extract the data. The RPA bot then logs in to Salesforce with its own credentials and pastes the data into the right fields on the opportunity and account objects. The RPA bot also creates a folder and saves the PO file into a shared storage drive. Lastly, it marks the opportunity "closed won" in the CRM.

Part 2: Invoice Delivery

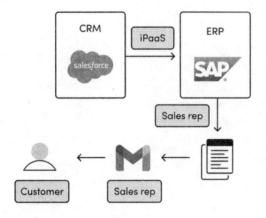

- Listen for closed won opportunity
- Create customer and order in SAP
- Assign product to order in SAP
- Move customer data from Salesforce to SAP via API
- Generate invoice
- Download invoice and send to customer

Tools Involved

- iPaaS
- Manual steps

The company knows the order exists. Now, they need to send the customer an invoice so they can get paid. All the work on the ERP is owned by the IT team at FusionSoft. They decided to use their iPaaS tool to integrate Salesforce with SAP. A listener picks up on the closed won opportunity, and data begins moving through a series of APIs to create a customer record in SAP, along with an order record. A product is assigned to the order, and data from the related Salesforce account and opportunity are synced over. Next, the iPaaS triggers the generation of an invoice in SAP. A sales rep then needs to download it and email it back to the customer.

Part 3: Provisioning

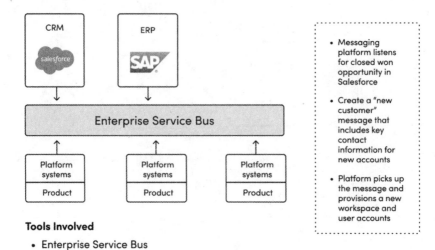

Tools Involved
- Enterprise Service Bus

After the customer is invoiced, they need access to the product they purchased. The product team has set up a custom webhook that listens for platform events in Salesforce. It creates a message in their messaging platform that includes the customer's name and email addresses for provisioning new licenses and a fresh workspace for the new user. That message makes its way to the various platform systems that make up the product. Onboarding emails are now sent out to the new users.

Part 4: Success and Support

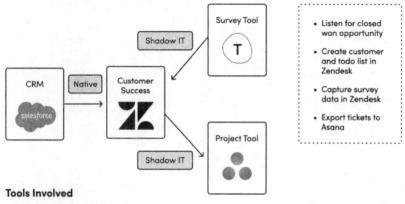

Tools Involved

- Native integrations
- Shadow IT integrations

Once new users are set up, the handoff between sales and customer support takes place. Data moves from Salesforce to Zendesk using a native integration between the apps. This includes account details, user details, and contract info to help CS track the life cycle and upsell opportunities. Since the support team uses a different system to manage their tickets (Asana, in this case), a shadow IT tool syncs cases to Asana. Since the team likes an online form tool for customer surveys, another shadow IT connection was set up to pull results back into Zendesk.

Part 5: Product Usage Analysis

- ETL/ELT to move bulk data from product to data warehouse
- Move transformed data to business analytics platform and PLG platform

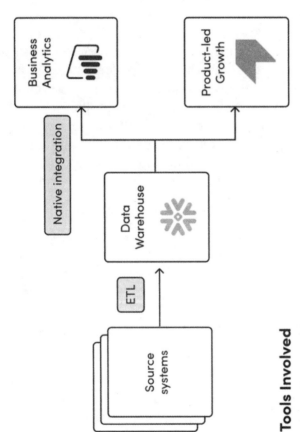

Tools Involved

- ETL/ELT
- Native integrations

Lastly, a few months into the contract, the product analytics team will be looking to conduct some in-depth analysis of the customer's usage. The amount of data is in the millions of rows, between user actions in the app, frequency, time in application, and user outcomes. To deal with this volume of data, a few months prior the team hired an external consultant to implement an ETL solution to pull all the product data out of the source systems into the data warehouse. They then connected a BI solution to Snowflake via native integrations so they could analyze and act on the data.

(The Not So) End-to-end Automation

Our hypothetical process is just a glance at what happens in a typical company. Of course, every company is very different, and the apps, steps, and requirements for each industry will vary. As we laid it out here, it may look and feel very reasonable. Like we said in Chapter 3, each of these automation decisions, when viewed in their context, makes total sense. The sales ops team saw a chance for some efficiency, and they built an RPA bot. The IT team brought in their iPaaS in a familiar way. The CS team wasn't getting what they needed, so they bought a shadow IT tool to help them meet their goals.

Companies get by with this approach, and it is the status quo for many. But we are looking at the picture of what happens when specialization is the norm. Let's talk through a few scenarios to unpack this further.

For example, let's assume a Salesforce admin unwittingly changes the layout of the fields on the opportunity record. Suddenly, the RPA bot, who was relying on field layout, no longer knows where to paste the data from the PO. It might be several days before the customer alerts their rep that they haven't received the invoice. Then, the rep has to check in with the sales ops team, asking why the invoice is not available yet in SAP. Maybe sales ops will figure out the problem and quickly fix it, and maybe they won't. Either way, the customer's experience is already off to a bad start. Provisioning is delayed longer than they expected, and the company looks bad.

What if a sales rep mistypes the email address for the new admin user who was supposed to be provisioned in part 3? In this case, the account would be provisioned to a nonexistent email address. Again, several days go by until the customer reaches out, asking what happened. In this case, it takes some serious detective work by the CS team to identify where the breakdown was. Again, a simple and likely common mistake resulting in the process crumbling and the customer impacted.

When automation is siloed and specialized, it is hard to figure out what went wrong and where. In other words, tracking down the problem is hard, and there is no built-in exception handling. When different teams are operating in silos and nobody can see the bigger picture, it can lead to the bystander effect.

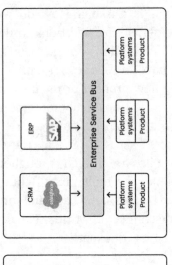

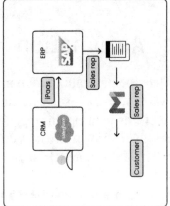

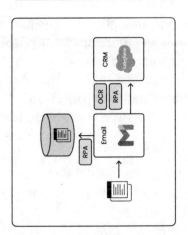

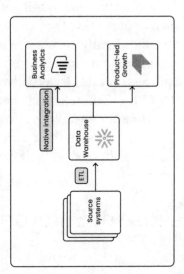

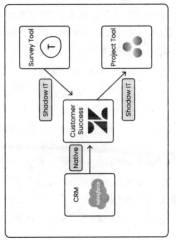

Perhaps more significant is what is missing. How do we find opportunities for iteration, improvements, and additions to the process? These integrations are rigid. If FusionSoft's market vanished in a pandemic-like event, they would have to rebuild. It's unlikely that it could be done in time to roll out a new product or pivot to another greenfield opportunity. These various solutions likely took months or years to build. Significant change is out of the question.

Salesforce is present and connected across nearly all these parts of the process. Yet this is deceptive—silos are littered throughout this flow. The ERP, Zendesk, and the analytics tools are all completely siloed from one another. With no data being shared back and forth, the teams start operating in their own disconnected worlds. They end up working alone, focused on their own areas of expertise.

The Rise of Enterprise Automation

Looking back at what we need to realize the new automation mindset and the multiple attempts of the software industry to solve the automation problem, it's evident we need something to bring this together. We need to move away from solving one problem only to create a different one. We need a robust, cohesive, and strategic approach to delivering on the promise of automation.

This strategic approach to automation requires the ability to democratize and enable broader teams to automate. It needs to act as the glue to bring our apps, people, and specialized automation tools together. It needs to orchestrate end-to-end processes while remaining easy to change such that we maintain our plasticity.

This may seem like a tall order, but the reality is that this is all entirely possible today. This is something companies are already moving forward with. It is what we call "enterprise automation."

CHAPTER 17

Enterprise Automation

"In the end, a strategy is nothing but good intentions unless it's effectively implemented."

—Clayton Christensen

In this chapter, we'll look at the technical and business capabilities we need for the new automation mindset. We've summarized the capabilities required for each mindset here:

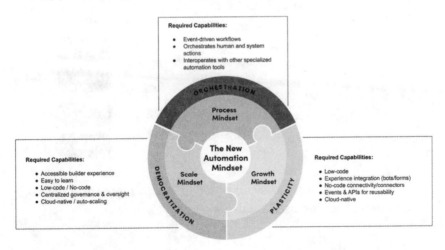

We can see that different technologies in this space cover different capabilities. But some of these technologies offer more *technical* value than *business* value. One might optimize for TPS (transactions per second), which measures how many "messages" or events are processed per second. This sounds cool when focusing on the technology, but what exactly does it mean for the business? The TPS rating of an integration tool has no impact on speed, agility, or effectiveness of a businesses. So why do we look at it?

Performance and capabilities matter, but only in the context of the results we want. A very high TPS might be important for certain scenarios, but does that mean we need it for every use case? If it's only applicable to two of 5,000, should it be a requirement? Or does it highlight the need for a specialized tool for those two use cases?

Companies fall into these kinds of tech-centric views of the world to their detriment. Many sacrifice capabilities that matter to the 5,000 use cases to address the edge cases. Today's automation ecosystem is rife with this approach. The new automation mindset calls for a broader view of the problem: one that aligns with the business outcomes we want, rather than the technology. This comes down to focusing on the "thing" we are looking to streamline: the business process.

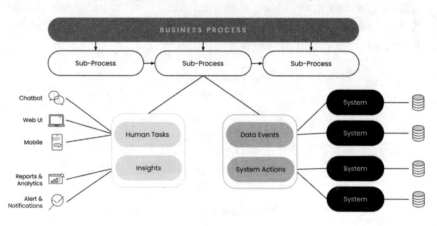

Every business process is composed of one or more sub-processes. Each of these subprocesses are made of:

- Human interactions:
  - Human tasks (reviewing an expense claim, approving vacation time, deciding on the budget for next year, etc.);

○ Insights (notification of newly signed contract, a weekly report of the top customers, etc.).

- System actions:

  ○ Data events (an invoice being received, a new employee hired, etc.);

  ○ System actions (updating a customer record, initiating the month-end process, etc.).

Automated processes need to work within the dynamic environments of the business. This means these human tasks and system actions need to interact:

- Through communication channels such as email, mobile, websites, chatbots, and other collaboration tools;
- With apps including on-premise apps, SaaS apps, and cloud infrastructure;
- With the data we have stored in our data warehouse, data lakes, databases, files, documents, and other locations;
- With our partners and suppliers to enable processes that not only include people and systems inside our company but also those outside.

Taking a closer look, we can identify three pillars of integration capabilities that we need to support to fully automate our business processes:

- **Experience:** capabilities related to integrating with people— Employees, customers, and other core stakeholders;
- **Data:** capabilities for integrating data across multiple systems for data consistency, system updates, and monitoring for business events in the data;
- **Process:** capabilities enabling us to tie these human and system actions together into an end-to-end flow with exception paths and leveraging event-driven actions.

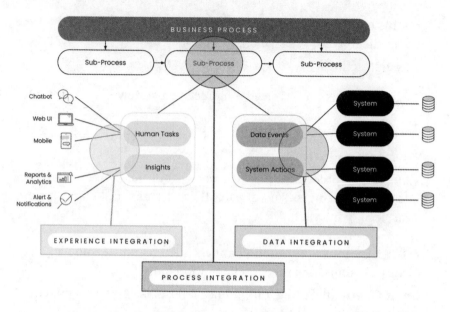

To support these integration requirements at scale, we need to allow for multiple architectural styles. These address the different needs of each use case and personas implementing them. Good architecture enables teams to build solutions that are easier to operate, test, and scale. It also enables them to share reusable assets to cut back on reinventing the wheel.

Reusable assets and capabilities are a secondary outcome of each problem we solve. These capabilities can then be further combined into "composable automations." Consider, for example, an automation that creates an active directory account when a new employee is hired. The logic that fires when a new employee is hired can be reused across other automations. Thus, it should be preserved as a reusable service or event. This problem is often naturally solved when our teams have the process mindset. A process mindset means thinking beyond the task of creating an active directory account. Rather, the priority would be automating the employee onboarding process. When we think of the entire process, the reusability of new hire logic becomes obvious.

We said that a technology-centric view of the world is what often limits us. Then, we've talked primarily about technology concepts—the irony! The key of successful automation programs is not the tech, it is the operating model. It is so important that the entire next chapter is a deep dive on choosing the right operating model. In short, the operating model defines:

- How your teams are organized;
- The processes for identifying automation opportunities;
- Designing automations;
- Building automations;
- Continuously supporting and evolving those automations.

The operating model is where we put in place concepts such as democratization.

Choosing the right technology and the right architecture is half of the battle. There are many examples of companies who have struggled, even after seemingly good tool and architecture choices. The following examples show this in action:

Example 1: FinanceCo bought the top-rated technology that their developers loved. They chose to build a cool-sounding event-driven architecture. They did not think through their operating model in the context of their business needs. Two years and tons of budget later, FinanceCo has automated some things, but the business is fed up with the pace. Then, they rethink their operating model, only to realize their expensive technology does not fit the new model.

Example 2: RetailCo sees citizen development as a promising idea. They go out and buy the latest low-code technology. They open the platform up to everyone in the company to start automating their work. But they didn't consider governance as part of their operating model. Two years later, they find themselves with thousands of automations. Those automations are either unstable projects or half-baked ideas. They are opening the company up to security risk and slowing the business down. When they realize their mistake, it becomes clear that the tool they picked does not have the governance capabilities they need.

These failures are not because of the technology, architecture, or the spirit of the operating model. The issue is that *these three elements were not aligned with one another* in support of the larger business outcome.

Getting the alignment right between these elements is called enterprise automation.

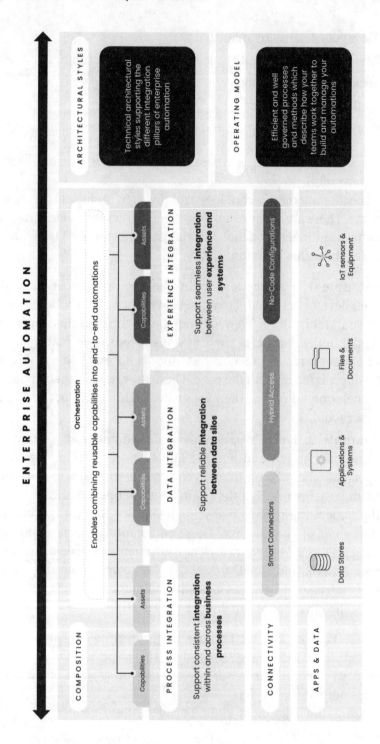

For a formal definition: *enterprise automation* is not a software category by a strategic approach to integration and automation consisting in a combination of methodologies, technologies, and a purpose-built operating model. It enables CIOs and IT leaders to address process automation, data consistency, and composition challenges such that they can address business automation requirements holistically with properly governed democratization.

For a deeper dive into enterprise automation approaches, check out this free course by navigating to the URL or scanning the QR code below:

discover.workato.com/enterprise-automation-certification

Enterprise Automation Platform

Where enterprise automation is the recommended strategic approach to automation, we still need to answer the question of "What tool(s) should I use?" We aren't talking about a tool to solve a specific use case or technical problem. We need something to bring together our people, systems, and specialized automation tools together so we can refocus on the business process we want to optimize. There are now new tools that enable us to do just this. We call them "enterprise automation platforms."

We'll start with one of the most important capabilities of an enterprise automation platform (EAP). As discussed in the prior chapters, low-code automation technology plays a critical role in enabling both plasticity and democratization. Low code allows us to rapidly adapt our automation landscape and in parallel enables more builders from across the organization to get involved in designing and building the automations. With all our builders using a common platform, we break down silos and eliminate the fragmentation of knowledge that we often see with siloed delivery teams. Our cross-functional communication, visibility, and troubleshooting improves, and ultimately our organizations begin to operate as one unified force. Without a technology that unifies our teams, we can't achieve our objective of a cohesive approach to automation. Therefore, low-code / no-code (LC/NC) is a central requirement of any EAP.

This core of a unified experience must be supported by a broad range of capabilities to address the needs for process, data, and experience integration. The following capability map outlines some of the core capabilities required to deliver on this objective and how they overlap with traditional integration and automation technologies.

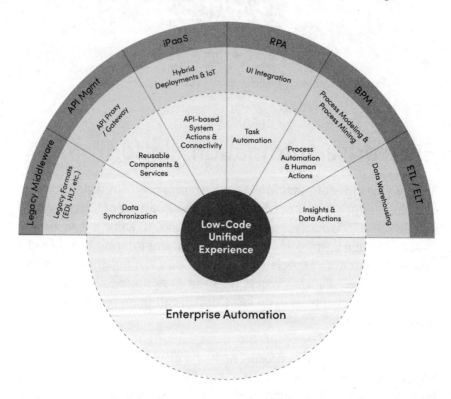

As shown, we believe that an EAP needs capabilities that traverse multiple software domains such as APIM, iPaaS, and RPA. However, at the same time, we acknowledge that such a platform can't or shouldn't try to be a superset of every other existing category. That is to say that specialized automation tools still have a very important role in your broader automation strategy but should be used for the specific use cases for which they were built to solve. It is critical to define where the EAP should be leveraged and where coexisting with specialized tools might be a better approach. The diagram above provides a starting point on how to draw this line and define when and where to use your existing tools.

If we take a slightly more architectural view of enterprise automation, it looks something like this:

Our EAP, supported by specialized automation tools where needed, provides the common platform to orchestrate our processes and create our process, data, and experience integration. The EAP, however, must also support our operating model and the various architecture styles we will need. Let's dive deeper into the architecture we need to make this successful.

Architectural Styles

This is one of the core tenets of a successful enterprise automation strategy and a key requirement for an EAP. The breadth of scenarios an EAP must support is immense and therefore could not be implemented using a single architecture paradigm.

For instance, if we look at scenarios like legacy data integration, where highly specialized resources will be involved in building these capabilities, then leveraging an architecture focused on reuse through microservices and APIs would be a no-brainer. The team's capabilities in this case match the solution and architectural approach.

On the other hand, if we have an automation democratization program in place, team members with arguably less technical expertise but with a wealth of business knowledge would align better with a point-to-point architecture. With this approach they can focus on

ENTERPRISE AUTOMTION

ARCHITECTURAL STYLES

- Point-to-point
- Event-driven
- Microservices
- API-led
- Data Hub

OPERATING MODEL

Centralized
Hybrid
Distributed

Delivery Team
Enablement Team

COMPOSITION

Orchestration

Low code/No code   Events   APIs/Functions   Zero-Ops

Capabilities   Assets   Capabilities   Assets

PROCESS INTEGRATION
Orchestration
Process Visibility • Process Orchestration

DATA INTEGRATION
Orchestration
Data Sync • Data Aggregation

EXPERIENCE INTEGRATION
Orchestration
Low-Code Bots • Low-Code Apps • AI/ML

CONNECTIVITY

Smart Connectors   Hybrid Access   No-Code Configurations

APPS & DATA

Data Stores   Applications & Systems   Files & Documents   IoT sensors & Equipment delivering value by composing systems and assets into end-to-end processes rather than trying to create assets that may never be reused.

Thus, multiple robust architectures have to be supported as part of your toolbox rather than enforcing a single architecture paradigm that may lead to overengineering or waste of resources. Statements such as "This is the holy grail of architecture patterns" are usually a red flag. These statements are usually combined with "By enabling reusability it will solve every problem in your organization," and they must always be taken with a grain of salt.

There is always a right tool or pattern for the right problem, and therefore if you are exposed to any "mantra-like" messaging, always go back and evaluate how the particular pattern handles the different dimensions of the new automation mindset. Moreover, check whether it provides technical support for:

- Orchestration;
- Plasticity;
- Democratization.

Chances are, like any other tech-centric solution, it will only cover certain aspects of your automation needs. It may be great for solving a specific problem, but no single architectural approach is a silver bullet.

Key Architecture Patterns for Enterprise Automation

The following are the most foundational architectures that should be supported by an EAP.

Point-to-point (P2P)

Point-to-point integration or automation solutions simply refer to cases where we are making basic automated connections between two or more applications. Typically, solutions that don't include any higher-level architectural patterns are put in the bucket of P2P. It's the default pattern when things don't fit elsewhere. P2P integrations are often considered an anti-pattern by traditional integration platforms due to integration problems of the past. These problems occurred when teams created hundreds of unmanaged and unmonitored integrations using a mix of complex and often custom technologies. This was an operational nightmare and is not the right way to implement the P2P pattern. Despite the bad name, P2P architectures have a time and a place in modern automation practices.

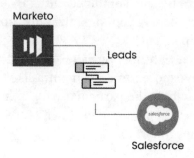

Think about the need for less technical personas who want to start building their own automations. They have to figure out how to interact with different systems, understand different data structures, and think through the various exceptions. This is needed to get a basic automation created. If on top of that we now expect them to also build reusable APIs or microservices, we would arguably be setting them up for failure. Instead, forward-looking IT teams within these organizations will typically create reusable assets and services for these automation builders to use. This enables services to be properly governed by a central team while still enabling these less technical personas to focus on delivering value through point-to-point solutions. When these solutions are built on a common well-governed platform, many of the traditional P2P issues of the past disappear.

Event-driven Architecture (EDA)

EDA is arguably one of the oldest forms of integration (right behind P2P, that is). For the longest time, event-driven architectures have drawn the attention of developers and architects alike. This is because the reactive and asynchronous nature of EDA is usually considered the most efficient, scalable, and reliable way to handle process execution.

Foundationally, event-driven architecture is all about converting different activities across your organization into "events." For example, we might have a system monitoring an accounts payable mailbox. When a new email is received, we check to see if there is an invoice attached. If there is, we generate a "new invoice received" event, which contains a reference to the invoice PDF file. From there another process can initiate every time a "new invoice received" event is triggered, and it might proceed to extract the data and upload this invoice to your ERP.

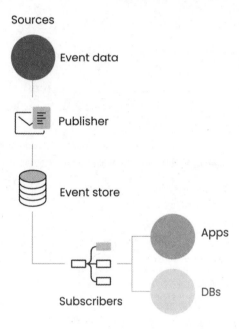

So how is that different from a simple point-to-point solution? The power of this pattern comes in when you now want to extend this automation. Let's say you also receive occasional invoices by mail. You can now scan your invoice and have the associated automation create a "new invoice received" event, which points to your scanned PDF. You don't need to worry about the rest of the workflow because that event will now automatically trigger the process of importing the invoice into the ERP. This ability to quickly plug in to and extend existing automation flows is what makes event-driven automation so powerful.

However, the fact that EDA typically requires the need for complex messaging systems and third-party components (e.g. AWS SQS), has historically made it too complex to use. Lucky for us, modern EAPs bring the benefits of EDA while commoditizing the associated complexity. They do this by managing the complexity of message queues, routing, and event processing by bringing it up a level to allow you to focus on the business event. This means your company can build event-driven architectures without the need for a degree in quantum physics.

Microservices and API Architecture

Microservices are a great way to clearly define reusable business capabilities either for system abstraction (e.g. API to orchestrate necessary calls to create sales order in Netsuite) or valuable business capabilities (e.g. a "create customer API," which in turn creates a customer record in all related systems). Microservices & APIs are usually concepts that go together as REST APIs are arguably the best way to expose microservice capabilities.

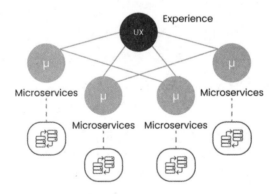

Using microservices/APIs enables companies to create building blocks to help encapsulate reusable logic, share data with suppliers/partners, drive modern user experiences, and even expose business processes as a service. Enabling the creation of APIs and the consumption of these APIs is a key requirement for any EAP.

Data Hub Architecture

The goal of a data hub architecture is to be the architectural equivalent of a lightweight master data management (MDM) solution. It has a focus on building "golden records" for core business data entities (e.g. customer, employee) as well as the corresponding business events associated with that data (e.g. new hire, customer onboarded).

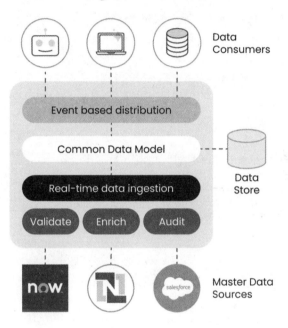

A significant number of automations are often linked directly to core business records (employee, customer, invoice, contract, product, etc.) and therefore it is important for the EAP to allow and enable this architecture pattern. For example, as a customer goes through its life cycle with the company, we may want to have other automated actions triggered (welcome email, billing, gifts, event invites, surveys, etc.). Instead of these automations triggering from the 10 different systems that contain various aspects of the customer record, we instead centralize this data using a data hub architecture. This enables all customer related automations from a single central data and event source.

This architecture can drastically simplify the process of creating future automations and thereby further promotes the ability for less technical team members to be able to get involved and automate.

Pillars of Enterprise Automation

As previously discussed, we define the three key pillars of enterprise automation as process integration, experience integration, and data integration. We will often find that individual components or steps of a process will fall into one of these categories. Here we will take a closer look at some of the key considerations needed for each pillar.

Process integration:

- **Orchestration:** The EAP should enable us to connect disparate processes, including the resources and applications they depend on. Handling the range of timing requirements and logical paths of typical business processes is critical.
- **Reliable processing:** Processes need to be executed with the certainty that business events will be delivered reliably. One missed record or transaction can significantly undermine confidence in the automation solution.
- **Transactional integrity:** Transactions need to ensure that in case of errors, proper rollbacks or compensation logic are supported to maintain the integrity of the transaction. Put more simply, the EAP needs to be able to clean up the mess if something goes wrong.

Data integration:

- **Connectivity:** Connectivity is key to capture all events happening at the application level and any data silo. Removing the complexity of understanding and connecting to different applications can greatly increase development speed and enable more builders to use the platform.
- **Metadata:** An EAP should provide the necessary metadata to understand the different systems, applications, and data stores we are working with. For example, an automation builder should be

able to see the record types and field names from the application they are connecting to. This greatly accelerates development and enables more builders.

- **Data transformation:** Given the plethora of applications and data structures, there needs to be a robust and yet simple approach to handling the required data transformations that we will see in all automations.

Experience integration:

- **Unified platform:** Some software vendors have tried to buy their way into having full-featured products. However, the customer reality was a "unified bill" but a completely broken user experience. The promise of a unified platform can only stem from a platform that was built from the ground up to embrace enterprise automation.

- **Low-code chatbots:** Experience is about meeting your customers (or employees) where they are. Nowadays, platforms such as Slack or Teams are becoming "the new UI" empowering much faster release cycles and ubiquitous access to applications. Therefore, an EAP should support chatbots as a first-class citizen.

- **Low-code applications:** Along the lines of chatbots, LC/NC development is increasingly permeating every aspect of software development, and UIs are no exception. Thus, an EAP should support low-code application building in the context of enterprise automation.

Unite Teams Through a Common Platform

The most important aspect of an EAP, and what separates it from other alternatives such as the traditional enterprise service bus (ESB) or robotic process automation (RPA), is the ability to democratize access by lowering the barrier to entry for a broader set of personas across the organization.

The fact that automations are directly related to business processes and business outcomes implies that the type of personas building these automations should have a wealth of business knowledge. In most cases, these people won't be specialized integration developers. Therefore, the only way to align your automation platform with the diverse skill sets of the team is by providing a low-code experience that allows builders of varying technical skill levels to come together.

Opening automation up to a larger set of builders is, however, not to be done without planning. It needs to be done in a controlled and well-organized manner. Defining efficient and well-governed processes that describe how your teams will work together to build and manage your automations is ultimately what makes for a successful operating model and successful automation practice. We will dive into this further in the next chapter.

Recently we've seen another interesting benefit to this approach. Having an EAP accessible to teams across the business is also becoming a job perk for some employees. Employees want to have access to tools to improve their jobs, they want to be united with their coworkers, and they want to help make a meaningful impact on the company. Over the next decade we will likely see this trend progress. Employees will no longer have patience or interest in working with companies that get automation wrong. The company who shows up with a fragmented and siloed approach to automating their business will be left in the dust. They will be inevitably outpaced and outperformed by those businesses that see automation as a cohesive strategy to truly differentiate themselves and unite their workforce. As with everything in business, advantage always goes to the first movers.

CHAPTER 18

The New Operating Model

"We are only as strong as we are united, as weak as we are divided."

—J. K. Rowling

"If you build it, they will come" is what Kevin Costner heard whispered in his cornfield in the movie *Field of Dreams*. It might have worked for his baseball field, but it is a terrible idea for technology projects. "Build it, and they will come" is a common misconception that new technology will instantly change our companies for the better. Unfortunately, millions of dollars in failed technology projects say otherwise. McKinsey found that 70% of large technology projects fail to reach their stated goals.[1] This is not due to a lack of technology but the lack of a well-defined and well-executed operating model, which is the subject of this chapter.

Choosing the Right Operating Model

Dan is an architect who works for an energy infrastructure company we'll call PowerCo. He delivered big technology projects in the past and now faced his next challenge. The company made an acquisition that had over 10,000 employees. His project was to integrate and transform the HR processes of both companies. There was a hard timeline for the project, which, if missed, would make tens of thousands of employees go without their medical benefits and possibly even their paycheck. No pressure, right?

The pressure ratcheted higher when recent headlines revealed a failed government HR payroll project. What was supposed to save the government $70 million per year turned into a $2.2 billion waste. It was clear that the approximately 100 HR processes that made up the project were a big deal.

Dan decided to look at basic changes he could make to ensure that this automation challenge would succeed. To find some inspiration, he looked at past projects the company had undertaken. As he looked through the history, he found something interesting. There was a long run of technology projects that had failed. The delivery of integration and automation was often the root cause. The same story seemed to play out over and over:

1. Project team chooses a technology to use for the integrations and automations.
2. Only a small number of specialists have the expertise to use the new technology, creating a delivery bottleneck.
3. Timelines slip, and stakeholders get frustrated by lack of progress.
4. The scope is cut to try to manage costs and timelines.
5. The project fails to deliver what was promised.

Dan didn't want to repeat the past.

"OK, so I just need to hire more developers, right?" Dan thought to himself. "I can probably get those from an outside consulting company." Unfortunately, he was wrong. While these kinds of specialists were available, the cost for that number and that caliber of consultant was far more than his budget allowed. There was also no way his company could afford to keep this army of specialists around long term to keep these processes running after they were automated.

The root problem suddenly came into view. Dan realized why past projects had failed. PowerCo had thousands of people with immense knowledge of the data, processes, and applications, and yet somehow none of them could help create these automations. It wasn't a lack of technical features of these platforms, it was that they were not usable by 95% of the team. A tool with nobody to use it provides very little value.

Dan needed to find a way for his company to deliver these automations using the people already on the team. When he thought about it that way, the answer was obvious. There were many people on the project with deep knowledge of the systems and processes that supported payroll, benefits, talent, and other HR functions. They had all the knowledge that was needed; he just needed a tool they could use.

He knew that giving such a large group of team members uncontrolled access to build anything they wanted would end in a mess. The work had to be done, but they also had to ensure the result was stable, secure, and easy to operate over the long run. He stepped back and thought through the different operating models he might be able to use to accomplish this.

Automation Operating Models

Most companies don't stop to think about how they will deliver their automations. They often simply default to the approach they are using today. You'll hear things like:

"Steve in IT builds our integrations and automations, so he can figure it out."

While Steve is likely an amazing and talented individual, automation is not the responsibility of a single person in the company. It must be built into the very DNA of the company. This requires a well-thought-through operating model to define how teams across the organization will work together to transform the company.

| Centralized | Hybrid | Distributed |

D = Delivery Team   E = Enablement Team

(continued)

(continued)

The centralized model is a common way companies choose to deploy automation. It starts with a central team that takes requests for automations from the rest of the company. This team then prioritizes, builds, and operates the automations.

The hybrid model still has a centralized delivery team but is augmented by a few additional teams who also deliver automation projects. The central team automates too, but they also take on a new role, ensuring all teams are building in a consistent way, enabling them to be effective, and providing governance.

The distributed model flips the typical central model around. It enables many teams to automate, and the central team focuses only on enablement and governance.

Each model is optimized for something different. Centralized is best for control. It does this by routing everything through a single central team. Distributed is best for speed, as you leverage a large set of people and teams from across your company.

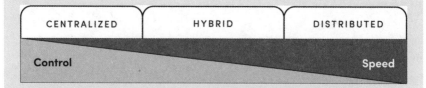

This does not mean that centralized can't be fast or distributed is disorganized and lacks control. It means that for a centralized model, the control will come more naturally, and the speed will require concerted effort and investment. With distributed, speed comes naturally, but investment and focus are needed to enable controls and governance.

We most often see companies use these models in stages. As you are just starting out, you may want to consider a centralized model. It gives you more control as you deliver on your first automations. It also gives you the ability to stand up your automation platform, establish governance, and learn from your first few projects. As your organization becomes skilled at this new discipline, you can now start to replicate it with more teams in the company. This transitions you to a hybrid model. As the company sees more success with automation and the demand increases, the central team can evolve from delivering automations to focusing more on enablement and governance. This completes the evolution by moving the company to a fully distributed model. By starting slow, the company is investing in controls and governance early and then later unlocks the speed of a distributed approach. Maintaining a strong central governance team is critical to a successful distributed delivery approach. This operating model is key to successfully achieving democratization.

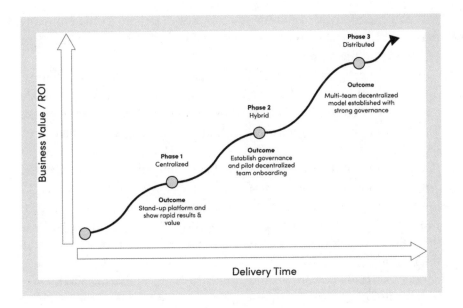

Dan decided to take the gradual approach to work PowerCo up to a distributed operating model. He implemented an automation center of excellence (COE) and began evaluating integration and automation platforms. He knew from their past project failures that choosing a platform that could be used by all teams was going to be critical to the success of this new operating model. After evaluating many tools, they found a platform that was low-code, easy to use, scalable, and had strong governance capabilities.

The team built the first automations for the HR program. In parallel they created strong governance processes and an enablement program to bring new teams onboard to automate. Once the program gained momentum, they began automating cross-functional processes such as payroll-finance reconciliations. They onboarded finance team members to help. This moved PowerCo into a hybrid model with multiple teams now building in the platform.

The team then doubled down on enablement by building an automation resource center. It was a webpage that any new team interested in automation could use to learn about how to get involved. They also created a community for people to share ideas and success stories with one another. This doubled as both a way for teams to learn but also a way to generate more interest in automation. Others in the company began taking notice, and he started receiving requests from multiple teams to join the automation movement.

The HR program was an epic success. The project came in on time, on budget, and modernized the HR processes significantly. Employee experience was greatly improved, and the HR team was ecstatic. They were able to start focusing on more strategic projects instead of working overtime simply trying to keep the lights on (as they did in the past). Dan and his team received a personal email from the CEO of PowerCo congratulating them on such a successful project and thanking them for the impact they had made on the company. As a result, Dan was promoted to take on a more senior level role in the organization and helped continue to drive automation across different parts of the business.

The story of PowerCo shows that the right operating model can be the difference between constant failure and widespread success. It is about how we automate. We have to execute faster with strong controls. The technology should not get in the way. If our technology keeps us from picking the right operating model, we need a different technology.

Leading the Change

Say we know our project, and we've picked the operating model that works for us. So are we automating yet?

Going from zero to hero with automation depends entirely on our ability to lead. It is a matter of guiding the company down a path of change. Applying automation to all corners of our business is a big deal and will almost certainly change the way employees do their jobs. It might be a good change, but it's change nonetheless.

People refer to the challenge as "moving the 600-pound gorilla." Imagine you're a zookeeper and you need to move a 600-pound gorilla from one room to another. It takes everyone working in unison. You can push on that gorilla by yourself—at best you'll get very tired, and at worst you'll have an angry gorilla. A crew is necessary, the zoo needs to be emptied of guests, and an empty exhibit needs to be ready. Most important of all, you need a willing gorilla.

Change in a company rarely happens through pushing or telling people what to do. Much like the gorilla, this will just result in anger and frustration. For this reason, after unsuccessfully trying to push the company towards automation, many give up and feel that the task is too big to take on. That's why a well-planned approach to the problem of moving the gorilla is critical.

The bottom line is that the gorilla will move but only if it wants to move. Therefore, you need to think less about forcing the gorilla to move and more about making the gorilla want to move. Maybe we pile the gorilla's favorite snack in the other room. Maybe we use peer pressure and get a bunch of smaller gorillas in the room to pique the 600-pounder's curiosity.

We may have taken a silly analogy too far, but the techniques to make a successful large-scale organizational change are exactly the same. A mix of the right incentives with the right social pressure will help any company move in the right way. With automation, we want to put the right operating model in place and fuel it with a culture of automation. This kind of change impacts many people across the company, and they need to be on board with the change. The key people you need to consider when looking to implement an automation strategy can be grouped into three categories:

1. **Leadership:** The widespread use of automation requires buy-in and support from the top levels of the company.

2. **Automation builders:** Those who build and maintain the auto-mations for the company will need to learn new skills and take on new challenges.

3. **Automation recipients:** When automating any business process, there is a wide range of employees and contractors whose jobs may change as a result of that automation.

Each of these groups has very specific incentives. Telling any of them what to do is typically not going to end well. Instead, we want to really understand their incentives and help show them how they will be better off. In the following table we list each group, their typical incentives, and the key messages we find resonate with these teams.

Team	Incentives	Key Messaging
Leadership	The leadership of most organizations will care primarily about costs, revenue, and speed.	Share insights into the impact of automation and how it can save money, allow the company to move faster, and in some cases increase revenue.
Automation builders	The automation builders want to make a positive impact on the organization and want to have the knowledge, tools, and control to do this.	Provide an easy-to-use tool, training, and guardrails so that all they have to do is bring their knowledge of the process they want to automate. Removing the barriers to entry is key.
Automation recipients	Automation recipients have their jobs to do; they don't want their daily processes to change unless it's going to change for the better.	Show how a post-automation world enables them to do more of the high-value work and less boring and repetitive work. Also, reinforce that the robots are not taking over.

As these key messages take root, you will begin to see a movement in the company. Reaching that point is not a matter of a quick email or PowerPoint presentation. These key messages can be met with skepticism and some degree of resistance. Therefore the most effective method of having these key messages resonate is not by saying it but by proving it.

Start your journey by automating a high-impact and high-visibility process. This success story gives you a credible and real-world example of how automation can change your company for the better. This enables you to support the message with evidence rather than just words. We'll call this first automation our "quick win." For the leadership team, you can use this quick win to show how much faster the process is after automation, the reduction in manual labor, and possibly the improved employee or customer experience. Showing the impact of automation to a leadership team using their own processes is by far the most effective way to demonstrate the business value that can be achieved. Even if you are the CEO, this approach can boost confidence that automation lives up to the hype.

This same quick win story can apply to other teams. For the automation builders, you're able to show both how easy it was to do and the kind of impact it had. When employees see their coworkers building automations and making a big impact, it gives them the feeling of "If they can do it, I can do it." Sharing this story also gets the creative wheels turning. Individuals will start thinking up new ideas of how they can automate processes in their respective departments.

Lastly, the quick win gives your automation recipients an example of how automation makes jobs easier. Maybe they got more time to focus on priority work, worked less overtime, or could take a vacation. These early wins can help overcome the fear instilled by anti-automation headlines. As silly as it sounds, it is a real concern. The quick win story can show that automation is not something to fear but something to be excited about.

The last and most important role is your role. Whoever you are, and wherever you sit in the company, you can be an automation champion. Every company needs someone to see the automation opportunity and paint a vision. The fact that you are reading this book and have gotten this far likely means you believe this is possible. Now you are armed with the knowledge of what it takes to make wall-to-wall automation a reality. This makes you the ideal champion for automation. It doesn't matter if you are an IT architect, a finance analyst, or the CEO. Organizations have seen people in all these roles initiate and drive major automation initiatives.

You now know why automation is important and how to make this change in your company. There's only one thing left to do. Start!

Note

1. Bucy, Michael, Adrian Finlayson, Greg Kelly, and Chris Moye, "The 'How' of Transformation," *McKinsey*, May 9, 2016, **https://www.mckinsey.com/industries/retail/our-insights/the-how-of-transformation**.

CHAPTER 19

The Future of the Enterprise

"Today, do what others won't so tomorrow you can accomplish what others can't."

—Simone Biles

"The internet is entering its Lego era" announced a *New York Times* article in 2006.[1] The article listed building blocks that developers used as they stitched together what became known as "Web 2.0." One of these building blocks was a recent announcement from Amazon called S3, or Super Simple Storage, the root of what became known as Amazon Web Services, or AWS.

Today, AWS is a cornerstone of cloud computing, but the platform had simple beginnings. It was new to the world in 2006, but the origin story goes all the way back to 2000. At the time, Amazon was trying to roll out e-commerce solutions for third-party vendors. As Amazon CEO Andy Jassy (who was Jeff Bezos's chief of staff back then) tells it. their developers were frustrated with the amount of time they were spending building and maintaining infrastructure. They felt like they were reinventing the wheel. What they were trying to build for their customers was not possible with their software stack. "Around the year 2000, we became a services company and really found religion around a service-oriented architecture, very quietly," said Jassy at a 2017 lecture.[2]

They asked all their technical teams to have well-developed APIs available for other teams to use at Amazon. That posture gave them the nimble structure to deliver services for **Merchant.com**. It also gave them an idea. If they were facing this problem, other companies probably were, too.

Amazon's innovation is the first known example of the new automation mindset. In a way, it is much like Lego, as the *New York Times* article described. With the building blocks handy, and no overhead work with infrastructure, all it takes is a few creative minds to come up with something special.

For Amazon, that special something was AWS. The AWS infrastructure is still used internally at Amazon, supporting the delivery of 2.5 billion packages every year. But the real story happened when Amazon rolled the AWS product out to the public. AWS made up 59% of Amazon's $22.9 billion profit before interest and taxes in 2020.[3]

Many companies have tried to emulate the Amazon approach over the years. But Amazon has an army of the best technical talent in the world to accomplish its vision. Companies that copied the Amazon approach have hired many expensive developers to make it happen.

In those early days of the internet, Amazon demonstrated all three elements of the new automation mindset:

1. **Process mindset:** Leadership compared what was built to what they were trying to achieve for customers. They realized they could eventually build what customers needed, but it was not a good long-term approach. They broke everything down to its component parts and rebuilt from the ground up by focusing on the outcome.

2. **Growth mindset:** The systems that Amazon was working with had eight years of history. Careers were staked on them. Billions of dollars of transactions were pouring through them. But Amazon embraced change and was willing to unlearn everything

they thought they knew to start again. They also did so instead of turning away from the plans they had for **Merchant.com**.

3. **Scale mindset:** Low code, as we know it today, wasn't around in the mid-2000s. Amazon still empowered people with creative ideas to build. Andy Jassy noted that the average company at the time spent 70% of its time maintaining infrastructure and 30% of its time creating. He figured if they could find a path to flip that on its head, it would be worthwhile. Today, required investments in infrastructure have dropped. More people than ever put their ideas to work and create.

Today, low code means the new automation mindset is available to everyone. Companies of all sizes no longer have to dream about becoming like Amazon—they can build processes and structures like Amazon from day one. Let's look at the stories of two real start-ups who did just that.

From the Brink of Extinction to an IPO

You'll remember the Toast story from Chapter 1: Thanks to their quick thinking, they saved themselves, and thousands of restaurants. In this chapter, we'll take a closer look at their story and impact.

Restaurants are a notoriously hard business. Restaurateurs overcome low margins, high turnover, and tough customers to follow their passion. Many do it with a love for food, and others with a passion for community. But one thing is for sure: no one ever went into the restaurant business for the paperwork.

Helping restaurants focus on their passion while simplifying busywork is one of Toast's first principles. "The restaurant industry is one of the most diverse and hardworking industries in the world. In many ways, it's been underserved by technology and financial services in regards to modernizing into a digital economy," noted Chris

Comparato, Toast's CEO.[4] Among other capabilities, Toast's point-of-sale (POS) platform enabled restaurants to easily accept credit card payments for in-person dining. Things were going great, and in February 2020, the company raised $400 million at a $5 billion valuation. Then, in the words of CNBC, "A month after that mega-financing round, it almost all came crashing down."[5]

In March 2020, restaurant revenue plunged by 80%, and Toast was left holding the bag. "I remember everyday going by thinking, 'oh my God, we're going to lose it.'" said Kent Bennett, one of the early investors in Toast.[6] Toast went from having the best strategy for the best market to having no market at all. Instead of closing up shop, Toast doubled down on their struggling customers in those early pandemic months.

In a public letter in early April 2020, CEO Comparato said "There is no playbook for navigating a global pandemic, but at Toast we will double down on our effort to support our community and become the leading platform for restaurants of all sizes."[6]

Over the next few months, Toast rapidly rebuilt. They launched products to fit the new pickup and delivery dining world. Two such examples are the introduction of the Toast Go 2 mobile POS device and Toast Order and Pay contactless payment. These offerings were designed to make it easier for restaurants to keep up with the rapidly changing health advisories and keep diners safe.[7]

Not only did they need to build new products, they also needed to change how they onboarded customers, as much of what used to happen live needed to be contactless. Toast's mission was to help restaurants. Restaurants needed help more than ever, so Toast stepped in to fill the gap. By the time Toast filed for their IPO in October 2021, they had generated $644 million in revenue that year, nearly 5x their 2020 revenue. They supported over 48,000 restaurant locations at that time, which was up from 20,000 in 2019.[8]

Because Toast truly embodied The New Automation Mindset, they could quickly react and respond to a market crisis while carrying thousands of other small businesses on their shoulders. It's an inspiring story.

It is tempting to think about The New Automation Mindset as an end goal. If we reach the magical peak of the mountain, we think our journey is complete. It's not true. Plasticity and the growth mindset mean we take on any new challenges and reinvent ourselves. It is a call to always be improving, and always be looking for ways to be more nimble. Toast could have rested on their laurels and celebrated an incredible IPO. But instead they are working harder than ever to build a different kind of company, an unstoppable company that hopes to thrive in the decades to come.

Using Pandemic Momentum to Push Upmarket

Navan (formerly known as TripActions) is another company with an amazing story. They also had a near-perfect response to the pandemic fallout. Before March 2020, business was booming. They had recently completed a funding round at a $4B valuation and were planning an IPO later in the year. Once the pandemic struck, business travel evaporated. Navan customers were cutting their travel budgets and trying to get out of their contracts. The crunch led to a 95% drop in revenue.[9] For a time, the company shifted to survival mode, saving customer contracts and convincing employees to stay.

Like the startup in the previous story, Navan had to pivot their product very fast to keep the business alive. Navan Expense, an experimental spend management product Navan had launched, had only 43 customers at the time. Observers were skeptical that Navan Expense could succeed in a crowded corporate card market. With the cliff Navan was facing, taking the risk and going all-in was the only choice.

Navan Expense was intended to help employees pay for flights, hotels, meals, and car rentals. In pandemic time, the spend shifted; employees were now looking for ways to buy work from home supplies, such as desks and monitors, or meal delivery. Because the company was built to pivot and evolve quickly, they could place bets in a crisis. It turned out to be a great decision—Navan Expense became the start-up's fastest growing business line.[10]

The success of Navan Expense helped Navan survive until business travel began to pick back up. At first, this was only happening upmarket, in the enterprise segment. While most small businesses cut travel spend, some large enterprises kept theirs. They also brought the budget back sooner as the pandemic wore on. Seeing this, Navan built more enterprise features to move upmarket.

Navan was not content to rest on their laurels. In mid-2022, I asked Navan CIO Kim Huffman what was next. She shared three priorities:

- **Resiliency:** continuing to build for flexibility and scale;
- **Maturity:** looking beyond tasks to enhance the overall company capabilities;
- **Growth:** enabling the company to pivot to new growth segments fast.

Reading this story, you might say Navan already embodies all these values. And compared to other companies, they do. But companies with the new automation mindset are not content to reach an end goal. They are constantly transforming. Kim still felt like the company had too many point-to-point integrations and not enough APIs. She wanted to keep building their service-oriented architecture and finding more ways to be nimble. They care about building on their success because of who Navan is as a company.

Today, as business travel has returned, Navan is soaring. They are stronger and more successful than ever. In many ways, the challenge of the pandemic strengthened them. While March 2020 saw a 95% drop in revenue, October 2022 saw them announcing a $9.2B valuation despite a historically tough market for SaaS.[11] The timing of their announcement is noteworthy, as it comes at a time where companies who were built for growth at all costs are tightening their belts and laying off employees. While the rest of the world is weathering a new market storm, Navan is unstoppable. They are an amazing example of the future of the enterprise.

The Future of the Enterprise and Becoming Unstoppable

The new automation mindset is a new way to think about technology and a different way to think about business, but at the heart, it is a path to building unstoppable companies. Earlier, we discussed the complex concept of antifragility. It is this concept that Nassim Taleb coined from his observations of nature and evolutionary processes. Adaptable or resilient things can remain the same despite challenges. But something that becomes stronger, better, and more powerful, resembles the Hydra of ancient mythology: If you cut off one head, two more grow back. Taleb says, "The resilient resists shocks and tries to stay the same; the antifragile gets better."

In the early 2000s, Amazon was on to something. While many thought they were reinventing the bookstore, Bezos had a bigger vision. Building a company on a services-oriented architecture was a better way to do things. It turns out, what they had built was so powerful that it became one of the most successful companies in history. AWS kicked off the cloud revolution, empowered the careers of millions of people, and propelled countless other companies to success. To build this, Amazon had to hire an army of engineers, and they built something no one else could. You could say Amazon is the OG of the new automation mindset.

The changing landscape of software, with the low-code/no-code revolution underway, means that companies such as these are taking the opportunity to become just like Amazon. The outcomes speak for themselves. Today, the chance to build unstoppable companies is more accessible than ever. The new automation mindset is no longer only reserved for companies that can afford armies of engineers; it is available to any company, from the car dealership down the street to a 100-year-old Fortune 500 behemoth.

Unstoppable companies will be able to respond to existential threats not by hiding in a hardened bunker but by embracing the threats and using them to become stronger. The potential outcomes are so exciting, and the possibilities are endless. But to get there, we have to change our mindset.

Notes

1. Markoff, John, 2006, "Software Out There," *New York Times*, (April 5), **https://www.nytimes.com/2006/04/05/technology/techspecial4/software-out-there.html**.
2. Statt Nick, 2021, "Meet Andy Jassy, Amazon's next CEO," *The Verge*, (February 3), **https://www.theverge.com/2021/2/3/22264425/amazon-new-ceo-andy-jassy-replacement-jeff-bezos**.
3. Long, Katherine Anne, 2021, "In the 15 years since its launch, Amazon Web Services transformed how companies do business," *Seattle Times*, (March 13), **https://www.seattletimes.com/business/amazon/in-the-15-years-since-its-launch-amazon-web-services-has-transformed-how-companies-do-business/**.
4. Ron, "Better Together: Thriving Through a Pandemic the Toast Way," *Tidemark Capital*, **https://www.tidemarkcap.com/post/better-together-thriving-through-a-pandemic-the-toast-way**.
5. Levy, Ari, 2021, "Toast Built a $30 Billion Business by Defying Silicon Valley and Surviving a 'Suicide Mission'," *CNBC*, (September 25), **https://www.cnbc.com/2021/09/25/toast-built-a-30-billion-business-by-defying-silicon-valley-vcs.html**.
6. Comparato, Chris, 2020, "Letter From the CEO on COVID-19 Impact," *Toast*, (April 7), **https://pos.toasttab.com/covid-19-impact-ceo-letter**.
7. Toast, 2020, "Introducing Toast Go® 2 and Toast Order & Pay®: Contactless Suite Empowers Restaurateurs to Keep Guests Safe and Grow Average Check Size to Navigate This Winter," *Toast News*, (November 16), **https://pos.toasttab.com/news/introducing-toast-go-2-and-toast-order-pay-contactless-suite-empowers-restaurateurs-to-keep-guests-safe-and-grow-average-check-size-to-navigate-this-winter**.

8. Schafer Brett, 2021, "Is Toast Ready to Take Over the Restaurant Industry?," *The Motley Fool*, (October 18), **https://www.fool.com/investing/2021/10/18/is-toast-ready-to-take-over-the-restaurant-industr/**.

9. Jeans, David, 2020, "Covid-19 Nearly Killed $4 Billion Corporate Travel Startup TripActions. Now It Has a $125 Million Lifeline," *Forbes*, (June 16), **https://www.forbes.com/sites/davidjeans/2020/06/15/covid-19-tripactions-funding/**.

10. Pimentel, Benjamin, 2021, "COVID-19 Bruised TripActions' Business. It Chose to Innovate," *Protocol*, (January 7), **https://www.protocol.com/tripactions-liquid-pivot**.

11. Mary Ann, 2022, "TripActions Secures $400M in Credit Facilities From Goldman Sachs, SVB," *TechCrunch*, (December 8), **https://techcrunch.com/2022/12/08/spend-management-startup-tripactions-secures-400m-in-credit-facilities-from-goldman-sachs-svb/**.

CHAPTER 20

The New Career Paths

"You stay elite by constantly moving forward."

—Bob Myers, 2-time NBA exec of the year

In 1908, Daimler Motoren Gesellschaft launched their first automobile. It was often hailed as the "car of kings." It took a factory of 1,700 employees to produce around 1,000 cars per year—hand assembled for the rich. It would later be known as the Mercedes, and it was a dream for car owners. It is still sought after by collectors today.

Despite their success, the Mercedes was not the car that revolutionized transportation. That distinction belongs to Henry Ford's Model T. Thanks to the assembly line, Ford packaged the innovations of the Mercedes into a product the average family could afford. David Hounshell observed that "Industrial society was highly advanced at the time the assembly line came into being. But once it came into being, it was so productive that very few things were made without the line after that."[1] In 1908, Ford produced 10,000 Model Ts. By 1925, production had scaled to an incredible 9,000 cars per day. Some analysts credit Ford for creating the American middle class. His workers not only could afford a Model T, but they had the time to drive it thanks to Ford's creation of the 40-hour workweek.

"Forget the Model T—Ford's real innovation was the moving assembly line. It didn't just usher in the age of the car; it changed work forever." And yet, "like a lot of [Ford's] other industrial production insights, the assembly line was met with hatred and suspicion by many of his workers."[2] It is striking that years after a revolutionary innovation, the fear of change is forgotten.

Fear of change is part of human nature. Today, many are concerned that robots, AI, and automation will make us all redundant. Some politicians and journalists are building careers on this age-old fear. The fear expands beyond tech, but even within tech with the rapid advances of generative AI, people start to wonder. When technology promises to change the way we work, we naturally react:

- What will this do to jobs?
- How will my career path change?
- What kind of new roles will grow in value?
- What can I do to stay ahead?

We spent this entire book discussing the benefits and approaches to automation. I think it is fitting that we conclude by answering these burning individual questions. We want to do our best to prepare you for the next technological revolution. We also want to talk openly and plainly about the inevitable changes that will affect all our careers. Lastly, we want to explore what these changes will mean for society.

Change is constant, but some innovations, such as the assembly line, have an outsized impact on society. The good news is that we have seen this before. History is on our side, as technology has created more opportunity every time. In fact, MIT research shows that 60% of all jobs today did not exist before the 1940s.[3]

The Explosion of Economic Value

A great example of the power of automation to create jobs is the automation of music.

Ambitious eighteenth-century inventors tried for years to automate music by creating robot violinists and other human replicas that would play instruments. Yet robot violinists did not transform music. Rather, the invention of recorded sound automated music led to a huge explosion of creativity and value.

In the late 1800s, there was concern that recorded sound would ruin everything. Colin Symes, in his book *Setting the Record Straight*, explains: "The musical elites . . . feared the phonograph threatened the aesthetic and moral conditions of music . . . its introduction provoked industrial unrest among Washington's civil servants, who feared that the phonograph would lead to numerous redundancies. Indeed, the first item for discussion at the inaugural convention of the National Phonographic Association in 1890 dealt with this issue and how to mitigate the fear of the phonograph generating 'technological unemployment.'"[4] After all, if you could just spin a record, why hire musicians?

It turns out, this was a really bad prediction. The successful release of recorded music today has the total opposite effect. Thousands of new jobs spawned from this one innovation. A sold-out arena concert tour after a popular album release is a great showcase of the sheer economic power unleashed by recorded sound. From roadies to concert promoters to merch booth managers, everyone can credit recorded sound for their career. New industries were created as new channels for distributing and monetizing music grew.

Without recorded sound, life would be much duller. Certainly, there would have been no radio, TV, Spotify, Alexa, or podcasts. Steve Jobs would have never launched the iPod. We can follow the thread of progress in all sorts of interesting directions. After all, without the iPod, would there have been an iPhone? Our world would look drastically different if the nineteenth-century elites had had their way and squashed Edison's innovation of recorded sound.

How Automation Is Changing Career Paths

While bots that mimic human work and generative AI models have been grabbing the headlines, an exciting career revolution has been playing out quietly in the background. Low-code/no-code automation platforms are fueling a new creative explosion in companies. If you have gotten this far in the book, you should have a good understanding of how the new automation mindset creates more opportunities for people and companies than ever before.

More business leaders are seeing the opportunities that low-code automation will create. For example, a recent article from David Peterson, titled "Why 'No Code Operations' Will Be the Next Big Job in Tech," captured it well: "If I were thinking about how to break into a startup right now, I would start building with these [low code] tools immediately. Even better, I'd start my own business on the side with only these tools."[5]

Roles focused on low-code/no-code technology are appearing in thousands of companies. Many of them have the word "operations" in their titles. IT is tasked with supporting and enabling these operators with more accessible technology. The growing capability of operators will continue to fuel demand for these types of jobs. Everyone has a new chance to position their careers for this change. Let's take a closer look at how operations careers are springing up in companies around the world.

Operation Roles and the Wonderful World of BigOps

The new operator (or ops) roles are appearing in every corner of the company, from sales to security. As software stacks grow in every department, these roles support them. The growing ecosystem that is emerging around these professionals is called BigOps.

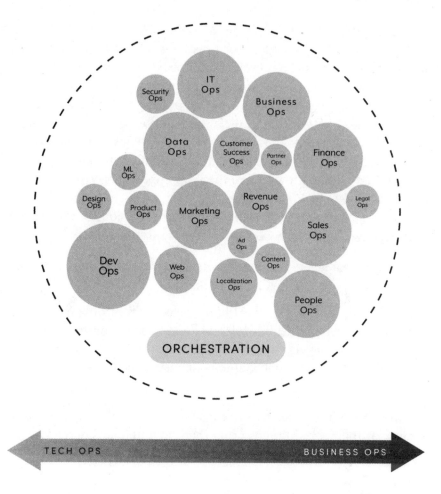

Not so long ago, the phrase marketing operations, or MOps, was meaningless. Now, it is a major and viable career path for thousands. The enormous marketing technology landscape has forced these roles to exist. Many marketing teams manage their processes from end to end without having to rely on IT. Demand for these professionals is only growing. At the end of 2021, more than 250,000 LinkedIn users in the US and nearly 600,000 worldwide included "marketing operations" in their profiles. The site also listed more than 15,000 open positions for marketing ops professionals at that time.[6]

BigOps is more than simply a job category, it's a bigger indication of how business is transforming and what is becoming critical.

The BigOps movement shows us how the process mindset and the ability to weave our people, processes, and technology together are becoming foundational requirements for nearly every business. If every business needs BigOps, operators will increasingly become critical.

In the early days of MOps roles, optimizing a variety of martech apps was the core task. Today, their roles have expanded. Automation is poised to become much more central to the MOps role. They are an example of potential innovators; with the right tech, they can make an impact. Their value grows when they can apply their creativity uninhibited by technology.

Similar opportunities exist in every company. Jobs in the BigOps ecosystem will grow in importance. Other examples include:

- HR ops managers will automate the entire HR process from hire to retire. New employee onboarding will be totally automated.
- SalesOps managers will automate lead routing, SDR compensation, and just-in-time sales call prep.
- SecOps managers will automate security alert management. They will run automated checks to ensure the security posture is up to date.

In each example, these ops roles are already experts in the technical aspects of their roles. Empowering them to automate company-wide processes will simply fuel their success.

How IT Roles Will Grow in Value

We have talked about how business roles are changing—what about IT? We mentioned earlier that IT needs to be elevated to a high-profile, high-impact guide role. This role is crucial for empowering the new automation mindset across the company. As a result, IT professionals will also experience some changes in their jobs as automation becomes more prevalent.

Big changes in IT are not uncommon. In the last decade, IT had to move from racking and stacking servers to cloud migrations. IT managers were no longer managing bits and bytes in their on-premise infrastructure but managing cloud vendors and compute environments. This led to IT setting up new DevOps pipelines to leverage the unique capability of the cloud to support a more dynamic application build process and architecture. By enabling developers to build better software and services, the value of their IT skills grew.

IT managers used to fight for headcount and budget to meet all the demands thrown at them. The pandemic turned that upside down for a time. The rapid mobilization of IT pros was key to keeping the doors open. Budgets were much looser to enable remote work. But as we enter the rough post-pandemic economy, these budgets are returning to normal. Demand is yet again outstripping resources.

Even though IT budgets may be shrinking again, the scope of IT is growing and evolving. Companies will become much more IT-focused as app builders and BigOps pros use low-code tools. This changing model means IT takes on a leadership role with security and governance. By democratizing the ability to create apps and automate workflows, bottlenecks that used to plague IT are being cleared by business experts. Work within the IT department is also changing. Automation is a force multiplier for the function. With more automation of tasks, IT time is freed up for leadership, and new careers are being born.

While workers throughout the organization can generate value from automation, a cohesive approach is needed. In many cases, automation experts may report to business line managers. It would be easy for them to go without contact with automation experts in other departments. To keep it all together and lead the efforts, there needs to be a central team. This team leads the center of excellence (CoE) to share knowledge across lines of business. These automation roles are becoming increasingly more important as well. We are now seeing roles such as director of automation and even chief automation officer popping up in different companies.

Become a Catalyst

Hopefully, by now, you are thinking about the exciting future ahead of us in automation. New opportunities, ideas, challenges, and efficiencies are just waiting to be discovered. All it takes is someone motivated and able to step up and build something that changes the trajectory of their company—and their career—forever. It can be an impactful story.

This is one of those stories. After six years of stocking supermarket shelves, a young woman named Jia Ying Lee decided it was time for a change. She started looking for a new job. Eventually, she found one at a start-up with less than 100 employees called Workato, in an entry level HR admin position. Over time, Jia Ying decided to tinker with the automation platform (the Workato product). She started teaching herself how to use it in her free time. Ideas started to come to mind for automating the HR processes that she was responsible for. This included the new employee onboarding process, made up of activities such as background checks, offer letters, and new hire provisioning. She took initiative and started automating. Soon, new hires at the company would comment on how their onboarding experience was different from any company they had ever worked for (in a good way!). "It just worked!" one person said. "I was able to get started on day one," said another.

Jia Ying was quickly noticed by the leadership team—and as the company began to scale, Jia Ying was promoted into new roles. As of this writing, Workato is nearing 1,000 employees. The overwhelming majority of them have been onboarded using automated workflows that Jia Ying built. She is now in her fourth position in the company, drawing a salary that is multiples of the entry-level role she joined at, and is the top automation expert in the HR organization, in effect, taking on an HR ops role for the company and joining the BigOps ecosystem.

In four short years, Jia Yang went from stocking supermarket shelves to being a catalyst for transformation. She had no fear that she was stepping on toes or treading on someone else's territory. She didn't worry about not having the right technical background. She simply stepped up, applied her creativity, and played a crucial role in building the company.

Perhaps your next unicorn employee is stocking supermarket shelves somewhere right now. Perhaps you are the unicorn employee wondering how automation will affect your job or looking to start a new career. As the new automation mindset takes hold in more companies, the opportunities for more stories like Jia Yang's are exciting. All we need to do is give potential innovators the chance. It is in our best interest as leaders to do everything we can to enable them. Change needs a catalyst. Over the next decade, automation catalysts who challenge the status quo will be the most valuable resources in the entire company. They will be instrumental in helping us compete in the new era of digital transformation. It is time we start empowering them now, by building the new automation mindset in our companies.

The Stakes Are High!

Businesses are important parts of the economy, but they are also an essential part of the societal fabric. The decisions we make in our companies have ramifications outside the company walls. For this reason, executives are under increasing pressure to lead companies that are good corporate citizens, contributing to society, and making the right decisions, from sustainability to inclusion.

Automation doesn't get as much attention. But the decisions we make with automation are impactful. They affect human livelihoods, families, and ultimately the outcomes that we see in the world.

Automation is surprisingly powerful. When applied in the wrong way at scale, it can damage society. It can push people toward bad political systems and beliefs that provide catharsis for their pent-up anger and frustration.

Economic scholars and think tanks have been tracking automation for some time. For example, Daren Acemoglu, a researcher at MIT, has coined the term "so-so technology" to describe low quality automation that saves costs for companies with no benefit to people.[7] So-so tech eliminates jobs and offloads the labor to customers. Examples include technologies that mimic humans, self-check-out lines, or automated customer service hotlines.

The Brookings Institute describes these so-so automations as command-and-control (C&C)-style automation. It keeps employees out of decisions and automates away their jobs with decrees from the top down. Their research links C&C style automation and the rise of autocratic governments around the world.[8]

Brookings contrasts it with the *opposite* of command-and-control automation: *the democratized approach that we have covered throughout this book*. Rather than acting as a blunt tool for human replacement, the democratized approach empowers people to change their own jobs. It also offers a positive ripple effect on society. If C&C automation makes societies bitter and populist, low-code, democratic automation leads to more democratic outcomes for society. "Developing low/no-code automation technologies means encouraging all digital users to become active participants in the digital world, thereby expanding the idea of a democratic digital citizenship."[9]

Connecting an automation approach to something as big as society may sound like hyperbole. But think about how society would have been affected if Henry Ford decided to maximize his profits and charge the same price Mercedes was charging for their hand-built luxury cars? Or what if eighteenth-century elites had their way and outlawed recorded sound to protect musicians' jobs? Society around the world would be worse off, no doubt.

The decisions of even one business leader can have real implications for how history unfolds. If we stick with the old automation mindset, not only are we setting our companies up for failure, but we are also eroding support for some of the most crucial institutions in our societies. Taking up the new automation mindset is the right path for every company; not only will it lead to dramatic business outcomes, but it will also empower individuals to accelerate their own careers—ultimately leading to happier people and a healthier society. The technology is there. We have examples of those who have gone before us. All we need to do is step up to our roles as catalysts—and the rest will follow.

Notes

1. Hounshell, David, 1985, *From the American System to Mass Production, 1800–1932: The Development of Manufacturing Technology in the United States*, Baltimore: Johns Hopkins University Press.
2. Eschner, Kat, 2016, "In 1913, Henry Ford Introduced the Assembly Line: His Workers Hated It," *Smithsonian Magazine*, (December 1), **https://www.smithsonianmag.com/smart-news/one-hundred-and-three-years-ago-today-henry-ford-introduced-assembly-line-his-workers-hated-it-180961267/**.
3. *Goldman Sachs,* 2023, "Generative AI Could Raise Global GDP by 7%," (April 5), **https://www.goldmansachs.com/insights/pages/generative-ai-could-raise-global-gdp-by-7-percent.html**.
4. Symes, Colin, 2004, *Setting the Record Straight: A Material History of Classical Recording*, Middletown: Wesleyan University Press.
5. Peterson, David, 2020. "Why 'No Code Operations' Will Be the Next Big Job in Tech," *Medium*, (August 27), **https://medium.com/@edavid peterson/why-no-code-operations-is-the-next-big-job-in-tech-b8bb886378ac**.
6. Elwell, Chris, 2022, "What is Marketing Operations and Who Are MOps Professionals?" *MarTech*, (January 3), **https://martech.org/what-is-marketing-operations-and-who-are-mops-professionals/**.
7. Sara Brown, 2019, "The lure of 'so-so technology,' and how to avoid it," *MIT Sloan*, (October 31), **https://mitsloan.mit.edu/ideas-made-to-matter/lure-so-so-technology-and-how-to-avoid-it**.
8. Ibid.
9. Bhorat, Ziyaad, 2022, "How to Democratize Automation," *The Brookings Institute*, (May 25), **https://www.brookings.edu/techstream/how-to-democratize-automation/**.

Appendix A: Key Roles for Democratization

While the concept of business and technical teams sounds straight-forward, we know that each company contains a complex mix of varying roles, skill sets, and organizational structures. To help clarify, let's look a bit closer at the key roles involved in healthy democratization.

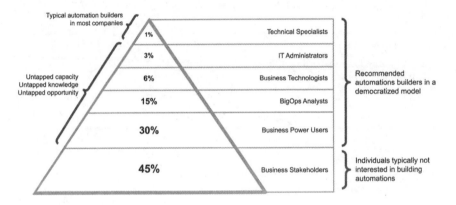

As shown in the chart, the roles in any given company are more complicated than simply "business" and "IT." We simplify throughout this book for readability, but when implementing democratization in your company, it is important to understand the nuances of the various roles and where to draw the line on who to include in your automation initiative. Here are some of the common titles for each of the roles we've identified in this view:

Role	Common Titles	IT or Business
Technical specialists Commonly the primary audience for traditional integration tools	Integration Administrator Automation Developer	IT
Business technologists Core roles supporting business apps and other business systems	HRIS analyst Workday Administrator Finance Admin	IT
BigOps analysts Support processes, systems, and data related to a functional area	HR PeopleOps Revenue Operations Specialist FinOps, ITOps, SecOps	Both
Business power users Team members motivated to automate business processes	Accounts Payable Analyst Marketing Content Creator	Business
Business stakeholders Recipients and users of automation	Mechanical engineer (*could be any job title*)	

You might notice that the titles for business power users and business stakeholders are the same. That's not a typo. The fundamental difference between those two categories of people is their drive and desire to participate in automating processes. For example, one accounts receivable accountant might be highly inclined to automate a process, but another may have no interest or desire.

Now let's look at how each role would participate in your democratized automation practice.

- **Technical specialists:** These technical experts should be elevated into a role that allows them to enable, guide, and support the broader community of builders. They should also be leveraged for the most difficult and most technically complex automation use cases. Technical specialists should also build shared services, guardrails, and other components to help other less-technical automation builders.

- **IT administrators:** These team members have a wealth of technical knowledge and with the right tools can streamline and automate a large number of IT operations. They can also be part of fusion teams to provide specialized technical expertise where needed.

- **Business technologists:** With such a strong business acumen and often detailed knowledge of the applications and data, these team members can both build automations and support business power users by providing the additional knowledge around concepts such as error handling, performance, and security.

- **BigOps analysts:** BigOps is a movement creating new roles, which are often the biggest drivers of automation in any company. These individuals understand the business processes inside and out. They also have deep expertise in the applications and their underlying data due to their frequent involvement with reporting. These roles can exist either in IT or in the line of business. We are seeing many individuals from both IT and the business transitioning into BigOps roles. More on BigOps in Chapter 21.

- **Business power users:** Business power users represent team members who could work in any department in any role. These are individuals with a strong drive to make positive changes for the organization. They want to improve processes, and they want to help do it. For them to be good candidates to build automations, they do need a basic understanding of the business process and potential data or applications involved.

- **Business stakeholders:** This group can also work in any department and in any role. They are primarily identified by the fact that they don't have the desire to personally automate any processes. This could be for various reasons, but our recommendation is to respect this wish. Forcing someone to participate in an automation program is not a recipe for success. Many of these people will eventually transition into business power users or even into BigOps analysts. These team members will often share ideas and requirements but will not build automations themselves.

There is another role that we haven't called out in the list because it's not actually a human role! Automation has now created the concept of "digital workers." A digital worker is a way for organizations to articulate the value being generated by your automations. You can use this concept to succinctly capture the headcount your automations are offsetting in a metric that the entire executive team will easily understand, e.g. our automations provide 232 digital workers—which means automated processes offset the time of 232 full-time equivalent (FTE) workers.

Beyond these roles, we also have leadership roles that are critical to any automation strategy. Let's quickly go over some of those:

- **Automation sponsor:** Every automation strategy should be sponsored by someone in the C-suite. Ideally, the CEO sponsors automation as a full-company strategy; however, it is also appropriate for a CIO (chief information officer), CDO (chief digital officer), or CAO (chief automation officer) to sponsor the initiative. It is this person's job to set automation targets, provide funding, and hold extended leadership accountable for the modernization of the business.

- **Automation evangelist:** While the sponsor will provide executive support and clear roadblocks, the evangelist's role is to build a culture of automation. This involves helping to share the mindsets we've discussed in this book, evangelize the benefits of automation, share successful automation stories, and create new champions for automation in all parts of the business.

- **Automation lead:** The automation lead is responsible for operationalizing automation across the company. They will typically lead the central automation team or center of excellence. This leader's team establishes the governance, owns and operates the automation platform(s), and has a primary role in enabling builders across the company.

- **Business leader:** Business leaders across the company play a pivotal role in automation. It is these leaders who ultimately own the business metrics that are being improved as a result of automation. These leaders must be educated on the impact automation can have on their business, and they must support and encourage their team to engage in automating their processes. Once a business leader understands how automation can fix some of their largest issues, they will often become automation's biggest champion.

With all of these roles, it can sometimes be confusing to understand how they would all work together on an actual automation project. When does each person come in, and what do they do? Let's walk through a quick scenario that demonstrates how these roles work together when using democratization.

Linda is an HR analyst (business power user) working for AcmeCo. She just got out of the quarterly HR all-hands meeting where they were sharing team updates. Tanya, the chief people officer (business leader) was telling the team that turnover was higher this quarter. She mentioned that people were primarily leaving the company due to a feeling that their careers weren't moving forward and that they had nobody to learn from. Linda knew there were plenty of people willing to share their knowledge in the company, but these people just weren't getting connected. She had an idea.

Recently, Todd from the IT team (automation evangelist) had done a presentation talking about how anyone in the company could build automations. Linda was a little nervous but decided to give it a shot. She reached out to Todd, and he pointed her to some quick onboarding and training on the low-code automation platform. She was able to complete it in less than a day. She knew now that building her idea was really possible!

Linda's idea was to build a way for team members across the company to use Microsoft Teams to self-identify that they would like a mentor. Others could identify that they would be willing to be mentors. The automation would then match up these people with one another and automatically schedule introductory meetings to get them started. She would call it MentorBot.

Before she dove in, she knew there were a few spots she might need some help with. Her training had told her that it was recommended she form a fusion team made up of a few key people who could help her out. She followed the advice and set up a meeting with Ray who was the Workday administrator (business technologist) and also June from the Automation COE (automation specialist). Ray thought her idea was great and helped by adding a custom "mentor" field to Workday to allow them to track the mentorship relationships in a central place. Ray also gave her some tips for using the HR data in Workday. June was there as a supporting resource in case she ran into problems and would also review her automation before it went into production.

With guidance from Ray and June, Linda created her automation in no time. June from the Automation COE reviewed the automation to ensure it was secure, built according to standards, and well tested. It was then deployed to production. Hundreds of employees began using the new automation. Jason in the Engineering team (business stakeholder) was so thankful for the ability to get connected with a mentor. He mentioned that it put his career on a new track and was forever grateful to Linda. Linda even thought of some neat enhancements to encourage previously mentored employees to become mentors themselves. She was able to quickly modify her automation and roll it out.

Two quarters later, Tanya (the chief people officer) presented the latest turnover numbers, and they were significantly lower. The previous complaints about lack of career progression were nearly eliminated. Tanya credited the automation that Linda created as the primary contributor to this significant improvement. She encouraged everyone in the HR team to think of other ways they could automate their processes. Linda enjoyed the process so much that she eventually transitioned into an HROps role (BigOps analyst) so that she could work on automating even more processes across HR.

Acknowledgments

To synthesize our idea and vision for a new movement in the coming era of automation and AI for all into a book is to embark on a journey that leans heavily on the support of a diverse community of experts. I am incredibly fortunate to be surrounded by a special group of people with unique talents and unwavering dedication. To each and every one of you, I humbly extend my deepest gratitude for your contributions to this project. There are so many people to name—that speaks to how much of a community effort went into the creation of this work, from ideating, to writing, to editing and rewriting.

Firstly, I would like to express my deepest appreciation and gratitude to Workato's customers and partners. You are our inspiration, our driving force, our source of ideas, and the reason we do what we do. It is your experiences and knowledge that underlie the concepts and strategies contained in this book. Thank you for always pushing us, collaborating with us, and motivating us.

I'm grateful to my co-authors Scott Brinker and Massimo Pezzini. Your insights, wisdom, guidance, knowledge of enterprise software, and encouragement were invaluable to me and this book. Your shared passion for what is possible in businesses is infectious.

This project also has two other key collaborators without whom this book would not have made it past the first base: Alex Lamascus and Dan Kennedy. It started in May 2021, when Alex Lamascus came to me with a proposal for turning a collection of ideas into a book. Over the course of the next two years, Alex led and managed this journey from inception to delivery and then launch. Dan Kennedy joined the project in January 2022 and brought his incredible polymath abilities to bear, from his deep knowledge of enterprise architecture, to his leadership, writing, and even design skills. Dan is someone you want on your team for many reasons, and I'm grateful for his help on this book.

I've been part of some big pushes in my time, but I'm speechless about this one. It is unbelievable how Alex and Dan helped wrestle this project to the ground. The amount of sheer work, all the smarts in creating so much new content in such a short period of time, while attacking all the big concepts and ideas we needed to (some of them required so much original creation) is stunning. So many people contributed so much, but these two were the engines behind this. I can't begin to thank them enough.

Special thanks go to our talented designers, Natalie Broussard and Cathy O'Malley, and our brand leader, Simmi Patel. They brought creativity and visual flair to this project, at many times working long hours to help us achieve our goals. I am truly grateful for their dedication, hard work, and keen eye for design.

I am also grateful to the following collaborators and reviewers, whose feedback, writing, and suggestions greatly improved the quality of this work: Andres Ramirez, Gaby Moran, Markus Zirn, Bhaskar Roy, Bharath Yadla, Carter Busse, Derek Roberts, Tridivesh Sarangi, Todd Gracon, Husain Khan, Karuna Mukherjea, Thomas Ream, Shail Khiyara, and Kristine Colosimo. Your willingness to share your time, knowledge, and expertise with us was core to the success of this project.

I would like to thank the founders and other leaders at Workato. Your dedication to and passion for our customers makes this all possible; I am so grateful for what you do each and every day. Many of the ideas in this book have come from working closely with my partner in crime Gautham Viswanathan, and our years working with our customers and honing the vision for this mindset.

I could not have done without the support and forbearance of my family, especially when I disappeared on them for pretty much the entire holiday season this past year to complete this project.

Thank you all for being a part of this journey.

—*Vijay Tella*

About the Authors

Vijay Tella

Vijay Tella is founder and CEO of the automation platform Workato. The company is the culmination of his pioneering work in both the enterprise automation and consumer-facing software spaces.

In the enterprise automation space, he helped found two multibillion-dollar products. This includes the industry's first middleware product, "The Information Bus" (TIB) at Teknekron, with the role of VP of Core Technology group when Teknekron was acquired by Reuters in 1994 for $275M. He went on to become the founding SVP of engineering at Tibco Software, which went public in 1999 and today produces over $1B in annual revenues with over 4,000 employees. He then became chief strategy officer at Oracle, launching and growing the Oracle Fusion Middleware (FMW) platform into a $2.6B line of business when he left in 2008. To this day, FMW is the technical underpinning of Oracle's business applications.

In the consumer-facing software space, Vijay co-founded a consumer video app called Qik, which was acquired by Skype in 2011. This deep dive into consumer technology sparked the realization that the user experience we all have come to expect from consumer apps was a crucial missing ingredient for successful enterprise automation.

In 2013, Vijay founded Workato, combining these two perspectives into a single enterprise automation platform. Workato's beautiful, approachable user experience (in Silicon Valley we refer to this as low-code/no-code) feels similar to what consumers expect from cloud apps but sports the strength and reliability under the covers that is associated with high-powered enterprise software such as Tibco.

Workato was recently named to the Forbes Cloud 100, the Deloitte Fast 500, the CNBC Disruptor 50, and the inaugural CNBC Top Startups for the Enterprise.

Scott Brinker

Known as the "Godfather of Martech," Scott Brinker has been ana-lyzing marketing technology for more than 15 years. He is the founder and editor of chiefmartec.com. He also pioneered the widely cited MarTec Landscape. He is VP of platform ecosystem at HubSpot, author of the best-selling book *Hacking Marketing*, and an advisor to Workato.

Massimo Pezzini

Massimo Pezzini is an independent IT strategic advisor and head of research, future of enterprise for Workato, the leader in enterprise automation. In this role, Massimo is a strategic advisor to the Wor-kato team, with a focus on how automation technologies will evolve to support a rapidly transforming business environment.

Massimo has over 45 years of experience in the IT market and spent 25 years at leading research analyst firm Gartner as vice president dis-tinguished analyst. At Gartner, Massimo played a leading role in some of the most groundbreaking research in automation and integration technology and has a profound understanding of the dynamics at play in these markets. He has advised hundreds of organizations worldwide, including Global 2000s, on how to strategically leverage integration and automation technology to support their digital trans-formation plans effectively and efficiently.

To bring this book to life in your organization, learn how you can ensure your colleagues get a copy, and learn more about your own automation mindset, head over to **www.workato.com/book** or follow this QR code:

Index

A

Accounts management (back-office task), 124
Acemoglu, Daren, 287
Actionable generative AI, platform, 212
Adaptability, process variance (contrast), 42–43
Adaptation, usage, 19–21
Advocacy (customer journey stage), 178
Agile, value, 41–42
Amazon
  automation mindset, demonstration, 270–271
  innovation, 270
  Super Simple Storage (S3), 269
Amazon Web Services (AWS), 269–270
  cloud revolution, 285
  SQS, 254
Antifragility, concept, 285
API management (APIM), 220, 225–227, 249
Apple (platform company example), 195
Applicant tracking systems (ATS), usage, 202
Application Programming Interface (API), 225
  architecture, microservices (relationship), 254
  religion, 227
  services, usage, 88
  usage, 201
Applications (apps)
  no-touch provisioning/deprovisioning, 133–134
  usage, 243
Architectural styles, 249–256
Artificial intelligence (AI). See Generative AI
  AI-assisted orchestration
    automation strategy component, 86, 89–92
    elements, reliance, 91
    low-code components, usage, 91
  AI-generated call summarization/field updates, usage, 150

AI-powered dynamic workflows, usage, 91
company-wide knowledge search (conversational answers), artificial intelligence (usage), 134
enterprise-grade AI platform, dimensions, 104
governance, relationship, 103–104
platform, 64
real value, 37
technologies, usage, 77
usage, 10, 77, 149–150
Assembly line, innovation, 280
Atlassian
  democratization, usage, 101–102
  workforce capability scaling, 106
Atlassian Foundation, Engage for Good, 102
Auto-discovery input capabilities, 213
Automated cash reconciliation, 131–132
Automated company review, 178
Automated fulfillment, 177
Automated identification, 177–178
Automated lead management process, appearance, 142, 143
Automated learning/development, usage, 166
Automated processes, 243
  IT communication, 105
Automated product review, 178
Automated promotions, 177
Automated social media monitoring, 178
Automation
  approaches, 71–74
  architecture, need, 85
  automation-centric LLMs assistance, 91
  back-office use cases, 124, 128, 129, 131
  benefits, 112
  Brookings Institute descriptions, 288
  builders, 265
  building, 245
  center of excellence (COE), implementation, 263
  changes, 17
  cloud-native automation, impact, 7–8

Automation *(Continued)*
  components, pillar classification, 87
  cost/effort, 219
  customer experience use cases, 171, 175
  design, 245
  discovery, 117
  ecosystem, 217
  employee experience use cases,
    157, 161, 164
  end-to-end automation, 245–247
  enterprise automation, 8–10
  evangelist (democratization role),
    294, 295
  front-office use cases, 141, 145, 146
  high-level topics, discussion, 117
  impact, 282
  initiation, 187–188
  innovative automations, 118–119
  inspiration, 119
  journey, mastery, 111
  lead (democratization role), 294
  links, 255
  manager approval request, 88
  notification, 88
  number, 23
  operating models, 261–263
  opportunities, identification
    process, 245
  overbuilding, 43–45
  platform, technical capabilities, 77
  process (hypothetical), 231–243
  real value, 37
  recipients, 265–267
  skills resource, wasting (avoidance), 45
  sponsor (democratization role), 294
  stakes, 287–288
  strategy
    components, inclusion, 86
    implementation, categories, 265
  supplier operation automation use
    cases, 182, 186, 189
  supply chain process automation
    opportunities, 182
  task-based automation, 71
  team sport/specialized experts,
    involvement, 7
  technical capacity, 44
  tools, 219–229
    interoperability, 77
    towers, 113–114
    unmanaged automation tools, 228–229
Automation mindset, 23, 62, 69, 241
  adoption, 85–93
  blueprint, 8–10
  capabilities, 112
  road map, 12–13
  unleashing, 23–24
Awareness (customer journey stage), 176
Awareness/demand generation (front
  office group), 139

B

Backcheck, service platform creation, 202
Background checks, performing, 161
Back office, 121
  fragmentation, overcoming, 37
  functions, business value
    (unlocking), 122–124
  importance, 134–135
  innovative automations, 133–134
  tasks, categorization, 124
Back-office automation
  benefit, 132
  power, 132–134
  tower, 113–114
Bank records, transaction iteration, 246
Bezos, Jeff, 269
Big iron software, 223
BigOps, 282–285
  analysts (democratization
    role), 293, 296
Bottom line/top line, improvement, 140
Building blocks
  approval building blocks, impact, 88
  orchestration building blocks, 75, 76
  technology components, 88
Business
  automation, stakes, 287–288
  business-reactive input capabilities, 213
  characteristics, 24–25
  consultant, impact, 44
  event services, usage, 88
  experts, impact, 99
  fresh thinking, input, 205
  information technology (IT),
    combination, 99–100
  leader (democratization role), 294–295
  operations, 283

power users (democratization role), 293
productivity, tech stack expansion
(relationship), 6
stakeholders (democratization role), 293
subprocesses, 242–243
technologists (democratization
role), 293
unlocking, 125
users (aptitude), technology (support),
105–106
value, 122–124, 241
Business process automation (BPA), 222
Business processes
automation, integration capabilities,
243–244
orchestration, 72–74
streamlining, 242
workflow, 244
Business process management (BPM),
35, 220
Business process management suites
(BPMS), 222–223
Business rules management system
(BRMS), 222–223

C

Cachet
announcement, engineer posting, 128
status dashboard, usage, 129
update posting, 129
Career paths, 279
automation, impact, 282
Catalyst, role (importance), 286–287
Center of excellence (COE), 296
implementation, 263
leadership, 285
Change, 39–41, 280
catalyst, impact, 287
culture, 20
embracing/fear, 5–6
scale, examination, 50–51
willingness, 20
ChatGPT-like interface, usage, 37
ChatGPT, usage, 209
ease, 211
Chorus by Zoominfo, usage, 149
Closed-lost reactivation emails, 150
Cloud, evolution, 229
Cloud-native automation, impact, 7–8

Cloud optimized, cloud native
(contrast), 229
Cloud platforms, 229–230
Collaboration
internal procurement stakeholders
(collaboration improvement),
technologies (introduction), 182
success, language (need), 105
supplier collaboration (improvement),
technologies (introduction), 182
Collective engagement, 20
Command-and-control (C&C)-style
automation, 288
Command-line tools, usage, 57
Communication channels, usage, 243
Community-powered platforms, need, 105
Company
empowerment, 58–59
impact, front office (connec-
tion), 139–140
reviews, automation, 178
rigidity, 83–85
Company-wide knowledge search
(conversational answers), artificial
intelligence (usage), 134
Competition, external pressures, 82
Compliance (back-office task), 124
Composable capabilities, 244
automation strategy component, 86–89
focus, benefit, 87
Conferencing bridge, opening, 128
Config tools, usage, 57
Connections, formation (automation), 176
Connectivity, 257
Consideration (customer journey stage),
176
Consumption, promotion, 204
Context shifting fatigue, overcoming
(automation use case), 161–163
Continuous feedback
impact, 216
loop, presence, 215
Continuous improvement, 82, 211
Contract management (front office
group), 139
Contracts team, internal notification
(sending), 188
Covid-19 pandemic, impact, 46–47
Culture, communication, 155

Customer
explanation/need, 44
frictionless customer check-in,
automation use case, 175
ID struggles, automation, 177
intent data, sources (finding), 149
portal, automation use case, 171–174
retention/expansion (driving),
automation mindset
(impact), 112
success/operation (front office
group), 139
Customer experience (CE) (CX), 92, 169
automation tower, 113–114
automation use cases, 171, 175
creation, 82
customer journey, innovative
automations, 176–178
designing, 171
enhancement, 140
fragmentation, overcoming, 38
future, 178
Customer journey
innovative automations, 176–178
stages, 176–177
Customer relationship management
(CRM), 137
platform, data entry, 53
processes, management, 140
system, 223

D
Dall E, usage (ease), 211
Data
analysis capabilities, expansion, 182
architecture, 84
capabilities, 243
cloud, usage, 88
hub architecture, 255–256
inaccuracies, removal (supply chain
challanges), 182
integration, 87, 90, 256–257
orchestration building block, 75, 76
pipeline tools, usage, 220
platform (platform-driven method),
196–199
"proof of vaccination" data capability,
creation, 90
transformation, 257

Deal desk
approval, Slack notification (trigger), 47
front-office automation use
case, 146–149
process, implementation, 148
Delivery team, enablement team (interaction), 261
Delivery time, problems, 42
Democratization, 62, 95, 204
balance, finding, 98–99
embracing, 106
potential, unlocking, 106–107
revolution, 59–61
roles, 291–296
support, 106
technical support, 251
usage, 63
usage (Atlassian example), 101–102
Deprovisioning
apps, no-touch provisioning/deprovi-
sioning, 133–134
implementation, 126
Development operations (DevOps)
pipelines, setup, 285
Digital economy, modernization, 271
Digital era, 10–12
Digital supply chain (DSC)
appearance, 187
automation use case, 186–189
Disjointed system/process, integration
(supply chain challenge), 182
Distributed delivery approach, 262
Distributed model, change, 262
Distribution team, internal memo
(sending), 188
Documentation, saving, 48
Docusign
involvement, 213
usage, 48
Doordash, front-office automation, 146
Dynamic content, automation, 176

E
Economic value, explosion, 281
Economy, external pressures, 82
Efficiency, maximization, 82
Employee. See New employees
compliance (ensuring), post-pandemic
return-to-work protocols (usage), 161

onboarding process, 244
PC-to-Mac migration, assistance, 133
request (receiving), low-code application form (generation), 90
retention/empowerment (driving),
automation mindset (impact), 112
volunteering opportunities,
matching, 165
Employee experience (EE), 92, 153
delightful experiences, automation,
154–157
elevation, 140
fragmentation, overcoming, 38
innovative automations, 165–166
Employee experience (EE) automation, 156
process, paths (building), 159
tower, 113–114
use cases, 157, 161, 164
Employee manager, approval delegation
(determination), 88
End-of-life parts, replacement
sourcing, 191
End-to-end automation, 245–247
End-to-end RMA process, systems
support, 184
End-to-end simplicity, 211
Engage for Good (Atlassian
Foundation), 102
Enterprise
central nervous system, 78–80
democratization, 22
future, 269, 285–286
requirements, 212
Enterprise AI platform, 64
capability map, 212
enterprise-grade capabilities, 216
need, 209
Enterprise application integration
(EAI), 224
Enterprise automation, 241
architecture platforms, 251–256
maturity model, 115–116
pillars, 256
rise, 247
usage, 8–10
workflow, 246, 250
Enterprise automation platform (EAP),
247–249
architectural styles, 249–256
Enterprise-grade capabilities, 216

Enterprise resource planning (ERP),
30–31, 41–42
invoice, uploading, 253
silo, 240
system, 223
Enterprise service bus (ESB), 224, 244
Event-driven architecture (EDA),
77, 252–255
Event-driven workflows, 77
Ever Given (Suez Canal ship
incident), 33–34
Execution engine
capabilities, 214
enterprise-grade AI platform
dimension, 104
versatility/power, 214
Experience integration, 87, 90
capabilities, 243
enterprise automation pillar, 257
Extract, Transform, Load / Extract, Load,
Transform (ETL/ELT), usage, 35,
220, 227–228, 244

F
Facebook (platform company
example), 195
Fadell, Tony, 202
Federal Express (FedEx), Dataworks
(platform-driven method), 198–199
File transfer service, usage, 19
Finance management (back-office
task), 124
Finance operations (FinOps) (back-office
task), 124
Fine payment reporting, 129–131
Flexible experiences (automation strategy
component), 86, 92–93
Follow-up reminders, usage, 88
Food delivery/loyalty rewards, automation
use case, 145–146
Ford, Henry, 279–280, 288
Fragmentation, problem (growth), 37
Frictionless customer check-in,
automation use case, 175
Front office, 137, 138
activities, grouping, 139
automation tower, 113–114, 137
company impact, initiation, 139–140
fragmentation, overcoming, 37
innovative automation, 149–150

Fulfillment, automation, 177
Functional areas, grouping, 180

G

Gartner
  composable enterprise, 204
  Hyperautomation framework, 231
Generative AI (GenAI)
  actionable generative AI, platform, 212
  adaptability, 215–216
  assistance, 91
  challenges, 210–211
  characteristics, 214–216
  data usage, 150
  enterprise-grade capabilities, 216
  explainability, 214–215
  impact, 7–8, 209
  input method capabilities, 213
  observability, 215
  usage, 8–10, 57
  utility-like characteristics, 215
Gift delivery, automation, 165
Gig economy, onboarding automation
    (use case), 164–165
Golden records, building, 255
Gong.io, usage, 149
Google (platform company example), 195
Go-to market (GTM)
  front office group, 139
  platform-driven method, 196, 199–201
Governance
  adaptability speed, myth, 100
  artificial intelligence (AI), relation-
    ship, 103–104
  enterprise-grade AI platform
    dimension, 104
  initiatives, IT leader misunderstanding
    (myth), 100
  usage, 100–101
Graphical user interface (GUI),
    usage, 220
Green screen scraping, 220
Growth
  driving, partner marketing
    (automation), 190–191
  Navan priority, 284
Growth mindset, 22–23, 39, 81
  action, 47–49
  Amazon demonstration, 270

change (embracing), plasticity
    (usage), 63
  opposite, 44–45

H

HipChat
  conferencing bridge, opening, 128
  room, automatic creation, 129
Huffman, Kim, 284
Human actions, system actions
    (combination ability), 77
Human-driven input capabilities, 213
Human interactions (business
    subprocess), 242–243
Human resources (HR)
  operations (HR ops), automation,
    284, 296
  program, automations (building), 263
Humble checklist, power, 31–33
Hyperautomation framework
    (Gartner), 231

I

Ideas
  leveraging, 204
  obtaining, 211
Identification, automation, 177
Improvement, ideas (requirement), 85
Incident management, streamlin-
    ing, 128–129
Information technology (IT)
  absence, 54–55
  administrators (democratization
    role), 293
  business, combination, 99–100
  limitation, absence, 55–56
  mobilization, 285
  operations (back-office task), 124
  roles, value (growth), 284–285
  rules/restrictions, (myth), 100
  service technology, automation use
    case, 124–128
  shadow IT integrations, usage, 243
Infrastructure management (back-office
    task), 124
Infrastructure team, responsibilities, 126
Initial public offering (IPO), 271–283
Innovative automations, 118–119
Innovative products/services,
    development, 82

Input methods
  capabilities, 213
  enterprise-grade AI platform
    dimension, 104
Instant answers, automation, 176
Integrated Operations, SWA usage, 73
Integration
  capabilities, 243
  framework, 35–38
Integration platform as a Service (iPaaS),
  35, 223–225, 233, 249
  usage, 219–220
Intelligent business process management
  (iBPM), 222
Internal organizational turmoil,
  refocus, 82
Internal procurement stakeholders
  (collaboration improvement),
  technologies (introduction), 182
Interoperability, 77
Inventory management (functional area
  group), 180
Invoice delivery, 233
IRregular OPerationS (IROPS), usage, 73

J
Jassy, Andy, 269
JIRA
  login need, 128
  ticket, creation, 129
Jobs
  execution, 74–75
  titles (auto-categorization), buyer
    persona (usage), 150

K
Kelley Blue Book (KBB) (platform-driven
  method), 198
Knowledge, fragmentation
  (elimination), 248

L
Large language models (LLMs)
  data, wealth, 211
  enhancement, continuous feedback
    (impact), 216
  usage, 37, 91, 209
Leadership (automation strategy), 265
Lead management (front-office automation use case), 141–145

automated lead management process,
  appearance, 142, 143
Legal operations (back-office task), 124
Light bulbs, security operations
  (connection), 133
Low-code applications
  form, generation, 90
  usage, 257
Low-code automation, impact, 282
Low-code chatbots, usage, 257
Low-code components, usage, 91
Low-code/no-code (LC/NC),
  usage, 57, 248
Low-code unified experience, 248
Loyal/high-value customers,
  automated identification/VIP
  treatment, 177–178
Loyalty (customer journey stage), 177

M
Machine learning models,
  leveraging, 162
Manager approval request, 88
Manual operational tasks, work
  expenditure, 3
Manual work (increase), app usage
  (increase), 3
Manufacturing management (functional
  area group), 180
Marketing automation platforms
  (MAPs), 137, 141
Marketing department, email
  (sending), 188
Marketing operations (MOps)
  roles, 283–284
Markets, entry, 82
Master data management (MDM)
  solution, 255
Material management (functional area
  group), 180
Maturity, Navan priority, 284
Messaging, 266
Metadata, providing, 256–257
Microservices
  API architecture, relationship, 254
  building, 252
Microsoft Teams
  notification, sending, 90
  usage, 88
Model T, production, 279–280

N

Nasdaq, Data Link platform (platform-driven method), 198
Native integration, usage, 243, 244
Natural language processing (NLP), usage, 149–150
Navan
    Covid-19 pandemic, impact, 46–47
    priorities, 284
Navan Expense, launch, 283–285
Nest, service platform, 202–203
Netsuite
    API, calling, 224–225
    bank files, loading, 131
    customer record, presence, 225
    involvement, 213
    sales order creation, 254
    transactions, mapping/posting, 132
New employees
    mentorship, facilitation, 166
    onboarding, automation use case, 157–161
Nominal EBIT, growth, 11
Non-technical stakeholders, discovery workshops (usage), 117
Nutanix, continuous evaluation, 45

O

Objectives, meeting, 82
Obsolescence, avoidance, 39–41
Onboarding
    automation (use case), 164–165
    process, background checks (performing), 161
Operating model
    automation operating models, 261–263
    change, 259
        leading, 264–267
    impact, 244–245
    selection, 259–264
Operational excellence (driving), automation mindset (impact), 112
Operation roles, 282–284
Operations platform (platform-driven method), 197, 204–205
Optical character recognition (OCR), usage, 232
Orchestration, 62, 69, 72, 204, 256
    acceleration, 63–64

building blocks, 76
engine, requirements, 77
layer, 185
technical capabilities, requirement, 77–78
technical support, 251
usage, 62–63
Organizational mindset, 21–23
Overbuilding, 43–45
Overspecialization/overgeneralization, problems, 219

P

Packaged business capabilities (PBCs), usage, 86–87
Packaged cloud offerings, 57
Pandemic momentum, usage, 283–285
Partner efficiency, fragmentation (overcoming), 38
Partner marketing, automation, 190–191
Partnerships, changes, 192
Partner/supplier relationships, innovative automation, 190–191
Past projects (maintenance/support), wasting (avoidance), 45
People (orchestration building block), 75, 76
Peterson, David, 282
Pfeiffer, Wendy, 45
Plasticity, 62, 81, 204
    achievement, composable capabilities focus (impact), 87
    automation architecture, need, 85
    improvement, ideas (requirement), 85
    technical support, 251
    usage, 63
Platform
    changes, 192
    community-powered platforms, need, 105
    company, definition, 195
    customer relationship management (CRM) platform, data entry, 53
    enterprise AI platform, 64
    integration platform as a Service (iPaaS), 35
    unification, 257
Platform-driven business, 195
    methods, 196–205

Plug-and-play, 87
Point-of-sale (POS) vendor
  principles, 271
Point-to-point (P2P)
  architecture, 251–252
  integrations, excess, 284
Proactive notifications, usage, 125
Process
  capabilities, 243
  improvement cycle, implementation, 45
  integration, 87, 90, 256
  manual effort, reduction, 161
  orchestration building block, 75, 76
  straight-through processing, 71–72
  variance, adaptability (contrast), 42–43
Process automation
  Amazon demonstration, 270
  technical capacity, 44
Processing, reliability, 256
Process mindset, 22, 27, 104
  orchestration, usage, 62–63
  task mindset, contrast, 28–31
Procurement/payments (functional area
  group), 180
Product
  databases, usage, 184
  registration management, usage, 184
  reviews, automation, 178
  usage analysis, 244
Productivity, focus/rediscovery, 36–37
Project
  requests, 53
  scope, reduction, 260
  team, technology selection, 260
Promoters/detractors, identification, 178
Promotions, automation, 177
"proof of vaccination" data capability,
  creation, 90
Provisioning
  apps, no-touch provisioning/
    deprovisioning, 133–134
  automatic provisioning,
    implementation, 126
  delays, 125–126
Purchase (customer journey stage), 177
Purchase order (PO)
  invoice delivery, 233
  processing, 232

product usage analysis, 244
provisioning, 242
success/support, 243
Pure-play limits, 226–227

Q
Quarterly performance, reporting, 53
Quote to cash (back-office task), 124

R
Rao, Mohit, 102
Real-time end-to-end supply chain
  visibility, supply chain challenge,
  182
Recommendations, personalization, 177
Recruitment technology, growth, 155
Redline management, automation, 177
Rehires (hiring process automation
  path), 159
Replacement sourcing, usage, 191
Reporting
  back-office task, 124
  inaccuracies, removal (supply chain
    challenges), 182
Reputation (customer journey stage), 178
Rescind/no-show (hiring process
  automation path), 159
Resiliency (Navan priority), 284
Responses, acceleration, 125
Restaurants, changes, 18–19
Retail convenience stores, robot
  automation, 189–190
Retention (customer journey stage), 177
  end-to-end RMA process, 184
Return merchandise authorization (RMA)
  design, navigation problems, 183
  end-to-end RMA process, systems
    support, 184
  goals, 184
  management, usage, 184
  process, ease/simplification, 186
  requests, submission, 185
  solution, 184
Returns management (functional area
  group), 180
"Return to office" experience capability,
  creation, 90
Reusable APIs, building, 252

Revenue
  growth (driving), automation mindset
    (impact), 112
  revenue-focused software applications,
    ecosystem, 137
Revenue.io, usage, 149
Revenue operations (RevOps)
  front office group, 139
  rise, 140–141
Rigid workflow/connectivity, 84
Risk operations (back-office task), 124
Robotic desktop automation (RDA),
    220–222
  success, 221
Robotic process automation (RPA), 35,
    232, 249
  bot, building, 245
  usage, 219–222
Robots, automation use case, 189–190
Robust architectures, support, 251
Role Based Access (RBAC), usage, 216

S
Salesforce
  API, usage, 224–225
  involvement, 213
  monitoring, 224
  new customer, addition, 225
  quote, account team creation, 47
  SAP, integration, 233
Sales management (front office
    group), 139
Sales operations (SalesOps),
    automation, 284
Sales order
  creation, Netsuite (usage), 254
  management (front office
    group), 139
Sapphire Ventures CIO index, RPA
    report, 221
Scale, embracing, 58–59
Scale mindset, 22, 53, 95
  achievement, democratization
    (usage), 63
  Amazon demonstration, 271
  democratization support, 106
Seamless self-service returns, automation
    use case, 182–186
SecOps managers, automation, 284

Security operations, light bulbs
    (connection), 133
Self-service analytics tools, usage, 57
Self-service mechanisms, automation, 177
Service level agreements (SLAs),
    adherence (improvement), 132
Service management, usage, 184
ServiceNow request, reading, 126
Service platform
  creation, 202
  language, sharing, 205
Services platform (platform-driven
    method), 196, 201–203
Setting the Record Straight (Symes), 281
Shadow IT integrations, usage, 243
Skill sets, balance, 97–98
Skills, impedance, 210–211
Slack
  message, receiving, 150
  notification, triggers, 47
  usage, 125
Smart phone, advantages/capabilities, 218
Social media, monitoring
    (automation), 178
Software as a Service (SaaS), core value
    proposition, 230
Software test automation, 220
Southwest Airlines (SWA)
  employees, meltdown, 72–73
  Integrated Operations, usage, 73
Sprints (work phases), 41
Stakeholder adoption/ratings,
    measurement, 205
Straight-through processing
    (STP), 71–72, 77
Strength, time (relationship), 4
Structured Query Language (SQL)
    queries, usage, 57
Success, skill sets (balance), 97–98
Super Simple Storage (S3)
    (Amazon), 269
Supplier
  base, data analysis capabilities
    (expansion), 182
  collaboration (improvement), technol-
    ogies (introduction), 182
  information, digitization, 182
  management information (functional
    area group), 180

relations (driving), automation mindset
(impact), 112
Supplier efficiency
driving, automation mindset
(impact), 112
fragmentation, overcoming, 38
Supplier operations, 179
automation use cases, 182, 186, 189
efficiency automation, 181
Supply chain
challenges, 182
digital supply chain, automation use
case, 186–189
efficiency, automation tower, 113–114
functional area group, 180
future, 191–192
innovative automation, 190–191
process automation opportunities, 182
risk management challenge, 182
route optimization, 191
Symes, Colin, 281
System actions (business subprocess), 243
Systems, following, 2–5
Systems thinking, application, 62–63

T
Taleb, Nassim, 285
Talent
acquisition, culture
(communication), 155
hiring, process automation paths, 159
negotiation processes, 155
Task-automation mindset, 104
Task-based automation, 71
Task mindset, process mindset (contrast),
28–31
Task thinking, following, 2–5
Teams
incentives/messaging, 266
organization, 245
project requests, 53
uniting, platform (usage), 256–257
Technical capabilities, requirement, 77–78
Technical experts, impact, 99
Technical skill, mental model (updating),
57–58
Technical specialists (democratization
role), 292–293

Technical stakeholders, discovery
workshops (usage), 117
Technology
components, usage, 88
interaction, ability, 203
operations, 283
recruitment technology, growth, 155
selection, 245, 260
Technology-centric viewpoint, 244
Timelines, problems, 260
Transaction
iteration process, 132
records, downloading, 131
Transactional integrity, 257
Transactions per second (TPS),
optimization, 242
TransferWise, usage, 184
TripActions, 283

U
Uber (platform company example), 195
Unmanaged automation tools, 228–229
Upmarket push, pandemic momentum
(usage), 283–285
UPS, company usage, 184

V
VictorOps
information, leveraging, 129
leveraging, 128
VIPs (hiring process automation
path), 159
VIP treatment, automation, 177–178
Virtual machines (VMs)
admin console, opening, 126
creation, 126
success, validation, 126
provisioning/deprovisioning, 125–126
requirements, determination, 126
Visual assets, ararival (impact), 188

W
Walmart.com, advertising (usage),
200–201
Wat, Joey, 40
Work
future, 166–167
phases, 41

Workato, product, 286
Workflows, 253
    AI-powered dynamic work-
       flows, usage, 91
    business user design, 105
    connection, benefits, 125
    monitoring/learning/improving, 77

Y
Ying, Jia, 286–287

Z
Zendesk, 48
    silo, 247
    usage, 184